Roger Cook's
Checkpoint

John Wilson graduated with a BSc from Liverpool University in 1958. After a period of teaching he trained as a pilot in the RAF before turning to writing as a career. His connection with *Checkpoint* began in the mid-seventies when he reported on several stories. He is the editor of the monthly professional journal *Consulting Engineer* and has written for a wide range of publications including *The Times*, the *Financial Times*, the *New Scientist*, *Penthouse* and *Forum*. He, his wife Marion and their two children Holly and Jemma live in Wandsworth.

Roger Cook's CHECKPOINT

JOHN WILSON

ARIEL BOOKS
BRITISH BROADCASTING CORPORATION

Picture Credits: The publishers would like to thank the following for permission to include their cartoons, David Langdon (page 17, reproduced by permission of the *Sunday Mirror* and page 58, reproduced by permission of *Punch*); Bryan McAllister (page 37, reproduced by his permission); Ken Pyne (page 141, reproduced by permission of the *Radio Times*). The photographs between pages 120 and 121 are BBC Copyright and the Punch cartoon belongs to Roger Cook. The Daumier cartoon is included by permission of the Armand Hammer Collection.

First published 1983

Published by the British Broadcasting Corporation
35 Marylebone High Street London W1M 4AA

Typeset by Phoenix Photosetting, Chatham
Printed in England by Mackays of Chatham Ltd
Cover printed by Belmont Press, Northampton

Set in 10 on 11 point Linotron Ehrhardt

ISBN 0 563 20194 0

Contents

Cases

The following cases are summaries of *Checkpoint* programmes, chosen partly because they represent clearly how a story is built up and presented and partly because they contain something particularly noteworthy or memorable.

This book is dedicated
to the
late Walter Wallich

PREFACE BY THE RT. HON. DAVID STEEL M.P.

I have always enjoyed the Checkpoint programme. I often tune in on my car radio on the way down from Scotland to the House of Commons. There is nothing more satisfying than to hear a good story of a blatant injustice, thoroughly researched and well presented!

The collection of cases set out in this book is wide and varied, ranging from feudalism in Scotland to heart transplants in Cambridgeshire, and make extremely enjoyable reading.

The various Checkpoint series have all confirmed my belief that grievances can often be redressed not by passing a wide range of new laws, but by highlighting and enforcing legislation which already exists. Checkpoint effectively plays its part in doing precisely that and I wish the programme every success for the future.

I am sure that it is the case, unfortunately, that the programme has never been hampered by a lack of material. It should therefore not be too long before a second edition of this book is required.

Foreword

'Keep it running' is a phrase familiar to those with experience of making radio and television programmes, but Roger Cook has given it a new meaning. He has shown that, by keeping a tape recorder running, silence speaks volumes, signifying someone's refusal to answer a key question or to refute a well-founded accusation. In effect, the silence says, 'There's no answer to that'. It is a technique of which Cook is, as far as I know, the originator. He is certainly the supreme exponent. But his brand of radio journalism demands more than technique. It calls for initiative and skill, painstaking research and preparation, personal courage, and sheer damned cheek.

Looking at investigative, or more properly, campaigning journalism in Britain over the past several years, I think immediately of Roger Cook and the programme with which he is primarily associated: *Checkpoint*. In other media, I also think of the Insight team of the *Sunday Times* under the editorship of Harold Evans and of Granada Television's *World In Action*, edited by Ray FitzWalter. Indeed, when I was faced, as chairman of the British Media Studies Association, with organising a national seminar on investigative journalism, I had the pleasure of bringing the three of them together. What a team! Fellow professionals and students learned a lot that day.

Being a journalist, I appreciate the value of a good story, maybe for no other reason than that it is a good story. But Roger Cook's 'good story' is much more than that. It is not just 'good radio' either, though it certainly is that as well. Its real achievement is more than this: it helps to dispense justice. That is the key. Roger Cook and the *Checkpoint* team expose cheats and afford some redress to the cheated. As in all the best dramas, from the Western onwards, the baddies get their come-uppance and the goodies get their own back.

The best investigative journalism calls for a commitment on the part of an organisation or the individual working within that organisation. That commitment is to be prepared to pursue a story, a cause if you like, right up to the point where justice is done, if that is possible, and not just to the point of publishing or broadcasting a 'good story'. In my view this should not be an end in itself. It is an important and worthwhile pursuit, and Roger Cook excels in it.

Philip Radcliffe
Director of Communications, University of Manchester.

INTRODUCTION

The *Checkpoint* cult

At twenty-past nine one September morning, I leapt into a taxi outside the headquarters of a large oil company in the City of London.

'Clerkenwell Road, corner of St John Street,' I said.

'How much of a hurry are you in?' asked the driver. 'Only, I want to hear the end of this.'

'This' was Roger Cook on BBC Radio 4's *Checkpoint* programme, exposing yet another intrusion into someone's peace of mind: a man and his partner made bankrupt after they failed to pay an estimated demand from the Inland Revenue.

'He really gets stuck in,' the driver said when the programme had finished. 'I'd like to know how he does it.'

A London taxi driver is not the first person I'd think of as a typical Radio 4 listener, which just shows how dangerous it is to generalise. Pop stars, housewives, bank managers, lawyers, construction workers, Members of Parliament, used car salesmen, librarians . . . these and many others are keen members of the *Checkpoint* audience, for one reason or another.

Since the first series began, on 6 July 1973, *Checkpoint* has established the highest possible standards of investigative journalism; so much so that this award-winning programme is regarded with admiration by journalists all over the world.

That London taxi driver is one of over a million dedicated *Checkpoint* listeners in the United Kingdom, and from his comments it was clear that he genuinely did wonder how Cook and his colleagues managed to produce the programme.

It struck me that other listeners might wonder the same thing, and that is how this book was conceived. It is written primarily for *Checkpoint* fans, but it should also be of interest to journalists and anyone concerned with the use of radio as a reporting medium.

Checkpoint programmes involve considerations of British laws, particularly with regard to libel and the operation of companies.

Whether or not someone could produce a similar programme in, say, the United States, Poland or Argentina is a matter for them to ponder.

Radio is a transient medium. *Checkpoint*'s parables of unfairness, injustice and downright villainy have no permanent public record. It would require a very long book indeed to describe all the cases dealt with over the years, but Roger Cook has spent a great deal of time helping to select those which he thought would be both instructive and entertaining. I am very grateful to him for his unremitting help in this.

I should also like to thank Alan Rogers, Hugh Purcell, John Edwards, David Perrin, Tony Jennings and Rhory Robertson for their practical help in bringing the book into being. Much of the material was originally researched by David Perrin, Andrew Jennings and John Stonborough. Latterly, Jon Danzig, Dina Gold and Malcolm Stacey researched the stories. Thanks are due to all these people and to former but long-standing team members such as Isobel James, Sally Diplock, Julia McLaren and Debbie Flemming.

Above all, the many people who contact the *Checkpoint* team with their complaints deserve a special appreciation. They invariably try to solve their problems through the 'usual channels'. For many of them, *Checkpoint* is a last resort, and they often display great courage in facing the microphone during what for them is a distressing time.

Clearly it would be impossible to acknowledge everyone who has contributed to the *Checkpoint* programme and therefore to this book, but my final thanks must go to the audience and in particular to that London taxi driver, without whom neither the programme nor the book would be possible.

CHAPTER 1

Checkpoint: What it's all about

Checkpoint is a twenty-five minute BBC radio programme created and presented by Roger Cook. It is broadcast throughout Britain on Radio 4 on a weekly basis. In ten years of operation, the programme has covered an enormous variety of topics, and although it occupies a 'consumer affairs' slot in the BBC's Current Affairs Magazine Programmes department (CAMP) it can only be labelled consumerist in the very broadest of senses. It is more accurately described as an investigative programme.

With some exceptions, each edition of the programme presents the case of one or several complainants against a person or organisation, labelled 'the villain' for convenience rather than as an act of prejudice by the *Checkpoint* team.

This simple description of the programme gives no clue to the difficulties faced by those who prepare it. The BBC itself imposes constraints with regard to such things as the use of foul language and the manner in which a *Checkpoint* reporter may record his interviews and then edit them for broadcasting. And the programme, like any written reporting medium, is subject to the laws of libel. It is a fact that the closer a journalist sails to this wind, the more entertaining and exciting his report is likely to be, as the fortnightly satirical magazine *Private Eye* bears witness. *Checkpoint*, with its audience of over a million, and its undoubted influence, has attracted many writs for libel, but at the time of writing only two cases have been successful, both having been settled for small sums. And the reason it is so fireproof in this respect is due to the meticulous research that precedes every story.

It must be said at the start that radio reporting differs in a vital respect from written or visual reporting. A newspaper journalist can – and often does – paraphrase an interviewee. Provided the result is not a distortion of what the person actually said, no harm is necessarily done. Television reporting can do wonders with no spoken words at all. Radio, on the other hand, is entirely dependent on what people actually say and how they actually say it, whether the broadcast is live or recorded. It is impossible to paraphrase a person's voice, without going to the most extreme lengths of technological editing skill. Having said that, certain relatively straightforward techniques can be used to 'editorialise' an interview.

Because of this, the *Checkpoint* team keep a master tape of all contentious interviews. This tape remains unedited to provide a check in the event of a subsequent dispute. (A brief description of radio editing techniques is given in Chapter 8.)

This and other precautions exist for an important reason: to ensure that *Checkpoint* is above all a fair programme. Here again, there are problems. If thirty people line up to complain that 'Villain Smith' has fiddled them out of their life savings with a phoney investment scheme, should Smith be allowed equal air time to explain that he did everything in good faith?

One of the enduring delights of the programme is that the team take a great deal of trouble to line up their 'villain' in front of a microphone. They telephone for interviews. They write numerous letters. They send telegrams. And, when all else fails, they 'doorstep'. Reactions of the 'villains' to a Roger Cook confrontation vary from genuine bewilderment that anyone could possibly be upset at what is an utterly honest-to-goodness effort to sell a first-class product or service, to bloody punch-ups. Cook has the unenviable reputation of being the most beaten journalist in Britain – sixteen times, so far, with broken ribs, concussion, fractures, lacerations and bruises to show for his doggedness. Not to mention the Ross McWhirter Award for Bravery, the Pye/Society of Authors Radio Personality of the Year for 1979 and a number of other honours. Because *Checkpoint* has occasionally produced joint stories with BBC television, some of the violent altercations have been seen by millions of viewers, as in the case of a certain gentleman whose carved Japanese miniatures were not as ivory as they seemed.

For its large and devoted audience, *Checkpoint* has become an established and necessary part of their listening lives. To understand how it was conceived, how it was born into the not-altogether-willing arms of the British Broadcasting Corporation, and how it has become an international yardstick for investigative reporting, we must first take a look at the man who started it all.

CHAPTER 2

The man who turns over stones

"His last words were 'I'm Roger Cook, of BBC Checkpoint'."

Roger Cook was born on 6 April 1943 in Auckland, New Zealand. His earliest recollections include a little boy called George Kadar, who didn't like him very much.

'He used to hide behind a water butt and smite me over the head with a stick when I walked by. This set the pace for many of the things that happened to me subsequently.'

Cook began higher education at Sydney University with the intention of becoming a veterinary surgeon, but soon changed to study the arts and literature. It was a course for which students paid their own way, and he attended the university at night while earning a living during the day. His first job was as a trainee announcer for a Sydney commercial radio station, 2GB, part of the MacQuarie Network. He was soon appointed as an announcer, and grew to like what he was doing to pay his way more than he liked what he was paying to become.

It was at this stage he had his 'Revelation,' when he realised that life wasn't always what it appeared to be – or what it was presented as being.

'The station used to broadcast something called the Ampol Show,' he recalled, 'which was sponsored by a well known brand of Australian petrol. As a lad, long before I joined the network, I used to listen to it with amazement. Winners of the show's quiz in the radio studio would be handed a golden telephone. Then the winner would be asked to give a number . . . "Ampol Treasure House. Number please?" And the winner would say, "Number 45907." "Number 45907!! You have won a wonderful Freezo Refrigerator . . ."

'I had this youthful vision of a huge warehouse full of thousands and thousands of marvellous goodies. . . . Until I joined 2GB, that is. Backstage they had a lady, who didn't have a golden telephone, or thousands and thousands of presents; just an ordinary telephone and a list with six things on it. No matter what number someone pulled out of the air, they got one of these six things.'

Cook next went to work for a firm called Eric Porter Productions. Porter was 'a marvellous man' who began a thriving animation business at roughly the time Walt Disney was becoming big in the USA. Cook worked, 'driving' an animation camera, recording documentaries and being a general dogsbody.

Following this he began work for the Australian Broadcasting Commission, the ABC, where he gained a reputation for doing things that other people didn't want done. He reported on a programme called News Review and also wrote for a magazine programme called Scope. Eventually the ABC shipped him off to Devil's Island in Western Australia ('A nice enough place, but the end of the professional world, as far as I was concerned.') where he still found he wasn't allowed to do many of the things he wanted to tackle.

'There was one particular documentary I was trying to do on the conditions in which some local Aborigines were forced to live. There was a suggestion that they should be shipped out to reserves, when they were fifth and sixth generation city-born. I got into a lot of trouble on that one.'

He also got into trouble by starting a satirical magazine called *Grot*, which was a contemporary of a similar one launched by Richard Neville in Sydney, called *Oz*.

'*Grot* became quite popular, and one of the local traders supported us by taking a regular back page advertisement. He called himself Tom the Cheap Grocer, and he let us get away with all kinds of things. I remember we prepared one ad for him that said, "Expensive food is for the birds at Tom's the Cheap Grocer", with a picture of two vultures tearing a carcase apart. It caused quite a stir in those days.'

Cook linked his literary efforts to a satirical insert called 'The Grot Spot' in a TV show on a rival broadcasting channel. He covered such stories as the fact that Western Australia at that time had one naval vessel whose duties included the defence of a huge ammunition store.

'We'd been told by one of the people who handled the stocks that the one thing this ammo dump did not have was ammunition of the right calibre for the ship that was supposed to be defending it.'

Eventually the magazine ran out of printers.

'The last straw was an article we did about censorship in which we carried a cut-out of the first magazine article in Australia to use a four letter word (fuck). It was a serious piece, but when we collected the printed copies we found that the printer had obliterated the word. We couldn't go on after that.'

Bill Warnock ran one of the biggest advertising agencies in Australia at that time, and he invited Cook to run the radio and television side of the business. This job lasted three years, during which Cook saved hard to get the fare to come to the UK. On one of his earlier sorties from Australia he spent some time in Viet Nam: a 'sad and unpleasant' experience that he doesn't like talking about.

He arrived in the UK in 1968 and began making film documentaries through his own small company. An early film was for the Reliant Motor Company, showing developing nations how they could start a motor industry and featuring a glass fibre bodied vehicle called the Anadol that was made in Turkey. He also began work for the BBC Radio's *World at One* programme at this stage.

'I was very brash. I walked in on Andrew Boyle, who was Editor then, and said, "I like what you do, and I think I can do it, with some different things that you'll like." He and the presenter, Bill Hardcastle, gave me the best kind of audition by sending me straight out with a Uher tape recorder on a job they wanted doing. I came back, and the piece was broadcast. Next thing, they offered me a contract. I think it was more a case of their being desperate than a measure of my ability.'

Apart from his reputation as the most assaulted journalist in Britain, Cook has gained amongst his friends the reputation of being accident prone, and an early sign of this unfortunate attribute occurred during one of his freelance filming projects, shortly after he had taken up this BBC contract.

'I'd bought a Reliant and was driving up the A5 outside Rugby with all my filming equipment in the back. A wiring fault developed, and as there was then no fire-retardant in the glass fibre body the whole thing suddenly became a Towering Inferno, with me standing by it in a layby, wringing my hands and remembering that the insurance on the equipment had just run out. I hailed a passing policeman who cordoned off the fire with his red plastic cones and radioed for more police and the Fire Brigade. They soon turned up and put out what was left of the blaze. We were all standing there tut-tutting about this and that, when a gentleman in an articulated lorry – having driven well over his regulation hours – fell asleep at the wheel and ploughed into the middle of us. The lorry crushed a policeman's foot and hit me square on, sending me flying forty feet into a ditch where I broke a number of vertebrae . . . Plus I landed in a bunch of stinging nettles, which I have always thought was the ultimate example of adding insult to injury!

'They carted me off to the local hospital and compounded the insult and the injury by putting me in the geriatric ward, where the old gentlemen amused themselves by showing me how their colostomy bags worked. Whenever I called for the Sister, she turned up with a new set of scripts she wanted me to take to the BBC. The people were very sweet, but I kept thinking, "What on earth am I doing in Rugby?" So I discharged myself, and a friend drove me to London in the back of his E-Type Jaguar, strapped to a plank, with my feet sticking out of the back window.

'I was pretty depressed about the damage to my body and the loss of my camera equipment, and it didn't exactly cheer me up to arrive home and find that my first wife had left me. The note more or less said that she just didn't really want to be married, and there was nothing personal.

'On the bright side: I did eventually get compensation from the lorry owners. But it would have been difficult not to, with six policemen and nine firemen as witnesses.'

Although this is told with immense good humour, the period was, in fact, a very low spot for Cook. He remembers with gratitude how everyone working on *The World at One* helped him to get over his problems, picking him up from hydrotherapy, sending taxis to occupational therapy sessions in Camden, propping him up in the studios to interview people. Once back on his feet, he began doing more of the programmes involved in 'turning over stones', but the accidents continued. He claims that his accident proneness is not linked to the beatings he has suffered in the line of duty.

'I certainly do not provoke people into attacking me. Mind you, I did manage to be physically damaged on an assignment that did not even involve a villain. Quite the reverse. I was interviewing a most respectable gentleman, the then as now Lord Chancellor, Quintin Hogg. One of his neighbours had an Alsatian that decided to turn me into an orthopaedic case, and I was rushed off to hospital pouring with blood and needing fourteen stitches in my leg and a lot more in my trousers.'

During one of the *Nationwide* co-productions, Cook was investigating a cure for blindness that involved being stung physically by bees and financially by a strange Middle European lady. One of the people he interviewed was a man who was becoming blind.

'Naturally, we handled this very sensitively. He lived in the Lake District, and we were filming him walking by the shores of Lake Windemere, which he shortly would not be able to see any more. Even then, unfortunately, he did not see as well as he thought he could, and he stumbled on some rocks. I made a dive and managed to stop him falling into the water, but although he stayed on the bank I flew straight past and landed in the lake, getting a badly wrenched shoulder into the bargain.'

Like other people who can't take too many holidays, Cook remembers his in some detail. One day he was walking down a street in Ibiza when one of the citizens who had been smoking an unorthodox substance decided that he'd had enough of life and launched himself from a third floor window, with Cook dutifully positioned directly beneath.

'Instead of ending it all, the guy landed on top of me. I got two broken collar bones, and he was undamaged.'

Then there was the case of the hotel chandelier. At the start of a holiday in St Lucia in the West Indies, he was enjoying himself at a welcoming party with a number of friends, when the above mentioned object detached itself from the ceiling. Once again,

Cook was strategically placed to receive maximum harm.

'I spent the next ten days lying concussed in a darkened room before returning to London and work.'

But not before he had discovered that 'Paradise Found' as the islanders call it had also been discovered by a large oil company called the Hess Oil Corporation, whose annual turnover was several times the island's Gross National Product. They moved in, promising the earth and delivering rather less.

'It was a good story for me,' Cook said, 'and I like to think that it was good for the Islanders, too.'

A more recent incident occurred during a film sortie into Scotland. Cook and a colleague were booked into a small hotel that had just been refurbished and extended. The manager proudly showed them into their new suites, and in due course they settled down for the night. But not for long . . .

'I had a bath, then sat in bed reading a film script. All of a sudden there was a hell of a row, and a bunch of people in stained overalls burst into my room shouting, "You've left your bloody bath overrunning."

'"Oh no I've not." I replied, with as much restraint as I could muster. "Go and look. It's empty." They had a look, and began to bundle out as quickly as they'd arrived, without a word of apology. "And if you do that again, you're in for trouble," I bellowed after them. Not a very gentlemanly thing to say, but I get grumpy when I'm tired.

'Eventually I turned the light off and settled down to sleep. I'd just got to that point of betwixt and between, when a hair falling on the carpet can induce a coronary, and these chaps turned up again, banging on the door and yelling something or other. I leapt convulsively out of bed, groped for the table light, found it didn't work, tripped over the bedclothes, fell headfirst over a chair, smashed my watch against a cupboard and lurched at Destruct Velocity into the wardrobe.' (Cook is a well built six footer!)

'It fell on top of me as I lay calling, "Help, help!", and a plaintive voice from the corridor said with a lovely Scottish accent, "We're not coming in, because you said there'd be trouble . . ." Eventually they sorted me out, and we discovered that my bath had not been plumbed into the drainage system, so when I pulled the plug the water had gushed into the dining room beneath. The manager was very nice, but the company he works for decided that the damage I suffered was no concern of theirs.'

Paradoxically, this was just the kind of situation people bring to the *Checkpoint* desk, and it highlights the dilemma facing the team if any of them are personally involved in a dispute: what do they do about it?

The answer is: absolutely nothing that bears upon their connection with the programme.

'I was really frustrated one time,' Cook said. 'I needed some new furniture, and it was a big expense for me, but I rather coveted a new settee and a matching swivel armchair that was for sale in a posh Scandinavian shop that's now no longer with us. I gave them a deposit with my order, but the furniture was not delivered. Eventually I received a bill for the balance which, naturally, I didn't pay. They sent me a number of rude letters, but didn't get round to sending the furniture. Then they sent a bailiff to repossess the furniture that I hadn't yet received. This went on for a year and a half, before I managed, for once, to contact the firm's managing director on the phone. He apologised nicely and said he'd sort it out for me. A couple of months later he called me and said that my furniture was in their warehouse and that it would be delivered on the Monday morning. That was Friday. On Saturday night the warehouse burned down.'

Although the *Checkpoint* team are scrupulous about not using the programme's name for personal reasons, sometimes a listener may not be so particular. Cook remembers taking one phone call . . .

'I used your name to a bent insurance broker the other day. Magic, guv'nor. Magic!'

CHAPTER 3

Getting started

Cook's work as a reporter for *The World at One* in 1968 covered many topics and he began to attract a lot of letters from listeners saying, 'Hey, that's the kind of thing that happened to me. And did you know . . .?', bringing new evidence to his attention. Ten years later the audience still provides over ninety per cent of the leads, which are carefully developed into the well researched revelations that have been the traditional foundations of *Checkpoint's* success right from the start.

As the ideas and information came rolling in, Cook went to see Andrew Boyle and William Hardcastle and suggested there was enough material to do a regular programme. Their reaction was to start a 'more or less regular feature' of Cook's brand of reporting within the existing programme at the weekend.

'The very first piece I did featured a systematic door-to-door deep freeze and central heating rip-off,' Cook recalled. 'And one of the last ones at this stage was an exposé of what had been done to Jess Yates, known in the popular Press as The Bishop, who was presenter and producer of a very popular Yorkshire TV programme called *Stars on Sunday*.

'For some years Jess had been having a relationship with an actress called Anita Kaye. This was a long-established relationship, but for some reason a few of the 'popular' newspapers decided that this wasn't really a good thing . . . He was presenting, after all, a religious programme . . . He was a married man . . . He was "Having it off", as they put it, with a lady many years his junior . . .

'The newspapers did all kinds of nasty things to Jess and Anita, such as inventing secret trysts as they did for Lady Diana and Prince Charles. They widened the age difference. They neglected to tell their readers that Jess had been legally separated from his wife for ten years. They said he'd been fired, when in fact he resigned because he thought he wasn't a very good presenter.

'So we took this up and gave the newspapers a little of their own medicine. Writs were issued. But one of the main newspapers concerned didn't even bother to check whether the quotes we attributed to their features editor were real. They didn't ask him if he'd spoken to me. So this writ was withdrawn, and the others followed.'

Cook and Boyle were convinced that the stories should be produced as a new programme, using additional reporters when necessary. Cook produced a pilot programme as a sample of the kind of thing they wanted to do.

'Nobody wanted to listen to it for a very long time,' Cook said. 'I never discovered why. The Controller of BBC Radio 4 at the time was Tony Whitby who used to call me The Colonial Pirate, for reasons that escaped me. He certainly liked what we were doing in *The World This Weekend*, and probably did not want to see the feature move from this spot. In any case, what we were proposing was fairly revolutionary, and I guess it caused a certain nervousness among the BBC's senior hierarchy.

'It was unlike, for example, *The Braden Beat*, in that we were not intending to treat matters humourously. No jokes, no sly nudges in the ribs, no "We didn't really mean it, Mr ICI . . ." None of that! Our idea was that something needed to be said, and we intended to say it, provided we could prove it and do it fairly.

'Eighteen months after we made that pilot we camped outside Whitby's office and refused to move until he listened to the tape. He did so, grudgingly at first, then came out and said what a splendid piece of broadcasting it was, that the network needed it and tnat the network was going to have it.'

The wheels started turning for the new programme, but for various reasons they turned slowly at first. William Hardcastle died at about this time, and Andrew Boyle was preoccupied with other matters. Then Cook returned from holiday to find that he'd been transferred to another department. The name *Checkpoint* had been chosen for the programme, and the powers that be had decided that it should be a consumer programme and handled by the same people that produced *You and Yours*.

Cook was still working a full shift on *The World This Weekend* and presenting *The World at One* on Mondays in rotation, with people like Bob Williams, when he began work on *Checkpoint*.

'I was given the corner of someone's desk to work on, and no researcher or proper secretarial help. This went on for some time, and then, as the audience increased, we had a fight over what sort of backing the programme should receive. Although CAMP, Current Affairs Magazine Programmes, stands by it now, I really don't believe they understood what *Checkpoint* was all about. They seemed to think that it should offer advice and 'point fingers gently'. I never want to offer advice, because if it is inappropriate, or if someone doesn't follow it properly, we get blamed. Then they appointed a researcher to the programme, but the person concerned was not a researcher, which is a highly-demanding job that requires training and experience. They clearly thought that someone, however bright, whose only training was as a secretary, would be more than good enough for *Checkpoint*.'

And so, amid a certain amount of internal squalling, the infant *Checkpoint* arrived, presented by a man who rejects the idea that he is a consumerist's Knight in Shining Armour but admits that he hates to see people being cheated or treated unjustly. The *Radio Times* billing traditionally describes *Checkpoint* as a weekly investigation into allegations of fraud, injustice and bureaucratic bungling – 'And that's what we go after!'

Checkpoint's impact and influence over the years has been enormous. Regulations have been dropped by governments. Rogue firms large and small have been put out of business. Malefactors have been tracked down and subsequently charged by the police. Other programmes, in radio and television, have sprung up around it. A popular television drama series was based upon it. And, most importantly as far as Cook is concerned, a totally new set of standards has been forged for investigative reporting on the air.

The programme's first producer was the late Walter Wallich, whom I interviewed shortly before his death in 1981. He joined the BBC's European Service in 1948 and transferred to Broadcasting House in 1952 to work in the News Division before moving into foreign news reporting in various parts of the world. In 1972 he was appointed Chief Assistant to Alan Rogers, Head of CAMP, and the appointment of such a senior man reflects the concern with which the BBC viewed the new programme. This is how he recalled the early days of *Checkpoint*.

> In 1973 the Editor of *The World at One* and *PM* programmes, Andrew Boyle, was using Roger Cook as a reporter. He proved to be a very efficient reporter, and he made the suggestion to Andrew that he should start a new kind of investigative programme with the help of producers from *The World at One*. I came to hear of this and suggested to Alan Rogers

that, in this particular case, *The World at One* was overlapping with what was, at that time, the preserve of Current Affairs Magazine Programmes; that is to say, programmes that could have a consumer interest.

We were producing *You and Yours* from 12.00 to 12.30 p.m., dealing specifically with some of the very affairs with which Roger was going to concern himself, although on what you might call a less hard-hitting, softer basis of enquiry and advice, rather than challenge and exposure.

I suggested to Alan Rogers that he should discuss this with Tony Whitby, Controller of Radio 4 at the time, which he did. As a result, *Checkpoint*, which had not yet gone on the air and of which only a pilot programme had been made, was transferred to us in CAMP.

Such changes do not normally take place without the creation of some bad blood. There was no doubt that Boyle was vexed at the takeover. In turn, Roger had experience of the 'go-go' style of *The World at One*, then presented by William Hardcastle, and he didn't think much of *You and Yours*, which he regarded as 'pussy-footing'. He was highly suspicious of working with our department. He was, however, determined to get *Checkpoint* off the ground and so accepted the handover. He came to see me, since I was to be the producer of what looked like being a ticklish and problematical venture.

It is fair to say that initially Roger did not believe in me or trust my ability to withstand Establishment pressure against what was an entirely new departure for the Corporation. Nobody had previously done investigative programmes of this kind. It was quite unusual, for example, for the BBC to mention names of firms or advertisers. The idea of making 'devious' researches behind the backs of firms we suspected of shady dealings was frowned upon, and it was quite clear that a new set of ground rules for this type of programme would have to be established.

We also had to establish a very strict observance of balance between accuser and accused to comply with the BBC's doctrine of fair dealing. Originally we tried to do this by eliciting information from both sides of a quarrel, but we soon discovered that 'suspects' were not willing to give information or interviews, and the balance would have to be provided by the presenter himself.

After initial mistrust, my relationship with Roger soon

became amicable and one of mutual confidence, a change aided, no doubt, by the fact that our very first programme was a baptism of fire.

Roger had decided to investigate the monopoly that opticians have in the supply of spectacles, the use they made of it (in selling spectacles that were over-priced and often unnecessary), and the alternatives available in other countries. This led to a letter from the chairman of the opticians' association to the BBC's Director General in which he complained vigorously of our style of presentation, of our 'unfairness' in the allocation of the time between the parties concerned, and of the imbalance in the programme in general.

There is no doubt that the Director General was gravely concerned by these allegations, since no similar programme had been done before, and part of my time over the next few months was taken up in drafting with Roger replies and refutations to the opticians' allegations for the signature of directors and controllers. I found that Roger ably defended his corner, substantiating his replies with chapter and verse, and he found that I was not easily persuaded to yield to pressure from above to do a second programme on the subject that would present the opticians' case in their own light.

It is interesting to see how this pioneering work of ours in 1973 is now wholly accepted, both by the Corporation and by the opticians themselves. Television's *Nationwide* programme subsequently examined the identical problem in a similar style to that which we then employed. This more recent investigation got full co-operation from the opticians, and as a result of the programme they decided to amend their code of practice.

This, of course, is not far enough, but it is quite clear that the opticians are now, as a result of this publicity, under considerable pressure to go further. The *Nationwide* programme and its outcome fully vindicates what *Checkpoint* had said eight years previously.

One reason for my appointment to *Checkpoint* was to represent it to the BBC Establishment and to defend it against any lingering fears and doubts that might exist among the hierarchy. A good example of the need for this was an investigation we did of the National Housebuilders Registration Council which is now called, I believe, the National Housebuilders Council. This was on the subject of their guarantee to house buyers of houses registered with them and their practical monopoly over the granting of mortgages by the building societies. The NHBC, after their initial protests to the Director General and the Chairman of the Board of Governors had proved fruitless, took their case to the BBC's Programme Complaints Commission, one of whose prominent members was Sir Henry Fisher, together with a similar complaint they had about an item done by television. The adjudication of the PCC tried to establish a number of ground rules that, in practice, would have made the production of investigative programmes impossible.

The Commission suggested that the same rules should apply to an investigative programme as are applied to a court of law, with regard to the investigation of witnesses, the taking and sifting of evidence, and other matters. They also demanded that the facilities given to both parties (accuser and accused) should be strictly equal and that neither should be assisted by the BBC in a manner that was not also provided for the other.

As far as the juridical requirements were concerned, it was clear that the BBC could not comply and still make such programmes. Whereas a law suit might go on for years, the BBC has a time limit within which a programme must be completed. And, as far as evidence is concerned, the BBC, unlike a court of law, has no right to *sub poena* witnesses, nor can a witness be sworn to give true evidence. Insofar as equality of opportunity was concerned, strict observance of the rules would, in fact, lead to gross inequalities. Take the case, for example, where the BBC receives a complaint from an old age pensioner widow against the gas board. It is now accepted that in the interests of equity we should pay for the widow to come to London, and that we should assist her, elderly and ill-at-ease, to make her case as best she can. We have no similar obligation towards the gas board, whose chairman is thoroughly briefed on the case by his staff before he is driven to Broadcasting House in a cavalcade of cars, to enter the premises with a retinue of experts who will check his every reply.

These arguments were accepted by the BBC, and, as the rulings of the Programme Complaints Commission were not mandatory in such matters of procedure their recommendations in this regard were not followed.

Other recommendations were noted, however. Among them was a requirement to balance as exactly as possible in the circumstances the time given to a complainant and a defendant; the recommendation to preserve all controversial tape-recorded interviews, including those parts not used on the air; and a requirement that the defendant's arguments should be given in the order in which they were recorded, without cross-cutting to other aspects of evidence.

I think that these requirements are fair and had already been observed. Their consistent observation has certainly helped to make *Checkpoint* more fire-proof.

My relationship with Roger during those early days was basically that of providing a brake for his tremendous drive and enthusiasm, which sometimes led us towards stories that I felt would be indefensible. It was not so much a matter of our disagreeing over the importance or the justice of a complaint as over the feasibility of defending it adequately on the evidence we had to support our case; a matter of degree, in fact. Our arguments were frequently lively and protracted, but did not detract from our mutual respect and liking. This meant that each new edition was tackled by each with confidence in what the other was doing.

It soon became apparent that the makeshift set-up that we had for *Checkpoint* from the beginning (which consisted of a part-time-researcher-cum-secretary, Roger Cook, myself and, from time-to-time, a reporter who worked on a subsidiary story to the main item) was inadequate. We acquired two full-time researchers, and I undertook the radical reorganisation of the filing system, which was fairly disorganised at the outset, but which was essential if we were to have a solid defence against attack. Records of all telephone calls were made. All materials concerning a given story were collated and indexed. And copies of tapes, together with parts that were not broadcast, were assembled. It is a system that has proved itself many times over the years.

One important problem we encountered was that of the recording of telephone interviews. Under BBC ground rules we were not allowed to record telephone calls except with the knowledge of the interviewee. This was undoubtedly an inhibiting rule, especially when we were dealing, as *Checkpoint* frequently does, with outright villains who are later apprehended by the police and convicted by the courts. The BBC was not prepared to deviate from these rules, except in quite exceptional circumstances to be directly approved by the Director General.

There were a number of occasions on which defendants were interviewed on the phone with the clear understanding that their calls were being recorded and would be used in a programme who subsequently denied this. It then became necessary to record the initial conversation in which Roger tells the defendant that the call is being recorded. This rather mundane 'chat' is also broadcast and preserved in our records, so that no misrepresentation of our intentions is possible.

We can all be satisfied that we did forge a totally new instrument in broadcasting that is now imitated throughout radio and television and accepted as the norm by broadcasters and, more importantly, by their superiors. *Checkpoint* is still the hardest-hitting of all these programmes and the one that concentrates most single-mindedly on investigations.

CHAPTER 4

The *Checkpoint* team

Since the early days, with a producer, a reporter/presenter and a part-time researcher, the *Checkpoint* team has developed into a small, highly-skilled bunch of experienced people. Roger Cook, in addition to having made many television programmes and other radio programmes, has remained the one person who has been the core of that team since the programme's birth in 1973. The current producer, John Edwards, a senior BBC staff man, has been with *Checkpoint* since 1977. David Perrin, senior researcher and co-producer until leaving in 1982, joined the team in 1978. At the time of writing there are three researchers, Jon Danzig, Dina Gold and Tim Tate, and a secretary. Over the years a number of people have researched and reported for *Checkpoint*, including Sue Cook (no relation), who went to BBC television's *Nationwide* programme, and John Stonborough, who left the BBC to front a help-the-consumer type programme on London's Capital Radio. Andrew Jennings, who researched many stories from 1978 to 1981, moved from radio to report on BBC television's *Watchdog* programme.

Checkpoint has a suite of four small offices on the seventh floor at the back of Broadcasting House, with windows overlooking Marylebone and Parliament Hill. The offices are linked by internal doors and a dozen telephone lines. A rough chart on one wall indicates in cryptic chalked notes the stories that are being researched and their broadcast dates. Other parts of the wall are covered with newspaper clippings about the programme, the odd award, telegrams and letters in congratulatory and condemnatory modes. Racks of telephone books ('Do not remove. These are vital'). Shelves of tape recordings. Bulky Ferrograph tape recorders, with splicing tape and Chinagraph pencils nearby. A huge bin, empty at the beginning of the programme process, fills to the brim with discarded lengths of working tape during the build-up to the Wednesday studio session, when the interviews are linked together by the presenter for the final recording.

Transmission times have varied, but the routine is now for a Wednesday evening broadcast with a Thursday morning repeat.

Throughout the week the team members spend a great deal of time on the telephone, listening to someone with a problem, checking out a lead, setting up an interview, double checking a point of detail. The desks are covered with letters from listeners . . .

> 'Dear Mr Cook,
> Please can you help. There is no one else left to turn to. I have been cheated out of my life savings and now face losing my home. . . .'

Notes of telephone conversations, contact books, legal documents, maps . . . The polite word for the office is 'busy'. A fly on the wall will have heard other words used, depending on the state of tension as a difficult edition nears completion or the message comes through that a story is lost, for some reason.

BBC Radio comprises a number of departments, such as News and Current Affairs, Current Affairs Magazine Programmes (CAMP), Religious Affairs, Schools Broadcasting, Drama, Talks and Documentaries, and Arts and Features. *Checkpoint* is part of Current Affairs Magazine Programmes. Various senior people in CAMP have an interest in *Checkpoint*, starting with the Head of CAMP, Alan Rogers, his Deputy who for a number of years was Hugh Purcell, and now David Harding. Others with a keen interest in the programme are Tony Jennings (see Chapter 5), the Corporation's Head of Legal Department, and Rhory Robertson, the lawyer assigned to consider the legal implications of each edition. In line-management terms, the programme's producer is the link between the team members and these people.

The role of the producer

As Walter Wallich pointed out, the nature of *Checkpoint* is such that members of the BBC hierarchy place a great deal of importance on the man who produces the programme. After Wallich the next permanent incumbent was John Edwards, who took over in 1977. Edwards joined the BBC in 1968 as a news reporter in Cardiff and since then has worked on a number of programmes, such as *Today*, and television's *That's Life* and the *Tonight* programmes. On transferring to Broadcasting House he became the editor of the weekend version of *Today*.

Edwards describes the *Checkpoint* producer as filling two roles: first, the day-to-day matters relating to staff, links with the BBC Establishment, money and 'all the boring things that must be done before we can achieve our prime purpose', and secondly the business of programme making. Tactically this is Edwards's responsibility – though he does work to the Editor of Consumer Affairs. Four people have filled this post since *Checkpoint*'s conception – Denis Lower, John Turtle, David Harding and latterly Leslie Robinson.

'Programme-making starts with the mail bag,' says Edwards. 'We currently get about four hundred letters a week from listeners, and I read them all. Only about forty per cent look good at this stage.'

If ten letters come in about one company, this is viewed as being extremely significant. The team assume that only one in a hundred of all listeners with a grievance actually put pen to paper. With an audience of one million (two per cent of the UK population) they believe that ten letters of complaint means that up to a thousand people will have suffered similar problems. This arithmetic was supported by an investigation into a mail order company. *Checkpoint* received nineteen letters of serious complaint and were told by the police that they had later collected two thousand general complaints against the company concerned.

'Almost all our input for programme ideas comes from the audience,' Edwards says. 'Without the letters, without this relationship, we have no rights and no purpose . . . no cause!'

Every letter sent to *Checkpoint* is answered, which means that there is a continuous two-way contact between the team and the audience. This is good, practical public relations as well as a real and valid basis for investigations. If the letters lead to the possibility of a story, four questions are asked: is it suitable for the *Checkpoint* treatment; will the telling achieve a useful purpose; is the story in the public interest; and will it be entertaining? In this context, Edwards views the programme as being a series of parables, because it is a way of teaching how people are caught in traps or unpleasant situations of various kinds. Rather than seeking to air the ills of a small group of people, the aim is to widen the message to all listeners, to bring out the reasons why the problems have arisen and warn the public at large of the dangers. Occasionally, even though a single complaint does not develop for the programme, the teams can 'lend support' to the complainant to try and get a fair settlement of a dispute. But the main effort is always to fill the twenty-five minutes of programme time with a fair investigation into disputes between complainants and 'villains'.

'Sometimes we find it difficult to go after our targets,' Edwards said, 'because we often deal with downright criminals, and we must never pre-empt legal processes or, indeed, break the law in any way. We also find problems arising because we deal with moral aspects of behaviour and standards of decency. It may sound pompous, but we do not consider *ourselves* to be arbiters of public morality. Our moral stance is controlled by the indignation of the listener.' Edwards pointed out that this has led the team into 'throwing stones at their own back window' with regard to what is called Chequebook Journalism, where substantial sums are paid for the exclusive rights to a particular story. 'We don't shrink from tackling our own organisation in this respect if we think it's at fault.'

Ultimately, the decision whether to run a story or not depends on personal standards, and on weighing the effect of doing it as opposed to not doing it. If, for example, complaints were received about a mail order company, it might be that the company was just going through a bad patch. While it is still perfectly proper to bring this to the public's attention, if the timing of the broadcast is 'wrong' it could lead to disaster for the company, with dozens of people losing their jobs. 'We agonise over this kind of thing,' Edwards said.

When all these considerations are made, the final criterion is that the programme must be 'a good listen'. Subjects are preferred that have a wide application to society, and complaints should not be simply repetitious. Such things can lead to boredom and the turning-off of thousands of radios.

Like Wallich, Edwards sees *Checkpoint* as having introduced a new kind of investigative journalism into the UK, not just for BBC radio but for all media, '. . . certainly bolder than any previous radio programme in naming names and making strong allegations against people.'

During Edwards's tenure of the producer's chair, *Checkpoint* has changed. Its resources have been increased, and even more importance placed on higher-quality research. As the programme has developed, the stories have become more complex, the subjects demanding more understanding, more double-checking, more interviews. Whereas there would sometimes be two or occasionally three items in one edition, time to deal with even one of today's stories is all too limited. As the stories have hit home, and as the audience has increased, public awareness of the programme has continued to increase, bringing prestigious awards and a great deal of Press coverage. In turn, this has placed greater constraints on the programme makers, in that the threat of libel actions has also necessarily increased. It is not unknown for a 'villain' to issue a writ against the BBC just so he can claim that he has done so, the implication being that the programme has been at fault. While many such writs may fade quietly away, some do not, and even though the team may regard themselves as 'fireproof' the extra work involved can be burdensome for all concerned. Yet, paradoxically, like most investigative journalists, the *Checkpoint* team would be uneasy if libel actions did not spring into being: this is, at least, a measure of how hard they are pricking someone. Needless to say, such an attitude does not always find sympathetic understanding in other parts of the BBC hierarchy, and the *Checkpoint* producer often finds himself in two firing lines in this respect.

'Putting it another way,' Edwards says with a wry smile, 'the *Checkpoint* producer acts as an interface between people whose views do not always coincide. But because we always work within the BBC's code of practices and standards, more often than not we find a way through such difficulties, and very few editions run into real trouble.'

But a persistent problem is that of fairness. The BBC rightly insists that the programme is both balanced and fair in the way it treats the subjects of its stories. While all those working on the programme respect this standard and work to uphold it, nevertheless they are biased in favour of the complainants because, as Edwards points out, they must believe that the complaints against someone are genuine, otherwise they wouldn't have a programme. As a result, they must be able to prove all the allegations made on the programme, and this is, of course, one of the areas most keenly scrutinised by the *Checkpoint* lawyer.

CHAPTER 5

Checkpoint and the law

I thought I was listening to Roger Cook's 'Checkpoint' but it turned out to be 'Yesterday in Parliament'.

Cartoon first published in *The Guardian* on 20/06/80 and reproduced by permission of Bryan McAllister

The BBC's Legal Division deals with all aspects of law, involving all activities of the Corporation, such as general solicitor's work, contracts and copyright. It is the solicitor's department that is concerned with *Checkpoint* and matters arising from the programme. Tony Jennings, currently the BBC's legal advisor and head of the Legal Division, was the first solicitor to be assigned to *Checkpoint*, in 1973. At that time there were six solicitors in that department, and now there are eight. They deal with conveyancing and major contracts, and they vet programmes for possible libels and contempts of court, providing a twenty-four hour cover for radio news programmes on a nationwide basis. Thus, a newsreader in, say, Manchester can call the duty solicitor at any time to clear any news item, if necessary.

When *Checkpoint* began it introduced a number of novelties as far as the solicitors' department was concerned, according to Jennings.

'It was the first BBC programme to have a solicitor assigned to it on a regular basis,' he said. 'In particular, one thing struck me at the time, in that the programme had consumer-based research as well as investigative work. Not only did it deal with scandals, in the sense that something had gone hideously and possibly criminally wrong, but there were areas where services were being provided within the law, or even by the law, that were of a poorer quality than they should have been. Thus, it was a matter of standards just as much as scandals that we were dealing with.

'This immediately raises the justified but thorny question of "what is fair?". If someone is working within what is accepted by their profession as a reasonable system, and if *Checkpoint* produces a complainant who says that the system is wrong, can you then accuse that someone of defrauding or short-changing the customer in any way? If you are saying, for example, that the standard of garages should be better, and yet they are all working to the standards set up by their professional organisation, you have some difficulty in naming an individual garage as being bad to its customers.'

An edition of *Checkpoint* that Jennings feels demonstrates these considerations dealt with the National House Builders Registration Council.

'I remember this well, because it gave us a great deal of trouble at the time. This organisation had, for people who bought new houses, a guarantee that ran for several years. Two *Checkpoint* programmes dealt with its activities and the way in which their guarantee did and also did not protect people. In other words, it asked the question, "Was the guarantee adequate?"

'The NHBC took their objections about *Checkpoint* up the line to the BBC's Programmes Complaints Commission, set up by the Corporation in the early 1970s to look at allegations of unfair treatment in BBC programmes. Their complaints were not upheld.'

The people on the original Programme Complaints Commission were all appointed by the BBC, and they tended to be very senior, often retired, such as High Court judges and even an omsbudsman. To every extent their opinions were independent of the BBC, yet however well-meaning such an appointed body may be, criticism can arise that they cannot be truly independent of the organisation that appointed them. The BBC Programme Complaints Commission was subsequently examined by the Annan Commission on Broadcasting, with the result that, in 1981, the Home Secretary appointed the first independent Broadcasting Complaints Commission, with powers to investigate all broadcast programmes from both the BBC and IBA. One novelty in the new BCC's Charter is that the Commission's members can look at matters of alleged unfairness even for people who are dead, an aspect, says Jennings, that could well lead to some interesting legal considerations in the future.

The BCC does not deal with general complaints about a programme, such as its technical content or whether or not listeners liked it. It is, like its predecessor, limited to matters relating to unfairness. An example would be if a reporter told an interviewee that the programme in question was dealing with one subject or a particular aspect of a subject and it finally dealt with another subject or aspect. The danger here is that the reporter would get the interview under false pretences.

By the time the old PCC was disbanded, only one case was brought to it against *Checkpoint*, and only two civil actions for libel had been successful against the programme. One of these was an inadvertent libel and was settled out of court for a small sum. The other concerned what later became a charity for research into child blindness that was settled for £15,000. In 1981, one of the first cases handled by the new and independent BCC was a *Checkpoint* programme that covered the activities of two people and a school for actors. The complaint was upheld, a decision that caused a certain bitterness within the *Checkpoint* team, who felt that the BCC members, few of whom had any broadcasting experience, had overlooked vital evidence that supported the programme complainants' allegations and that they had tried to impose standards that were unrealistic, in much the same way as had been those proposed by the BBC's own PCC. Cook pointed out that there was gratifying support for the team's reactions from among senior BCC staff.

A subsequent complaint to the BBC from a man who made a considerable living from selling phoney university degrees was examined in greater depth – and rejected.

Like his colleagues, Tony Jennings emphasises that the

extremely careful research of the *Checkpoint* team is one of the reasons that so few successful libel actions or complaints have been brought.

'Another reason is that, despite their colourful and hard-hitting approach, scripts are never intrusive or over-written. For example, if they have clear evidence that someone has committed one offence, and then they write it up as if he or she constantly did that, they would be guilty of over-writing. This would open the door to a possibly successful legal action. They must be scrupulous in not generalising from a particular incident.'

Bearing in mind that the BBC is by its nature a part of the nation's 'Establishment', the role played by its lawyers in the development of *Checkpoint* is refreshing. It would have been very easy for them to take the safe, soft option on many occasions and advise against broadcasting, but the infrequent times at which they have given such advice have been when there is a clear-cut legal reason for doing so. Even then, the advice now given is to make a programme broadcastable whenever possible, not to stop it outright. Cook remembers that one of his early programmes seemed likely to draw fire in this respect, and he went over the script and interviews carefully with Jennings who told him, 'The question isn't whether you'll get a writ, but how many and when! However, I think the issue is an important one, and I think you should go ahead and broadcast.'

Jennings says that many people who are exposed by the programme are almost obliged to issue a writ, so that they can say, 'Sure *Checkpoint* did a programme on me – and I'm sueing!' The fact that they subsequently withdraw their action, or lose it, may not get the same emphasis, of course. There could also arise occasions on which the possibility of a successful action might not take precedence over the editorial need to publish.

'If we unearth someone who is so crooked or preying in such an evil way on the public . . . the possibility of a writ, successful or otherwise, is, in a sense, irrelevant from a journalist's point of view. There is a clear editorial duty to expose such a scoundrel.'

With a smile no doubt prompted by recollections of many a late night hassle over some of those early *Checkpoint* programmes, Jennings agrees that Cook and his team have been responsible for a degree of innovation in the relationship between 'the law' and investigative journalism.

'I think we can say that, because the programme has broken new ground and continues to do so. It constantly challenges accepted ideas, and what I find particularly interesting is that, after so many years of intense operation, the programme is still stimulating. It hasn't become "Show Biz". More importantly, it still goes after real targets, not soft options.'

Since October 1977 the weekly legal responsibility for *Checkpoint* has been largely in the hands of solicitor Rhory Robertson, a law graduate from Southampton University. His main impressions of the programme include the observation that it has developed from being mostly an insight into back-street villainy to a programme that delves very deeply into major stories, often involving international operations of major companies as well as individuals, big company frauds and bank scandals.

'I joined the BBC because I was interested in libel law,' he says, 'but rapidly I found myself becoming enmeshed in intricate company webs. The programme now covers a great deal of ground, and I think this is in part due to the enormously high quality of the research, and in part due to the careful selection and preparation of material. All the people involved work extremely hard in getting down to the nitty gritty business of unearthing the facts behind the facts in complex major stories.'

As an investigative programme, *Checkpoint* gives Robertson a number of 'special considerations' each week.

'To begin with, the programme is consistently good. In my view the best example of investigative reporting in the media. It's worth reflecting that a *Checkpoint* spin-off programme critically examined the De Lorean venture two years before there was even a whisper about the propriety of that operation. And in the programme's ten-year existence there have been almost no errors of fact. The few that have got through the fine sifting have been matters of detail rather than substance. If we are sued, our defence is primarily that of justification: what we say is true. If we can't prove it, we don't run it. It's as simple as that. What can be difficult is the nature of the proof itself. When the programme seeks to show that someone is a charlatan or a fraud it pulls no punches, and the only worthwhile defence against a libel action in such cases is that the allegations are true. We have to show that the person concerned is a crook in the way that we allege.'

Robertson makes a distinction between the research he and his legal colleagues might be called upon to do compared with that done by the *Checkpoint* team.

'The programme staff are always working to strict time schedules, not to mention budgets,' he says, 'whereas we might find ourselves with a legal case that gives us years to work on. Therefore we often find we can dig up a great deal more than the original programme. This can be of great assistance in a successful defence against a writ, bearing in mind that the onus is always on the BBC to *prove* that a story is true.'

The BBC's legal staff sometimes assist in the development of a story by advising on a particular point of law, but their main objective is to judge each programme before it is broadcast to see if it is libellous in a way that cannot be defended.

'My real involvement starts on the Wednesday morning, when the presenter and production team assemble in the studio,' Robertson says. 'Because of the nature of the programme, often all a lawyer can do during the hectic recording is to try and pick up an unwitting libel, one that can be removed by changing phraseology rather than programme content. Of course, we can never remove the risk of the villain sueing, because we are out to expose him, to show him to be what we believe him to be. So I don't sit there as a researcher or as an editor. I acknowledge that the researcher is a professional who knows what he or she is doing and has properly documented the facts that are being alleged on the programme. If I was to work any other way, we would have to start recording three days before transmission instead of the same day.'

As an example of an unwitting libel that no one spotted, Robertson quotes the case of the solicitor in which *Checkpoint*, in investigating one partner of a firm, mentioned another partner who promptly sued.

'Taking into account the ludicrous level of damages now being awarded by juries, we settled for a very small sum indeed,' he recalled.

Although Robertson has sat through scores of *Checkpoint* recording sessions, his mind tuned to the legal aspects, he still finds himself staggered by the programme content.

'You can sit in that cubicle while Roger's recording, with all the hullabaloo going on, and a sort of numb shock comes over you. *Checkpoint* believes in calling a spade a spade, and so every week you hear detailed allegations made and every week you think "How am I going to justify this?" It's a source of constant surprise to me that so few people do bring libel actions against us. They would certainly be entitled to, in the sense that they have been libelled, and if we get the facts wrong they would certainly have a case.'

Robertson referred to the story about St George's School (see Case 15), with its allegations of brutality and homosexuality. By 29 November 1982, several weeks after the broadcast, no writ had been issued, although a government inquiry had been announced and the principal concerned had made denials in the Press.

'Frankly, I would have expected one in this case,' he said. 'On the other hand, we covered a story in 1980 about a school for English run by Salam Lawrence Blackmore who, two years after the broadcast, personally issued five writs against people in the BBC. I am afraid that litigants in person are the one thing I dread. They have no idea how to plead their case, and they can make the most extraordinary and incomprehensible allegations. I had Blackmore's action struck out of the Lists.'

Another case that produced writs was that of Chief Nzeribe (broadcast in November 1982), self-professed international businessman and arms dealer, joint plaintiff with Alhadji Shinkafi, director of security in Nigeria. The latter's action highlights one of the special problems of 'lawyering' *Checkpoint*, in this case a problem that started when the programme alleged Nzeribe had made a payment of money to Shinkafi and his wife.

'There is no doubt that the payment was made,' said Robertson, 'and we can prove this. But the mere inclusion of this fact in *Checkpoint* has a significance that may not necessarily apply in other programmes. It can raise questions of bad dealings, corruption or fraud, for example. Because of this, it is usually not good enough for a lawyer merely to argue that the fact itself is true. The motive behind the fact must also be proved, and in order to win a case the motive may have to be shown to be quite different from, say, simple charity.'

Those who continually see the BBC in the role of 'Auntie', with all that this implies, can only be refreshed by the way the labyrinthine legalities of the programme are handled by Robertson and his colleagues. When a senior staff member heard a pre-broadcast recording of one story and exclaimed, 'My God, that's libellous!', Robertson snapped back. 'Of course it's libellous. It wouldn't be *Checkpoint* otherwise.'

CHAPTER 6

The ethics of broadcasting *Checkpoint* – How far can we go?

In practice, editorial concern over *Checkpoint's* content lies mainly in the ethics of the programme as a whole, the manner in which the villains are dealt with and the use of bad or abusive language. In this latter case, the general attitude is that they are dealing with reality, unpleasant as it sometimes might be, so it is normally justified and therefore acceptable.

The heading of this chapter was the title of a lecture given by Cook to an audience at the Edinburgh Radio Festival in August 1980. The rights and wrongs of what the *Checkpoint* team itself does are a constant underlying concern to the team members, and each week's events, each programme, presents new circumstances and new ethical considerations. The programme might include material that is distressing not only to the complainant but to the audience. Another might justifiably present a company's wrongdoings and simultaneously threaten the livelihood of perfectly innocent workers in that firm. Is it *right* to broadcast?

The lecture's content was discussed in great detail between Cook, producer John Edwards and senior researcher, David Perrin. None of them could have predicted the dramatic way in which it was to be presented at Edinburgh. Cook's schedule that day included an early morning interview in London with the owners of a string of rogue plumbing companies. (See Case 4.) As he was obliged to explain to his lecture audience, the interview degenerated into yet another assault. He was given hospital treatment and flew to Scotland later in the morning, to appear at the Radio Festival swathed in bandages and unable to bend down to perform the simple but necessary task of picking up the notes that he dropped, halfway through the proceedings. Here is the lecture, lightly edited, dealing with the difficult concept of the programme's ethics. How the lecture audience reacted to the visual proof that ethics play a vital part in *Checkpoint* must be left to the imagination!

Checkpoint is sometimes outrageous. It makes, or is a vehicle for, accusations that range from statements that someone is lying to those that allege serious crime. How far can we go in this respect? The simple answer is: as far as the law and physical or ethical considerations will let you. On the purely factual front, we go as far as the degree of proof will allow. By and large we look for the same standard of evidence that would justify our story in a court of law. We rely heavily on detailed and painstaking research, on closely cross-checking details. Such work can, on occasion, lead us to reject a story. More usually, after having collected our evidence on tape and in documentary form, we have to distinguish between what is and what is not permissible in law. For example, the Rehabilitation of Offenders Act may preclude reference to a prison sentence that is both factual and relevant. There are also the considerations of what is or is not *sub-judice*, and we sometimes must decide if a writ issued against the programme is an attempt to shut us up, a 'poor man's injunction' that will never be proceeded with.

As far as physical considerations are concerned, if the person we're after has a record of violence (and they often do), is an interview worth the risk? I take the view that, in the light of the circumstances in which these confrontations take place, it is. *Checkpoint* may be the closest thing to redress that our complainants ever get. I don't expect to be attacked. I'm no braver than the next man, and if I *knew* that I'd be at the wrong end of an iron bar I wouldn't go. I just hope for the best.

But the question that exercises us most is the ethical one. If we are accusing companies or individuals of malpractice, then we are obliged to treat the accused fairly. But it's not just the accused whose fair treatment must be considered; so must that of the complainants. Sometimes they have to tell us very moving and disturbing stories of loss, injury or death, and a programme such as ours runs the risk of being accused of parading people's misfortunes and misery before millions of listeners, just for the sake of a good story. Would that be a fair accusation? Well, though we might object to the word 'parading', it is our job to broadcast good stories, stories that some might find obtrusive. But we don't do this *just* for the sake of the story; nor do we see ourselves as staging trials by radio. Our objectives are often to get redress for someone, or to illustrate how a system fails to provide redress. Sometimes we aim to help people by putting a stop to a rogue company's business or by warning, through a kind of parable, others who might suffer as those on the programme have done. We have other aims (and I hope we don't sound self-righteous) of public benefit, such as examining a proposed law and, maybe trying to effect a change. (See Case 10, Stan French)

An important ethical point is that complainants come on our programme *voluntarily*. It would be wrong to force or trick people into telling their stories. And, as I have indicated, we do not hold people up to ridicule by letting them tell how they were deceived or tricked in ways that might make them sound stupid or by letting them reveal details of their lives that might be very private. We don't think they are ever ridiculed. *Anybody* can be tricked or fall into misfortune, however simple, however sophisticated or intelligent they are. We tell the story on *Checkpoint*; with all the benefit of hindsight, it might *seem* that people were stupid to have been caught. But at the time some of them *were* caught, I would defy anybody to have been clever enough to have spotted what was going on. People are not getting more gullible: the 'con' tricks are getting more sophisticated.

Are there some tales of misery or woe that should not be told or investigated? Is there a limit there? Questions of taste will always apply, of course, to how a story is treated, but as far as we are concerned there is no limit here. If something fraudulent, criminal or unfair is being done to the public, why should it not be told? If a person is willing to reveal even the most private details of a wrong they have suffered, and of the consequences this has had, why should they not be allowed to describe it in their own way – as long as there is evidence to support them and as long as they do not exceed that evidence?

The person should not be humiliated in the way they are asked to tell their story. They must be allowed to choose the way they want to tell it, with all the help, coaching and support they need from us. We feel that such help is permissible; furthermore, we try to keep in touch with witnesses after the broadcast, to give them support and sometimes to receive support from them. When we started *Checkpoint*, the BBC didn't agree on this point, but that was a while ago!

These days, as our cases become increasingly complicated, we often know more about a complainant's problem than he or she does. And on matters of legal fact, we sometimes find ourselves briefing victims on their own stories. What we choose to let them say *on the air* is subject to a simple test: does it allow us to expose and possibly stop someone doing wrong; does it show how a government policy or law or any aspect of the legal system fails to meet the objectives set for it; and so on?

In addition, we meet cases in which redress might not be possible, where the lessons to others might be minimal, yet where the mere telling of a story can bring relief to someone who has had no help from those responsible for giving it.

We are sometimes asked if we should not restrict ourselves to matters that cannot be put right by the police, through the courts, or by some other statutory method. The answer is: definitely not! Even if such organisations could stop all malefactors or always gain redress, the telling of the story to the public has a good effect as well: we hold the view that people have the right to know what is going on in their society, and telling them is part of our job.

But what of things that can't be put right by the police or the courts, etc? It's hard to categorise them, because all things can *theoretically* be put right, through the courts if there is a civil wrong or stopped by the police if it is a criminal matter. But that doesn't mean that it *will* be put right. The police are too busy, or they may not realise what is going on. Maybe a person can't afford to go to a solicitor and doesn't qualify for legal aid. Maybe a solicitor doesn't press the case. Perhaps there happens to be a genuine miscarriage of justice that should in theory be caught by, say, the ombudsman. . . . So, although in principle many of the cases we broadcast stand a chance of being put right officially or judicially, we can't stop dealing with them.

It's a different matter, of course, with what *has* been dealt with officially. If a person has already won a court case, or if the police have successfully prosecuted a wrongdoer, from a journalist's point of view there will probably be better cases to deal with. And here I am talking about malpractices, frauds, or unfairnesses on which the police or courts can act. There is also that batch of stories which are precisely *about* the failings or the wrongdoings of the police, the lawyers or the courts.

A key question in determining how far we can go in all this is: what can we fairly say and do about someone who is accused?

I talked before about ethical limits. Our ethics are basically journalistic ethics; that is, being fair in what we publicly disseminate about a person and being fair in the means by which we unearth information or give a person the chance to reply to accusations. But should we be doing our sort of programme at all? Is it 'trial by the media'? Have we already gone further, ethically, than we should go? While our ethical considerations are those of journalists, we meet ethical problems such as these in their sharpest form. We say things that defame, things that can put people out of business, and so on. So we must be even more careful with our facts and even more scrupulous about fairness than is usual in our profession. But having to be fair does not lead to the conclusion that we should not do our sort of programme at all, just that we must be more alert in this matter. And we are approaching here a fundamental principle.

There are those who argue that people like us have no right to broadcast as we do. They refer to the point I have already raised and say, 'After all, there are police to catch criminals and courts to try them properly. There are solicitors to handle things and civil courts to arbitrate in non-criminal matters'. In practice, this argument does not stand up to scrutiny, because, as I have said, the system is fallible. Some wrongs fail to receive police attention, however hard people might press their problems. Some people may not be able to afford a civil remedy in the courts. And even if they get a court judgement, they may still fail to receive the money due, for example. *Checkpoint*, like other media, is a possible form of redress.

On a number of occasions, people whom we have examined have subsequently been brought to book by the police and courts, sometimes only because they *were* examined on *Checkpoint* with the result that the officials concerned got themselves moving. In addition to this point, if our investigation does harm an accused person, is this not justified in the light of what that person himself has done? If he sets out to harm the public, does he not deserve a public come-uppance?

The real issue, it seems to me, is this: Given that the media have the right to accuse people of malpractice or of crimes, how fair is the method used to do this? Investigative programmes or articles must not be or seem to be kangaroo courts. On *Checkpoint* we make accusations and give the right of reply, but we must not set ourselves up as judges. If we seem to, it is only to the extent that we regard as wrongs what other people regard as wrongs. We act on behalf of those who, faced with the clear facts would say, 'That's not on!'.

The word 'fair' crops up a great deal in our considerations, and how 'fair' is 'fair' depends on the circumstances of each case. But there are guidelines. It is obviously unfair to accuse someone falsely, even assuming that the accusations are accepted by us in good faith. If they are not, the person concerned can always sue, which is an important check on what we do. Secondly, the accused person must always have the right to reply and to know in advance to what they are replying. Thirdly, others besides the person accused should not be harmed; for example, a wife or any children, except to the extent that their reliance on a livelihood that is criminal or unfair is curtailed. Fourthly, the privacy of the accused should not be unjustifiably invaded. What is justified here takes us to the question of what is fair in seeking replies from accused people *who don't want* to give replies to legitimate questions.

People we accuse frequently don't want to reply. Sometimes they are simply guilty and have no reply to make. Sometimes they turn away because they have been caught out. Sometimes they have already run away before we try to trace them. Whatever the circumstance, when we first manage to communicate with them we explain why it is in their own interest to give a reply. Some realise, too late, after a programme that it would have been better to say something in their own defence. But what if, despite our best efforts, they still refuse to reply to questions? Is it fair to broadcast the accusations?

We think that it can be, and our view is based broadly on the same reasoning that maintains that a court case can sometimes proceed in the absence of the accused: it is in the public interest to do so. In any case, it boils down to the facts: we can't do without them, but we can sometimes do without the accused. More to the point, if the rule is that we cannot broadcast when an accused person refuses to reply to our questions, then all he has to do to avoid exposure is to keep quiet, and stories that should be told for the public good would not be told.

Which is more important: the rights of the public or the rights of the accused? The rights of the accused, although indeed important, can, in our view, become less important the graver are his wrongs.

Another problem arises here: in such a case should we reveal wrongs without identifying the perpetrator? Usually such a course would be impossible in the sort of wrongs we uncover. What we are exposing is what an individual or company is 'up to'. What use is an anonymous warning? Besides, if we don't identify them clearly others who are innocent might be defamed because listeners wrongly think we're talking about them.

To summarise this important aspect of our work: we will broadcast without a villain's contribution, but we try very, very hard to get him or her to speak. We telephone, we write, we arrange interviews, only to have the arrangements broken, and as a last resort we 'doorstep'. The chances are that his business success depends on avoiding people, whether they be his customers or journalists, so how right would it be to abandon a broadcast or not seek answers to questions, just because the villain carries on being evasive? We will take whatever steps are necessary to give him the opportunity to make a defence and to give ourselves the opportunity to put questions that are important. But unless the matter is unusually serious we do not believe it is fair to pester a villain daily week after week. One or two attempts are as far as we normally like to go.

When we eventually meet the accused, microphone in hand, we tell him immediately that he is being recorded, and why. If he resorts to violence we do our best to protect self and equipment and make the most dignified exit possible. It is not our way to fight back, either physically or verbally: that would reduce us to his level. *Checkpoint* is not concerned with 'bear baiting'. Furthermore, the job of making accusations and trying to get answers and, if possible, redress does not give us the right to assume the powers of the Customs officer or the methods of the spy. Trying to get an answer is a matter of asking our questions courteously. How he responds is up to him, and it is usually at this stage that he shows his true colours, with no prompting or hectoring from us.

Finally, we try never to forget that the accused may have his own problems, too. It would be going too far to make a fool of somebody, or humiliate them, if they have perpetrated wrongs without being a fully responsible person.

As a general rule, it's not really a case of how far we can go, but *mind* how we go.

CHAPTER 7

Story development and investigation techniques

For the first few years of operation, *Checkpoint* stories came from a wide variety of sources, 'gleaned' by Cook from his contacts and colleagues within and outside the BBC, with the occasional lead supplied by a listener.

'But never did we follow up a major story in a newspaper,' Cook insists. 'We took the line that we ought to make the news.'

On the other hand, stories were sometimes sparked off by an apparently straightforward item in the Press, and this is how the first *Checkpoint* story was unearthed, triggered by a short paragraph saying that people's eyesight in the UK was getting worse. Cook contacted a friend who was working in Moorfields Eye Hospital and asked if this was the case, perhaps due to an industrial hazard. The friend pointed out the glaring difference between the results of eye tests at the hospital and those done by High Street opticians. In short, anyone visiting an optician was much more likely to be told that he or she needed expensive glasses than if they took exactly the same test at Moorfields.

'I thought that was very interesting,' Cook recalls. The result of his interest was a sparkling start to the new programme and the first of many unsuccessful writs.

Sometimes a story lead came totally out of the blue: 'When Ian Breach was reporting for us he happened to be reading two annual reports. One was for a credit card company who said they had received 2,100,000 cards from the manufacturer. The other was from that manufacturer saying they had shipped 2,150,000 to the credit card company. A discrepancy of 50,000 cards! As far as anyone can make out, a number of cases quite literally slipped off the back of a delivery lorry, to be picked up by a sharp operator who realised the potential. Not long afterwards, you could buy one of these unsigned cards for £50 in Oxford Street.'

A bonus for the *Checkpoint* team is that nowadays the people who write to them have a reasonably clear idea of what the programme is all about. Many of them will include not just the factor that is bothering them, but also the information that 'something like this seems to be going on in such-and-such a place'. The programme's files are now extensive, and such a letter can ensure that a number of previously recorded incidents are made into a coherent pattern.

Once a promising lead appears, the next step involves checking with anybody who might be able to throw more light on the subject. For example, if a complaint comes in about a firm offering double glazing or cavity insulation, the researchers will contact Trading Standards officers, local newspapers or local building contractors – anyone who might have heard of the firm concerned. Quite often, more complaints emerge during this process which, Cook explains, is not merely a matter of digging around to see what is there. It is part of a planned and logical process, and if nothing is discovered to turn a single complaint into a general story the chances are that it won't be broadcast.

Before the 1981 Companies Act, the team could turn with a reasonable degree of confidence to Companies House for details of people who had set up a private company or those who had registered a business name. The new legislation will make this increasingly difficult, as there are now fewer requirements for this to be done and virtually no checks on whether anyone has conformed to the more relaxed requirements. Cook covered this important topic in the third *Checkpoint* of 1981 (see Case 17) and the result was that a number of people and organisations questioned the detailed clauses of the new Act.

This particular edition was conceived and completed by the team 'working in hyperspace', because the planned programme had been jettisoned for legal reasons the night before it was due to be recorded in the studio. (Scarce resources and the need for topicality militate against there being a programme 'in the can' for broadcasting in such a circumstance, so heads come together with thinking caps on.) The idea was bruited that, as the team know a great deal about company law, this topic might make a good standby programme.

'I hope we aren't arrogant about things like this,' Cook said, 'but there can't be many people around who have the experience of "bent" companies that we have. We thought we'd be able to conjure up a good, solid story quite quickly *and* say something about the ways in which companies operate in the UK. We phoned the Department of Trade and Industry and asked them if we could talk to someone authoritative about company law. At this stage we were aware that the Companies Act was due to be discussed by the authorities, but when we spoke to the Press officer he rather surprised us by saying, "You'll be coming to our Press conference, of course."

'Amazingly, they had not told the very people in journalism with the most experience about their conference. Regardless of this hiccough in the scheme of things, the story fell into our lap, because the Bill was published that day.'

It is a matter of pride to the *Checkpoint* team that, whatever hysteria might prevail in the office to get a programme on the air, the transmission remains cool and, indeed, impersonal. Their main aim is to let people tell their own story, be they complainant or villain, without exaggeration, with a minimum of editorialising, with courtesy and with politeness. One of the stories dealt with a man who was making and selling a range of motor caravans that were technically dangerous. He had taken a lot of money from people by the time Cook interviewed him. After the item was broadcast, Cook received a memorandum from within the BBC chastising him for raising his voice during the interview.

'What they didn't know,' he said, 'was that halfway through the interview the gentleman concerned produced a panel-beater's "dolly" – a large horse-shoe-shaped piece of metal weighing many pounds – that he held over his head in what even an impartial observer would describe as a threatening manner. At that stage the tone of my voice did indeed change somewhat. It went up an octave or two.'

The *Checkpoint* team has a good deal of contact with two important organisations outside the BBC that are themselves concerned with many of the items covered by the programme: the police and the Office of Fair Trading. The aim is to strike a balance in what can be a sensitive situation.

'Some of our complaints come from people who believe that these and other organisations have not properly looked after their interests,' Cook says. 'I believe that over the years we have established sensible relationships, and we often find that there is a mutual benefit to be gained by a degree of cooperation. But at no time do we behave in such a way that our editorial independence or our informants are compromised.'

Research

Since its first broadcast, *Checkpoint* has been based on impeccable research which, as Walter Wallich pointed out, has helped to make the programme 'fire-proof' against legal actions.

Research has a meaning for journalists that is different to that applied to academicians. It means digging out information, then checking. And then double-checking. If necessary, triple-checking. *Checkpoint* is based on this principle, but the practice of it has been developed by the team, with successive researchers, since 1973. In the early years, Cook did much of his own research. Now he is able to devote most of his time to recording and editing tape, and of course, to writing the script. That doesn't mean that he can't still be found on the end of a telephone or buried in a pile of documents when the occasion demands it. There is, of course, no such creature as a 'typical' researcher. They come from a variety of backgrounds and with a variety of qualifications. As the programme entered its tenth year, senior researcher and co-producer was David Perrin (who subsequently left to join Thames Television). Perrin graduated in philosophy from York University and went to Oxford for post-graduate studies in that subject. He began his career as a debentured journalist for the *Harrow Observer* in 1963, and after graduating he joined the *Oxford Mail* as a general reporter.

In 1974 he travelled to New Zealand where he worked in Wellington on radio programmes such as *Viewpoint*, a magazine programme. In 1978 he moved back to London and joined the BBC, and then the *Checkpoint* team in August of that year.

Perrin explained that the process of turning a letter from a complainant into a programme follows a well-proven path. The answers are sought to several questions: Is the letter true? What else is there to the story? Have other people previously complained about the same thing? Has the complainant tried all possible avenues of redress before writing to *Checkpoint*? Will he or she talk to the team and record their stories? Can the other side be contacted and also persuaded to talk?

After this, and after all the checking is done, arrangements are made for the reporter to visit and record interviews. At the same time, the final shape of the edition is considered, while the researchers carry on their checking to establish complete accuracy of allegations and facts relating to the story.

'At this stage it's important to get every salient point into the edition, to ensure we don't leave anything out that materially affects the issue, and to keep everything in context,' said Perrin. 'And while we're asking ourselves, "Will this be believable on the air?" we're also checking such things as possible court appearances or any other changing circumstance. And always: Is it of public interest, and is it entertaining?'

As far as the techniques of research are concerned, the team will approach any individual, firm or organisation whom they imagine, believe or know has information that is relevant, making no distinctions between the chairman of a State industry, a bent antiques dealer, or a little old lady from Macclesfield. All are dealt with courteously and firmly, and the first task is to find other people who have suffered a similar experience to the first complainant. This can be done in several ways.

'You can discover a great deal from a simple telephone number and a conversation with the switchboard,' Perrin explained, 'and an accommodation address, chosen to hide a trail, can still be a source of useful information. We may get a lead on a former business of our villain, for example, and this can lead to more complainants. If we unearth an address, we visit the neighbours. We contact firms that are in competition with the person or firm we're investigating or that supply goods and services to them. Then we contact various trade debtor agencies, County and other Court records, bankruptcy registers, Companies House and the Register of Business Names, the Office of Fair Trading (where they may have records of complaints and possibly of an undertaking a person may have given to trade properly). It can all add up to a substantial amount of information on what may turn out to be a dubious man or enterprise.'

It's a path down which the journey is painstaking rather than exciting, but there have been moments of high drama and revelation, often when two or more separate lines of work converge and point towards the same miscreant.

'We were looking into a kitchen and hotel cleaning franchise,' said Perrin, 'and this led us into a whole bedlam of activities run by one man. It started out with a number of allegations of non-payment of bills. Some of the complainants recollected that the gentleman concerned had boasted that he owned a night club and a travel agency in the Hitchin area. One remembered him pointing at a certain street and another that he sported an ashtray on his desk from the Association of British Travel Agents (ABTA). Someone else thought that the night club might be in a certain road. We checked the phone book and called the one likely number. A man answered and said he knew about the person we were looking for, and he added to the list of dodgy activities by mentioning a central heating company and a brewery. We were put onto a firm of estate agents, and they also knew the man: he had never settled their bill. They recalled he ran a catering company and that his son's school had used it for one of their functions. The school said that they'd had to call on this gentleman several times to collect money he had taken at the entrance to the function.

'Finally, one of the people we talked to told us that the man had owned a string of limited companies that had gone bust in turn, and we figured the time was ripe for him to be setting up another one. Then one of our listeners contacted us with information about an advertisement with a Box Number that seemed to be the same kind of business as the previous ones that had "failed". When we checked into the company we found that it was indeed the same man who was behind it, and we managed to get an interview with his new partner about the business.'

In another investigation, into a private security firm called Security Task Force (broadcast on 21 January 1981), one complainant led to another, and another, until the team had four good leads, an example of the 'cascade' process. In all this there is a distinct absence of any 'modern' information handling. No computers or micro-fiche data storage in Room 7073! The researchers have access, of course, to the BBC's own extensive news library or to any of the others run by national newspapers. They could, if they wanted, make use of international switching networks and linked data bases, but they never have need of such methods. The most sophisticated information devices in the office are the UK telephone books. The point is that their work takes them into areas that are totally novel, so it is most unlikely that they would unearth anything of value in other publications, for example.

David Perrin sees *Checkpoint* as an evolving programme that has set a number of important precedents. In particular, by persistent and accurate research it has proved to the BBC and others that names can be named and that reporters can stand up to senior people, certainly with politeness, but with the determination not to be swayed or put off by the trappings of that seniority or specious threats, and this in an environment far removed from the Greek Street home of Pressdram or the sometimes less scrupulous byways of Fleet Street.

'When the *Checkpoint* researcher digs into a story,' he says, 'he or she is dealing with people who want to keep secrets. But persistent enquiries will unearth a great deal of information from other sources, so that the interviewer can approach his subject with enough confidence to do a very "hard" interview. The programme is concerned with adversary journalism, and it will go ahead in the public interest even if the other side refuses to co-operate.'

Perrin believes that *Checkpoint* has proved vital over the years in dealing with stories that had never been covered before, particularly in the area known as Twilight Trading, where people operate on the fringe of the law and libel actions are always around the corner. And above all, the programme team is prepared to believe the 'small person' who can't win his case by orthodox means.

'*Checkpoint* will take on the Establishment, because the team is not prepared to swallow reasons from governments or large organisations without checking them out. They'll question the way the law is operating or how a council works, and if necessary they'll challenge the system.'

Throughout this process of research, checking and eventual interview, Perrin says that an abiding principle is never to lose sight of the fact that the cases involve people. Thus *Checkpoint* will take on stories that from a Fleet Street point of view would be utterly unnewsworthy. In his four years on the programme Perrin earmarked a number of topics he feels will provide a continuing fund of injustices and unfairnesses of the kind central to *Checkpoint* investigations. He cites banks, government departments, auditors, solicitors and architects . . . inpenetrable, secret, powerful . . .

'We have complaints against judges, commodity brokers, registrars, the police and MPs who don't pursue a case for political reasons,' he said. 'We try to check them out, only to find that things don't add up, or we can't penetrate the defensive wall. But even though we have this difficulty, we can still break through, maybe by making the two-hundredth phone call three hours after we should have been home for dinner.'

CHAPTER 8

Recording the interviews

"I didn't realise the new 'Checkpoint' series had started, Mr. Cook."

Once the researcher has finished his or her brief and contacted all the witnesses, it's time for the interview. The ideal arrangement (although not always in terms of sound quality) is for the interviewee and the interviewer to meet on the former's home territory. This usually leads to a more relaxed and natural result. Next best is for the interviewee to come to a BBC studio, once again to meet the interviewer face to face. This studio can be 'self-operated', with the recording equipment and microphones all in one room, or it can be the more usual manned studio. Here the recording equipment is operated by a studio manager (the 'SM') from an adjacent cubicle. It is part of the SM's job to adjust the recording levels to the required standard and to balance the 'level' or volume of each person speaking. In the self-operated studio this is done automatically. *Checkpoint* operates throughout a wide area, and this means that a third method of recording is sometimes necessary. This involves the interviewee going to a remote studio in a BBC building linked by a special British Telecom line to Broadcasting House.

Interviewer and interviewee hear each other through headphones, and the recording quality is the same as that of a single studio interview. However, this 'artificial meeting' is least likely to achieve best results. In the case of *Checkpoint*, many people begin with the disadvantage of having to admit publicly that they have been deceived or have made fools of themselves. People often find the experience of an interview nerve-wracking, and the first thing an interviewer must do is put them at their ease.

Once the interview is ready, the story must be checked through with the witness before the recording can take place. This is an important step, because on occasion an interviewee will have only a vague idea of what exactly has happened until it is explained. *Checkpoint* witnesses are coached and encouraged to speak naturally rather than supply the answers to a lot of questions. Their broadcast contributions to the programme contain no interruptions from the interviewer, and this helps to make it more 'their' programme and obviates accusations that they are guided down a biased route through leading questions. Sometimes many 'takes' are necessary before the interview acquires the accuracy and naturalness for which *Checkpoint* strives. According to Cook it took some time initially for the BBC to accept this principle of 'fairness through coaching'. But now the logic is accepted that inexperienced contributors, uncoached, usually do themselves and their cases less than justice, whereas, say, the chairman of a large company may well have been on a number of the expensive courses available on 'how to deal with the media'.

Similar care is taken whenever possible during 'villain' interviews. If the villain is non-violent the interviewer may make several takes so that the finished interview presents the villain's case as fairly as possible. Each major allegation must be put clearly, and his response clearly heard. Regular listeners will be aware that not all *Checkpoint* villains are willing to respond this way, of course. In any case the programme protects itself against accusations of unfair or biased editing by keeping an uncut 'guard copy' of the interview.

So in practice a *Checkpoint* interview takes place where possible on location. An additional benefit in this is that the local atmosphere can give the listener a feeling of 'being there'. Of course, background noise can sometimes be obtrusive. This calls either for a 'close mike' approach or for the separate recording of a sound effects track that can be dubbed under the interview later, after it has been edited. Loud background noises make the latter approach difficult, and microphone technique is always critical. It will vary with the subject, the location and the type of microphone. A strongly directional microphone used close up, for example, can sometimes reduce unwanted background noise to a barely discernable minimum.

Outside recording requires a portable tape recorder. Standard issue for BBC Radio is a German machine called a Uher 4000 Report. This is the size of a shoe box and weighs about twelve pounds. It uses five-inch reels of standard quarter-inch magnetic tape. When handled properly, these Uhers deliver recordings of broadcast quality, far better than recordings produced by, say, a cassette player. *Checkpoint*, however, prefers the Swiss-made Nagra E recorder. Although this is slightly heavier and larger than the Uher, it is capable of producing much better quality and of using larger reels of tape to give longer recording times. The Nagra E is generally used with a good quality omnidirectional microphone. Sometimes a special microphone is used; for example, a lapel mike or the so-called gun mike, capable of picking up sound over a considerable distance.

Cook often uses another kind of Nagra, the miniature SN. This is the size of two cigarette packets and weighs barely two pounds. Its great advantage is manoeuverability in the kind of difficult situations that can arise during a 'villain' interview. The full-size machine can not only be a dangerous encumbrance but is also a target. Many is the villain, says Cook, who has attempted to destroy the evidence by destroying the recorder. Like its larger brothers, the Nagra SN produces high-quality recordings, but it uses a special tape. The recording must therefore be transferred to standard tape before editing can take place.

Editing is done for both technical and editorial reasons. Dealing with the technical point of view first, we start with the quarter inch magnetic tape on which interviews are recorded. As the tape passes over the recording head of the tape recorder the tiny particles that make up the coating are magnetised in a pattern that corresponds to the sound waves picked up by the microphone. When the tape is rewound and passed over the playback head, the magnetic 'message' is detected, amplified and turned back into recognisable sound in the loudspeakers or earphones.

Part of the recording process almost inevitably introduces unwanted noises, such as clicks, rumbles from the microphone cable, the buffeting of wind during outside recordings, telephones ringing or the hum of an air-conditioning system. Many of these can either be physically cut out of the tape or electronically filtered out as one tape is dubbed or re-recorded onto another.

There are various ways of editing tape for editorial reasons, ranging from the relatively crude linking together of untouched recordings to really sophisticated electronic manipulation of the recorded material. In *Checkpoint*, as with most BBC news and current affairs programmes, tape editing involves physically cutting the tape with a razor blade to remove or insert material. The points at which cuts are to be made are carefully marked on the tape against the machine replay head with a chinagraph pencil. An angled cut is made in the tape at these points using a metal editing block, a kind of template that keeps the tape in place. The cut tapes are rejoined as appropriate using a self-adhesive editing tape.

Editing for *Checkpoint* involves several stages. In the first, a relatively crude selection of material is made, perhaps from a number of takes. What each contributor will say in the finished programme is assembled in rough order. Each band or 'insert' of tape is then assembled in the order in which it will appear on a master insert tape. This tape is then 'fine edited'. Repetitions and verbal stumbles are removed and mistakes corrected. A good deal of broadcasting time and listener annoyance can be saved by getting rid of this extraneous material. The entire editing process can involve hundreds of physical cuts in the tape and helps to reduce what may have started as three or four hours of tape closer to the eighteen minutes normally required for the twenty-five minute programme.

Checkpoint contributors usually get more time 'on the air' than contributors on other programmes of similar length. It has always been policy to keep the presenter's own involvement (which is scripted and linked into the contributor's tapes in the studio) to a minimum. Stories told by the people involved are almost always more interesting to hear, and the main purpose of the presenter's script is to provide a framework for the programme, to link and to introduce each piece of edited tape or insert. *Checkpoint* often has up to twenty such inserts and links. 'Keeping the script in between both concise and uncomplicated can be a mind-bending process', says Cook, 'especially when the stories are often anything but simple.'

A major problem during the programme-making process is to decide which part of a witness's story is most relevant and which is told best. Something near to the contributor's heart may not give much to the programme. Some aspect of the matters that have been aggravating him over the years may not be germane to his story. Sometimes what he says may not be legally correct and must be paraphrased in the script. In most cases *Checkpoint* can give only an outline of a complex story, but each major aspect must be fairly and accurately presented. Paraphrasing may also be necessary to ensure that the programme fits into its allotted time, although every effort is made to minimise the effect of programme duration and programme deadlines.

Editing in an information-intensive programme such as *Checkpoint* is, of course, essential. But it is never done in such a way as to exclude colour and feeling. However, even the villain can benefit from the tidying-up process accorded every taped insert in the finished programme: a point more succinctly made is a point more easily followed, especially in broadcasting when there is no opportunity to re-read part of an item that may be unclear.

There are other constraints in tape editing that to the layman or even the newspaper journalist would go unnoticed. Some desired edits may be impossible to make because of sudden background noise. Or maybe a speaker's intonation is such that an editing cut would be ludicrously obvious. For example, imagine that Mr Innocent tells the *Checkpoint* reporter about a cheque he had been given by Mr Villain that bounced. The interviewee might say:

'Well . . . er . . . I sent this cheque to, er, my bank, and . . . er . . . well . . . it came back marked Refer to Drawer.'

The newspaper journalist would have no problem with this. It would appear in print as: 'I sent Mr Villain's cheque to my bank, and it bounced,' complained Mr Innocent.' Note that in addition to removing extraneous sounds he has legitimately paraphrased the statement to make quite clear what had happened.

The radio reporter cannot normally do this.[1] He has a strip of recording tape on which there are some sounds that do not add to the story and, worse, take up valuable air time. Fortunately for the listener, he can physically remove most of them by cutting them out with his razor blade at the (⋆) marks as shown in the following paragraph (although he is usually much more limited by his 'raw material' than a journalist in the printed media).

[1] It is possible, with sophisticated equipment and techniques, to edit a recording so as to make an interviewee say almost anything, provided the editor has enough material on tape to work with. It is also true to say that an experienced editor can do the most extraordinary things with his simple razor blade and splicing tape.

'(★)Well . . . er . . . (★) I sent this cheque to (★) er, (★)my bank, and (★). . . er . . . well . . . (★) it came back marked Refer to Drawer.'

After cutting the underlined sections are removed and the tape rejoined with two splices as shown. This leaves the editor with: 'I sent this cheque to (★)my bank, and (★)it came back marked Refer to Drawer.'

It looks simple on paper. In practice, the editor has to judge to a fraction of a millimetre where to make his cuts, otherwise the interviewee's statement will sound dreadful. It is at this point that much of the tape editor's skill is applied, because he must make a decision that is based on experience. It is almost impossible to indicate to someone else how they should make an edit, and even the most experienced editor sometimes has to attempt a difficult edit several times. He checks the edit by playing it back, and if he is satisfied he continues the process throughout the tape.

'The secret of good editing,' Cook says, 'is to do it fairly and accurately and, above all, to make the finished tape sound as if it hasn't been edited at all!'

CHAPTER 9

The scope of *Checkpoint* stories

During its ten years of transmission, *Checkpoint* has covered a huge variety of stories, from the shattering but unnecessary personal tragedy of a real-life *Cathy Come Home*, through a number of multi-million pound frauds, to a programme about the plight of kidney patients. This latter episode, evocatively entitled 'Selected to Die', was credited with persuading the Chancellor of the Exchequeur to allocate an additional £80 million for much-needed kidney machines. No one planned any of these stories to fall into specific categories, but Cook points out that there seem to be eight main recurring groups: business empires; medicine and health; finance; the law; bankruptcies and liquidations; business opportunities; property problems at home and overseas; public and private transport; and bureaucratic bungling. There are also stories that cannot be categorised, which he labels 'oddities'.

'One of the things that has interested us most over the years, because it gives us a considerable challenge, is the Big Business transaction,' says Cook. 'We have dealt with a number of business empires, some of them quite extraordinary, and some discovered in odd, unusual ways. An outstanding example was an enterprise set up and run from Lymington in Hampshire, by a man called Peter Victor George Newton and his son Richard, and this particular story was brought to our attention by Dennis Woodman who was having trouble getting money out of a company called Camargue Motors. This was one of Richard Newton's companies. The money was for rented space where cars were to be stored and where a lot of papers and documents were also stored.'

It became evident to Woodman from enquiries that he had made in the area that he was not the only person who was owed money, and Camargue Motors was certainly not the only company involved. This is an excellent example of how a story can grow from a seemingly small incident, to reveal a huge network of activities. (See Case 1)

Another business empire investigated by *Checkpoint* that has since collapsed was run from a number of addresses by two families called Randal and Sumner. They also went by such names as Green, Grey and Brown. This group specialised in mail order for hair loss treatments, business schemes, jobs in the States, working holidays abroad and other attractive opportunities . . . They offered extremely varied goods and services, but the *modus operandum* was the same in each case: they would take the money sent by respondents to their advertising and not deliver what they had advertised. Their speciality was to take only small amounts of money so that it wasn't worthwhile for any individual to complain, but to do it on a very large scale. But there are always people for whom the loss of even a relatively small sum of money, coupled with the feeling of being let down over an attractive opportunity, is too much to bear. (See Case 2)

One of the stories jointly investigated by *Checkpoint* and BBC television's *Nationwide* programme was run by Raymond Hill, a one-time tobacco salesman turned business tycoon and property speculator.

'This is an example of how we follow ourselves up,' said Cook. 'We'd picked Hill up on one aspect of his activities as part of another programme that covered the way he dealt with employees and former employees, summarily dismissing people, and refusing to give them holiday pay and other entitlements. Following the first programme, we received more material and were able to go into his business empire, which was mainly in the property development field. At the time we estimated that he'd cost people about £1 million, but subsequently learned that this was an underestimate. In addition, he caused untold misery.' (See Case 3) After the first of these programmes, Cook's car was attacked with paint stripper, and after the second it was 'hot wired' by someone and burst into flames as he was driving ('Not that any connection can be proved!').

One of the most spectacular businesses in terms of gall if not size was run by a man called Harris. The hub of his group of companies was an office above an off-licence in North London. He'd managed in the five months before his eventual disappearance to mount a national advertising campaign for a firm called Premier Glass, a 'division' of Premier Engineering, offering new windows, doors and double glazing. Then he rolled that over into another company that he called Tudor Stone, a 'division' of Tudor Stone & Cladding. Like Premier Glass, this was allegedly owned by Peter Harris, according to the papers he produced for people, but no details were registered in Companies House.

His extensive advertising netted tens of thousands of pounds in deposits, when the companies simply did not exist. Harris surrounded himself with misleading information, such as an accommodation address in Kingston that had never heard of him, so that any queries petered out into thin air.

'The police don't normally give us interviews,' Cook explained, 'but they were looking for Harris as hard as we were, and in this case they agreed to see us, because they were amazed at the way Harris managed to cover his tracks. They couldn't find any trace of him at all. He's the one who got away, although the businesses we reported on ceased to operate.'

Home improvements

Harris was active in one of the worst areas for conning people: home improvements, such as wall coatings, cavity insulation, double glazing, central heating and loft conversions. In one of these companies alone the extent of the indebtedness ran into millions of pounds. None of the guarantees could be met, and the product had been sold all over the country.

All the companies investigated by *Checkpoint* made a number of false claims; for example, that they had painted the Dounray atomic reactor or the Forth Bridge . . . absolutely untrue, but, according to Cook, the more outrageous the claim the more likely it is that the intended victim would think, 'Surely they wouldn't say that if it weren't true?'

'This is something we notice quite often,' he says.

A common trick in these businesses is that the sales people say they will turn the customer's house into a show house and give him a discount (which is, in fact, non-existent) if he will let others come to see the work. People have often been encouraged to buy a poor product in this way. A relatively short time after the treatment, a sub-standard wall covering, for example, might peel off, or the preparation for the treatment might be inadequate, with the same result.

Many of the problems arose through the financing. A customer would be put in touch with a finance company (usually specialising in the business concerned and having very high rates of interest) and end up having to continue paying even after the work done had collapsed.

'There was a company called Setonic Ltd and another called G. H. Coatings that had done particularly awful jobs,' Cook recalls. 'They had addresses in Barnsley and Leeds, and people got absolutely nowhere, even after taking out County Court judgements. The man behind all this was Harry Hepworth. We tried five times to get hold of him, without success, but as a result of one programme we had a roll-over effect, and people began to write to us about other things that Hepworth might have been involved in. A nation-wide hairdressing school, for example, in which his people would teach you how to cut and tint. This was the Charles Baron School of Hairdressing, run out of the same address as the wall coating company. Pupils got next to nothing in return for their inflated fees, and many teachers were not paid their salaries.

'After having done a programme on this hair dressing project, that had cost a lot of people a lot of money, we received even more letters and did a complete programme on his many nefarious activities. The West Yorkshire police were keenly interested in him, at the time.

'There was a lot of internecine warfare between the people operating these companies. I remember a Michael Wiggins and John Penniston, both operating in the home improvement field. Penniston was running a company called Fleethead Ltd, and there was another associated company called, Roof Maintenance Services. Penniston alleged that Wiggins 'stole' the company and took it over. They did badly by their customers all the way through, and we came across about ten different names. This was another co-production with *Nationwide* on television, and we did a 'biblical' sequence . . . this company begat another that begat another, and so on . . .'

The programme has included a number of investigations into loft conversions. One company, Yorkhome, was run by a man who seemed to be not so much crooked as totally incompetent. He said he didn't answer letters because he didn't like getting them, and he didn't apply for planning permission because he knew very well what would stand up and what wouldn't.

'People had an awful lot of trouble with him,' said Cook. 'And that company is now out of business. And there was yet another company run on similar lines, long gone now, but with a name unfortunately like a reputable company – as it was deliberately meant to be – which did a loft conversion on a house facing the sea on the Dorset coast. It didn't seem to be very solidly built and creaked rather a lot when people went up to it, and the first day they had a storm the whole lot actually blew away. It was discovered that it was only held on the house by a few wire nails.'

Many of these companies that advertised to do work on your homes promised all kinds of services that they didn't deliver. They'd claim to have got planning permission and sorted out all the building regulations. A large number of them didn't. One, in particular, took a number of people for a ride, went into liquidation, and simply changed the name from Elite Loft Conversions to Elite Loft Conversions (Northern) and Elite Loft Conversions (Southern), trading with the same people from the same premises.

In the early and mid-1970s, a number of companies sprang up to supply plastic wall and roof coverings, treatments that were supposed to last for at least fifteen years and eliminate maintenance, leaking roofs and all house painting.

'A lot of cowboys got into this,' said Cook. 'Apart from the Harry Hepworth ventures, there was the Wall Coating Group of Companies, from Hartley Wintney in Hampshire. They went out of business, but their managing director boasted to me over the phone that he'd had more companies than I'd had hot dinners and said that at the last count he could remember fifty-three!

'We visited them with a camera crew at their HQ, a magnificent rented period office in Hartley Wintney. It had a great front door sporting one of those lion door knockers with a big ring through its mouth. I marched purposefully up to the door, picked up the knocker, and gave it a smart 'rap' . . . and the entire thing disintegrated in my hands and fell into two pieces. You have to remember that at such a time we're all pretty keyed up, because we're facing an interview that is the climax of a great deal of hard work. But one after the other we began to laugh, especially after the sound man made the obvious comment about having a wonderful pair of knockers there.'

Plumbing can eat up a sizeable chunk of the home budget, and Cook remembers the case of the brothers Hetmanski with a sense of amazement. They were operating plumbing companies in and around London in the late 1970s and early 1980s. In this case, several of the people who used to work for the Hetmanskis came forward to give information to the programme, having become extremely disillusioned with their bosses.

'As *Checkpoint* has developed we get more and more insiders coming to us,' Cook said. 'What often happens is that we research one story about somebody, and after it's broadcast we get people phoning or writing to say: "Did you know they were doing this, as well?" The interesting point is that it's not just people who have suffered as a result of malpractice who are prepared to do this. We are often able to link this extra information with facts that we already know but needed to follow up.'

The Hetmanskis ran their empire by setting up a number of false addresses, so anyone looking for them would end up running around in circles. Their real address was protected by a wired-glass door and entry phones, with no business identification of any kind.

This was another story with a violent ending. 'There wasn't much of an interview,' Cook recalled. 'A large ruckus . . ., and afterwards I was threatened and told I'd be killed if the programme went on the air. Having made that promise publicly, they're not in any position to get away with fulfilling it, so it's not really that frightening. If I did go missing, the finger points fairly obviously in one direction.' (See Case 4)

In the autumn of 1980, *Checkpoint* covered a series of complaints about 'home improvements' that turned into one of its most difficult assignments. This was in Belfast, Northern Ireland. At that time there had been a moderate reduction in terrorism, and though the evidence of destruction was still to be seen everywhere, the team discovered that in many of the scarred streets people were trying to improve their standards of living, with the aid of grants from the Housing Executive towards the cost, with life savings and with bank loans. Residents, Cook reported, seemed to have the confidence to extend and modernise their homes and bring them up to the standards most of us expect, on the 'other side of the water'.

'It was one of the most extraordinary investigations into building problems we had ever done,' said Cook, 'and it concerned a number of complaints from people living in the heart of Republican territory about a man called Sean Mallin, a man with alleged Republican para-military connections and a record of uttering forged cheques and stealing credit cards, who had been ripping off "his own" people in Belfast. He picked on those who were trying to give themselves decent homes, and his technique was brutally simple. He took substantial sums for starting work on a property, work that was never finished, with devastating results for his victims. For example, they would get approval for a grant, have the work started, pay Mallin a huge deposit out of their own money or with a bank loan, and then find that the grant wouldn't come through because the work wasn't finished. And of course he was concerned with other schemes for making money out of the community. Some ended up with debts of ten and twelve thousand pounds that they could never hope to pay, plus a house they could no longer live in.'

This man had changed the names of his operating companies several times, and, when it suited him, he used other people's names, without restriction. He would order goods in their name, and they would receive bills they knew nothing about. He sold company cars that did not belong to him. 'Quite amazing,' said Cook.

At the end of the investigation, Mallin twice agreed to a meeting, but did not keep the appointments, so Cook had to resort to the persistent phone call.

'It was getting rather hairy, by that time,' he recalled, with large shadowy people following me about in hollow, empty streets in the less fortunate parts of the city.' (See Case 5)

Health and medicine

An important area of public concern is medicine and health, and one of the main problems encountered by the *Checkpoint* team in matters concerning health is the way that Local Area Health Authorities act as their own judge and jury, making it difficult if not impossible for anyone with a problem or complaint to get satisfaction.

'One of our saddest cases was that of eleven-year-old Helena Bye, from Wales,' said Cook. 'This showed how medicine in the National Health Service can go wrong for parents who believe their child is not being given the attention it deserves. In this case the poor child died, and there was no way the parents could initiate a proper enquiry.

'Another example we came across, in a joint *Nationwide* story, was that of a surgeon's brother who died during a routine operation, and once again there was no way the complainant could get an explanation that satisfied him, although it certainly satisfied the Local Area Health Authority. They were able to say, more or less behind closed doors, "It's all right. We've looked at this. Now go away."'

After showing that there were faults with conventional medicine, the programme received a large number of complaints in which people had tried to get relief through the National Health Service and had then turned, often in desperation, to fringe medicine.

'There was the extraordinary Mrs Janet Pitman (See Case 6) who lived in a little village in Somerset,' Cook recalled. 'She claimed she could cure absolutely everything by dietary means, and her diagnosis was effected by swinging a pendulum over a length of your hair. We had letters from people who had sent off for a diagnosis and been told they had the most horrendous diseases, some of which were hereditary, for which there was no cure. I sent off some of my hair and was alleged to have had cancer of the throat and to have been beyond help.'

In this, as in other such cases, conventional doctors were worried about the practice involved, because their patients were being told to come off conventional medicine, thus taking a great personal risk. The alternative treatment was often bizarre or even dangerous, such as eating five pounds of grapes a day, and nothing else.

'Mrs Pitman was obsessive, rather than deliberately misleading. She would quote at length from all kinds of books, even bringing magical practices into her arguments. If anything, she misled herself as to the efficacity of her diagnoses and treatments. She did appear to believe in what she was doing, and she was outraged if anyone suggested that she was doing any harm.'

The 'Case of the psychic surgeons' was another matter, according to Cook. (See Case 7)

'These were people brought to the UK by the Spiritualist National Union to operate on people. They claimed to be able to plunge their hands into your innards and remove whatever nasty growth is causing the trouble, wherever it is in your body.'

In another joint radio-television investigation the team demonstrated that what they were doing was fraudulent, by filming some of their operations. In this case, says Cook, the filming was possible because the Spiritualists themselves believed that the operations were genuine, and once again there was a great deal of sadness in the fact that many of the 'patients' also believed in the validity of the treatment.

'It was particularly harrowing to see a young boy with paralysed legs in a wheelchair who had been convinced that he could walk. As we watched he was dragged by a friend, out of the chair and back, leaving two furrows in the ground, desperately claiming that he had just walked.'

After the filming the team arranged proper forensic analysis of swabs and tissue samples they had managed to get from the operations. One of these had been performed on the chairman of the Spiritualist National Union, Gordon Higginson. While they waited for the laboratory results they scrutinised the films they had made, in slow motion, and then made contact with an American magician who had an interest in exposing this kind of fakery, called James Randi. They persuaded him to come over to the UK and to demonstrate on Cook the same kind of operation.

'He did the operation, producing various growths and blood from my stomach,' said Cook. 'And it was done by using a rubber condom filled with appropriate substances and palmed at the right time to make it look as if the contents were being drawn from my insides, from an indentation made with the fingers in the soft flesh of the tummy. The condom was ruptured during this process, and the whole convincing-looking mess was thrown into a bowl and removed.'

The laboratory results from the 'real' operation on Gordon Higginson showed that the 'surgeons' had used chicken giblets and pig's blood. When Higginson was confronted with this evidence, Cook had the impression that Higginson, having originally believed in the validity of the operation, became embarrassed at the possibility that it was a fake. In any event, the tour planned by the 'surgeons' was cancelled.

Following the broadcast the newspaper, *Psychic News*, launched a campaign claiming that *Checkpoint* had manipulated the evidence.

'As in many of these cases,' said Cook, 'we were facing perfectly genuine people who simply did not want to believe that someone had indulged in malpractice. In fact, the main part of our evidence was the film we made of their own operation, together with forensic reports from people of the highest calibre.'

Cook still expresses amazement when he recalls the story about an alleged relief for arthritis, called dimethyl sulphoxide, which also happened to be a powerful industrial solvent (See Case 8). This was being sold by the former MP for Grantham in Lincolnshire, Dennis Kendall, who had already been involved in a number of extraordinary business ventures going back to the Second World War. He was alleged to have ripped off the War Office to the tune of £1.7 million over guns for the Spitfire fighter plane, a sum that he was obliged to pay back. There was a 'people's car', a project that came to nothing (prospectuses were issued, finance arranged, and three were built). He then went to California, where Cook found him living 'in some splendour' in Beverly Hills. He had many connections with people running clinics in the USA, and he was the sponsor of a clinic in the UK where people were charged £350 for a course of injections of dimethyl sulphoxide.

'It's dripped into the body,' said Cook, 'and it's supposed to bring relief to sufferers of arthritis, but we couldn't find anyone who would agree that it had done so, except for people who we believe had been offered a fee to recommend it to others. On the other hand it had produced some horrifying results.'

The programme raised questions as to how this substance was being used, whether it ought to be used in this country, how it got round the Medicines Act. Section 6 says if a doctor thinks it is to the advantage for a patient he may, on his own account, prescribe treatment that may not in fact be approved. Kendall had the help of a General Practitioner to administer dimethyl sulphoxide, under Section 6 of the Act, without a prior consultation.

'People just went to this GP, lay down and got injected,' said Cook.

Checkpoint's interview with Kendall in California revealed a man who could not be shaken in his belief of the treatment's value, planning 'bigger and better things' for his miracle relief.

In February 1981, *Checkpoint* broadcast a story about Papworth Hospital, the main UK centre for heart transplant operations. (See Case 9) This was at the time when the Panorama television programme was in the middle of a controversy over the issue of brain death. At the time this involved sixteen possible heart donors. After receiving information from a number of people in the Papworth area, the team decided that this might not be the most important issue. *Checkpoint* received complaints that the care offered to them for the entire East Anglian area, for which Papworth was the major heart and thoracic surgery hospital, was being jeopardised and that they were paying for a national transplant programme that did not relate to the area's true requirements. They didn't see why they should. Waiting lists for operations other than heart transplants were growing, because there was no money available. They made the point that, although it was a splendid achievement to develop heart transplant techniques, in the economic climate 'now was not the time to do it'.

'We were caught up in the cross-fire,' Cook said, 'because Papworth was in the public eye as a prestigious hospital. Yet we believed that the problems of the Many were more considerable than the problems of the Few, vital though the individual need for a heart operation might be. There are, after all, other equally vital operations, and the people concerned felt things were badly out of balance. We agreed.'

This edition generated a great deal of reaction, and the team received many letters, some being congratulatory and some not.

'It's a very emotive subject, and a lot of people who wrote hadn't really listened to the programme. They hadn't heard our careful qualifications. We quite often find that this happens, that people only hear what they want to hear, or they get something wrong. For example, one of the people we interviewed was the chairwoman of the Local Area Health Authority, and we opened two letters, one after the other, the first of which said: "How dare you interview the chairman like that. You didn't know what you were talking about, and she sent you away with your tail between your legs."

'The next letter I opened began with the same words: "How dare you interview the chairman like that . . . You made her look absolutely stupid." Another letter, from a senior member of the Papworth surgical team, said what a responsible programme it had been.'

Cook makes the point that, quite apart from the considerable and self-imposed discipline relating to the team's reporting standards, plus the ever-present need to consider possible criminal or civil legal repercussions, in such emotive cases as this they are even more careful to present a balanced report.

The attraction of money

Firms that deal in money and various aspects of finance often come under the *Checkpoint* magnifying glass. Many of them operate successfully simply because of the age-old attraction of money, and they don't care how they break or bend the rules to do business with their unsuspecting victims. In April 1975 a Liverpool firm called Glenn Securities was offering what seemed to be a very good deal; in effect, a 'home money making scheme'. The company took advertisements in many reputable newspapers, offering a commission to people who would act as agents in setting up loans. No name was given. Just a telephone number. The first response was usually a recorded message that gave some more information and asked the caller to phone back at a specific time. Then a company employee expanded the theme: applicants would merely have to answer the telephone to prospective customers, ask for details, fill in a form and pass this to the company. This sounded reasonably simple – and attractive – to many callers. The next step was a visit from a Glenn employee whose function was to translate the enquirer's interest into the signing of a cheque for £35 to cover the setting up of the new commission agency. And that was that. Once the money was paid over, Glenn Securities effectively lost interest in their new 'agent'. *Checkpoint* received over thirty complaints and, after checking them out, tried without success to interview the people who were running the company. David Tench, then working in the legal department of the Consumers Association, explained to listeners how Glenn Securities could get away with this 'pretty shameful' practice.

'This is the sort of fringe activity that will be controlled by the law eventually,' he said, 'when the 1974 Consumer Credit Act is in full force.'

(The Act is *still* not in 'full force' at the time of writing. New money brokers can still obtain a licence to operate very easily. If they transgress, the authorities can, of course, take their licence away just as easily, but by then it can be too late.)

Tench explained how the Office of Fair Trading would operate the licencing system that would oblige all firms in the loan business and fringe activities to register. He pointed out that it was the OFT's job to find out which firms are respectable and which are not and warned people to be careful in responding to this kind of advertisement.

'A firm operating an agency in the loan business should not require money to be paid into it. They should be paying *you* money, your commission as and when you earn it, and there shouldn't be any question of your having to pay for the privilege of getting an agency.'

Sound advice, but Glenn Securities continued operating, and a few weeks later *Checkpoint* once again tried to get to the bottom of the problem. One ex-employee, having acquired copies of the company's books, came on the programme and said that he thought as many as 1,200 agents might be involved, and 'I would say at least 1,000 of these are dissatisfied.' Another former employee estimated that a mere £6,000 had been lent to borrowers through this 1,200-strong network of agents. Once more Cook tried to interview the principals, Peter Kearney and Brian Hanlon. At one point he managed to have a telephone conversation with Hanlon, who put up a dense smokescreen, offering to answer questions that were put in writing. The interview ended inconclusively, to say the least.

HANLON: '. . . well thank you very much Mr Cook for allowing me your time, but if you wish to know anything further as regards any enquiry which you want to raise, please don't hesitate to contact me in writing, when I shall reply.' He never did.

Listeners then heard that the men behind Glenn Securities were starting other companies, Mill Glenn Finance and, on a grander scale, Centre-Face Limited, where the agency fee was raised from £35 to £600. They also learned that the Merseyside CID had become interested in the three companies and their directors. The effect of *Checkpoint*'s publicity and the subsequent Press coverage put paid to Kearney and Hanlon's finance activities, and in October 1979 both men were imprisoned for conspiracy to defraud. Other charges involving forgery and uttering were ordered to lie on the file.

The *Checkpoint* team constantly hear of cases in which unscrupulous people can obtain a licence to operate a finance business, eight years after this particular broadcast. The problem is that they can perpetrate a fraud or other misdemeanour at least once with impunity and sometimes on several occasions due simply to the inertia and inefficiency of the monitoring system.

A particularly complex finance firm was investigated in April 1979. This was Barnett Christie, a fringe bank that had collapsed owing £4 million in fixed deposits to more than 2,000 people (see Case 9). The attraction here was a 'tax free eleven per cent interest rate on relatively small deposits' that proved of particular interest to retired people with a few thousand pounds to invest. In this case Cook succeeded in having an interview with the man behind the bank, Frank Christie, who argued insistently that he need not accept blame for anything that had gone wrong.

This case is interesting for a number of reasons. It had many complainants, all of whom had exerted considerable effort to sort out the problem for themselves. It is a good example of how skilled and thorough research can equip an interviewer to respond critically to responses from an intelligent interviewee, Frank Christie. Finally, after this confrontation, the listener is left to draw his or her own conclusions. At the end of the programme Cook had some trenchant things to say about the authorities and the new Banking Act that came into being just a few days before the broadcast.

CHAPTER 10

Problems with the law

Many complaints to *Checkpoint* concern the police, courts and other aspects of the legal system. In a transmission on 3 September 1976, Cook commented that one of the fattest files in the *Checkpoint* office contains complaints about solicitors. In his introduction Cook said that they had chosen two cases, not because they were by any means the worst the team had received or because they wanted to pillory the solicitor concerned but because they illustrate how daunting it can be to sort out a mess of your solicitor's making. On that day in September *Checkpoint* explained what happened to Harry Prest from Hull. Having budgeted very carefully he had bought a new house but was horrified to discover that he was responsible for carrying the cost of repairing the road outside. Ian Whitty, his solicitor, had not told him about this, and the first indication he had that something was wrong arrived in a letter from the council. This stated that ten feet of roadway was to be torn up and renewed. Prest contacted Whitty who found out that no mention of this was revealed in the searches carried out. He admitted liability and offered to pay the bill when Prest received it.

When the £110 bill arrived, Whitty could not be found. He had ceased to practice and, in the week of the programme, had been struck off for misappropriating at least £67,155 of his clients' money. He had entered a rest home in York. Prest contacted the Law Society and was introduced to another solicitor. Unfortunately, as Whitty was not available, Prest could not take his claim further in that direction. He went to the council and explained what had happened, pointing out that he was unemployed and could not afford to pay their bill, a considerable amount under the circumstances. Not unnaturally Prest did not see why he should have to pay anything, as he was not at fault.

'My feelings are very, very sore at this moment,' he said. 'I don't know where to turn from here.'

In fact, his only legal redress was to sue Whitty for negligence, but even with Legal Aid he saw no point in suing a man who apparently had no money.

The next case concerned Paul Medforth from Sheffield who had a motor cycle accident in 1971 when he ran into some unmarked road works. He spent a week in hospital with his jaw wired up and a further eight weeks off work, during which time the contractor, a Mr P. J. O'Donnell, came round to see him and admitted liability. At about the same time Medforth's father introduced him to Mr Whitty who suggested that he sue O'Donnell for damages. He assured the young Medforth that he had a 'cast iron' case and that he, Whitty, was just the solicitor to pursue it. But this proved not to be the case.

'It dragged on for almost three years,' Medforth said, 'with Legal Aid forms and other things, but he kept assuring me that I had a good case. I kept in contact with Mr Whitty by telephone and letter, but I didn't get very far . . . I don't know whether some letters were lost or ignored. Eventually he said he'd have to issue a writ. Over the next few months I kept writing, and he wrote the odd letter saying "Mr Medforth, don't despair! Things will be all right in the end." In 1975 I lost contact with him completely, and in 1976 I phoned and a secretary told me that the business was closing and everything would be passed to another solicitor.'

At this stage Medforth was still fairly confident about his claim, though disturbed by the changes and delays. However, he was totally unprepared for the bombshell dropped by the solicitor appointed by the Law Society.

'He contacted me, saying that the action had been dismissed due to lack of prosecution,' Medforth said. 'I was liable to pay the costs, which amounted to more than £500. Bearing in mind the pay I'd lost being off work, plus the damage to my motorcycle, the result is that I'm nearly £1,000 out of pocket and with injuries to the jaw that still trouble me. All for something that wasn't my fault and for which the other side admitted liability at the time.'

He felt shocked and disgusted about the affair, and so too did Robert Briars, the new solicitor. He carefully traced back into the documents and explained how yet another firm of solicitors had been appointed by the Law Society to act as Whitty's agents in an appeal to a judge in chambers to allow the prosecution to go ahead. This appeal was dismissed, and Medforth was ordered to pay both the costs of the action and of the appeal. The original bill of over £500 was reduced by the court registrar to £442.17, still a huge sum for Medforth and his £30 a week income. Determined not to let the matter rest, Briars continued enquiries.

'Mr Whitty had been sole proprietor of his practice and had been admitted to a private nursing home,' he said. 'Like most solicitors at that time he was not in possession of an indemnity policy, which would have covered any damage suffered by a client as a result of his negligence. I then made enquiries to the Law Society to see if Paul Medforth would be covered by their compensation fund. He wasn't, because this applies only to cases of dishonesty. This is clearly not a case of dishonesty but one of negligence.'

Catch-22 for Medforth. *Checkpoint* tried to interview someone from P. J. O'Donnell Construction Ltd, who had originally admitted liability, but they declined. The firm's insurers, Commercial Union were still pressing for costs, pointing out that Whitty should have been insured for the consequences of neglect. Whitty also declined to make any comment on the record.

'So,' Cook said, 'we're left with the solicitor's professional body, the Law Society. How can people like Messrs Prest and Medforth find themselves in this kind of situation?'

The Law Society's senior assistant secretary, Graham Lee, addressed himself to the question: 'It's really quite simple for it to happen in certain cases. A matter can be lost sight of, and time limits in personal injury cases are very, very strict. If a solicitor over runs the time limits, his client is out of court, and the only remedy is to sue the solicitor for negligence.'

A daunting prospect, commented Cook. But how can this be prevented in the future? Lee revealed that, as from that very week, solicitors were required by new rules to insure up to a certain limit against the consequence of their own negligence. When pressed to say how quickly this might be brought into practice, Lee pointed out that a client would still have to prove negligence before he could claim. Then he would be assured compensation, if only up to the limits of the compulsory cover.

Lee's advice to people who believed that their solicitor is making a mess of things is to sack the solicitor and find another one. Cook found this a questionable course, reinforcing the way solicitors always seem to make money out of tribulation. Perhaps the Law Society rather than the courts should be the arbiters. He put it to Lee that the Law Society is only able to shut the stable door after the horse has gone. Lee explained that the Society has its functions and duties laid down by Parliament and that these limit it to considering matters relating to a solicitor's conduct, not negligence. Cook thought the difference between bad conduct and negligence would mean little to the aggrieved client. He put it to Lee that the Law Society had an image of being an organisation whose job it is to stop the legal boat being rocked. Unfair, said Lee, because all allegations to the Society against solicitors are properly investigated. But the client who suffers as a result of a solicitor's negligence is best served by going to court, which puts him right back on the legal treadmill.

Another serious legal problem concerns the arrest and treatment of people who are suspected on the flimsiest evidence of 'trifling' offences. In some cases, said Cook on 19 April 1979, there has been no offence at all, as in the case of Peter Orde, then a twenty-nine-year-old factory worker from Coventry. His story is frankly chilling, told with complete conviction. He was awakened at about 5.00 a.m. one morning in 1978 by the sound of a car starting. It sounded like his own car, so he grabbed some clothes and ran downstairs. Sure enough, his car had been driven away, and he began to run towards a neighbouring telephone box. At the same time he saw a police car cruising away from him, so he tried to attract the occupants' attention. After running a short distance he heard someone shouting to him to stop. He turned round to see two policemen running after him, one unleashing a dog. He stood completely still.

'When the dog reached me it leaped straight for my chest, and I tried to side-step it. Then the dog landed on me and took hold of my arm, sinking its teeth into my forearm. All this time I was shouting, "Get the dog off me! I haven't done anything. My car's been stolen."

'The dog handler reaches me, throws the dog off and immediately knocks me over a garden wall onto my back. I tried to get up. My feet are still over the wall, and when I'm trying to get up I'm hit in the face twice and knocked back down again. The dog then jumps into the garden and attacks my right shoulder from behind. While this is going on another police officer has arrived, then suddenly he bends down and holds me and starts hitting me about the face and head with what appears to be a torch. Again, during all this, I'm protesting my innocence, who I am, that my car's been stolen. Eventually the policeman who was holding me was dragged off by another policeman who must have arrived in another police car. I was spreadeagled on a police car and searched.

'At this point I asked them to check with my wife. I said, "Look, that's the house, with the light on." And then I was asked to get into the Panda car. As I was getting in the sergeant noticed the blood on the roof of the car and said, "The dog's had him. Give him a dressing." To which the officer who'd been hitting me said, "Well, that's what the dog's here for, and I'm not here to act as nursemaid." While this was going on there was some comment from an officer outside the car saying, "Oh, you're lucky you're not in America. We'd have shot you."'

Eventually the police checked his story and released him. He went to hospital to have his wounds dressed. Later, at home, a policeman arrived to tell him his car had been found. He made several official complaints which, said Cook, resulted in several excuses ('The police dog wouldn't have done it unless you gave it cause.') but neither disciplinary action nor an apology. A 'rather grudging one' was subsequently given through his Member of Parliament.

Another case concerned Moota Utim, a Post Office international exchange telephonist, who went voluntarily to his local police station to assist in their enquiries about a manslaughter case involving someone he vaguely knew. The police officers began by being 'quite friendly'. They then suggested he had received a phone call from this slight acquaintance in which he (the acquaintance) had confessed that he had beaten up his wife very badly. Utim told them he had not received such a phone call. This denial resulted in his being incarcerated all day and overnight, with no refreshment or food. He had no idea what his rights were, and the police did not tell him. The following lunchtime they asked him to write down a statement.

'After twenty-four hours in that place I was ready to say anything that they wanted.'

He was released that evening after his flatmate had successfully traced him and made contact with his own solicitor.

'I thought they were friends of the public,' Utim said. 'I don't feel that any more.'

Cook reported that the officers concerned had no comment to make, as there had been no official complaint. But Utim was 'more than a little scared of the police' by this time. So was a lady from the Midlands, held in a cell and denied access to a solicitor for five hours on a shoplifting charge while her children were left to wander around unattended. After nine months the case was summarily dismissed, but 'following suggestions from her solicitor that complaining on *Checkpoint* might result in police harrassment of her husband' she withdrew from the programme, as for similar reasons did a twenty-year-old social worker who happened to be in a pub when it was raided for drugs. She suffered the pain and indignity of a 'heavy-handed' internal search by a policewoman wearing old kitchen gloves.

Another case involved a girl who used to work as a housemaid in a leading London hotel. Her problem started innocently enough with the seeming gift of a make-up bag and 20p from a guest, left with a note saying, 'For the maid'. The guest made a complaint that she had stolen the make-up bag. This resulted in her arrest, with finger printing, photography and undressing at the station. An officer tried to force her to make a statement admitting theft, but she refused, all the time in tears. After four hours the police drove her home and looked for stolen hotel property. They found nothing, but the charge of theft went ahead. She had to appear at court three times and was eventually acquitted. She received no compensation, merely fares for travelling.

'It still affects me,' she told listeners, 'because they've still got my photograph and my fingerprints, and they never even said sorry. They've disgraced my whole character.'

Once again the authorities, including the hotel management, refused to comment. Cook pointed out that such cases were not in the majority and were part of the ground to be covered in an imminent Royal Commission on Criminal Procedures. One of the bodies that presented evidence was the National Council for Civil Liberties. Peter Thornton, a barrister who helped to prepare their evidence, analysed the procedures in practice and commented that there seemed to be an increase in this kind of complaint, where people are taken 'unnecessarily' to a police station and subjected to methods that should not be used. Thornton suggested that instead of arrest for minor cases the summons procedure should be used, as in the case of motoring offences. Such a procedure, he said, was used in parts of the UK for shoplifting. He advocated that the initiative for deciding whether to prosecute or not should be taken away from the police, as in Scotland, where there is an independent and publicly accountable prosecutor.

Cook also interviewed the president of the Association of Chief Police Officers, Philip Knight, Chief Constable of the West Midlands. His first question was: What is *supposed* to happen when someone is first arrested and taken to a police station. Knight gave a clear account of the procedure and included the point that at some time during the proceedings the prisoner would be told his or her rights. He discussed with Cook the ins and outs of police station procedure, but found it difficult to accept that some of the complaints were well-founded. In his area and in a good many forces, he stated, arrestees are handed a printed copy of their rights. As to the matter of what might be a minor, as opposed to major, offence for which the police might choose a summons procedure rather than an arrest, Knight made a fair point. Some so-called minor offences carry quite large jail sentences. Shoplifting, for example. There is a difference between someone who takes 'the whole shop away with a van' and someone who takes a tin of beans. Where does one draw the line?

Knight accepted the general point that things were not always as they should be in the matter of arrest procedure but stressed the existence of the complaints procedure. Cook, in turn, pointed out how this is a 'fairly daunting' exercise for some people. He mentioned the woman who withdrew from the programme on the advice of her solicitor.

'I'm very sorry a solicitor should think that,' Knight replied. 'If that were thought by any solicitor about my force I would dearly love to see him and talk to him, because that is not what policemen are for. That is not what police procedures are all about.'

'And you would hope that, if procedures can be improved, the police wouldn't be wrong as often.'

'I accept that,' Knight said. 'Ideally we would never be wrong but, if that were the case, we should all be angels, and I don't think there are many of those on this earth.'

One of the most celebrated *Checkpoint* cases involving the law was that of Bernard Saltman. (See Case 11) Among the many ramifications to this affair was the astonishing verdict of Guilty brought in by the jury after the judge's summing up clearly pointed in the other direction. It involved a fire in a warehouse, an insurance company that paid part of the compensation then changed their attitude after they had sent in a forensic 'expert', an accusation of arson and gaining money by fraudulent means, an arrest and conviction, two years in jail, a rejected first appeal, a strenuous campaign on the part of Saltman's wife, family and friends and, not quite finally, after two *Checkpoints* on the subject the quashing of the conviction after intervention by the Home Secretary. At the time of writing, the Saltmans had still not settled things with the insurance company, nor had any compensation from the authorities.

Another aspect of British justice was highlighted on 2 March 1983 when *Checkpoint* broadcast a programme partly recorded in Brixton Prison. It illustrated in dramatic terms how unfair Britain's system of keeping accused people on remand in prison can be. It concentrated on the stories of people held without bail for up to two years before finally being acquitted of all charges. Quite apart from the appalling destruction caused to their private and business lives, there is no system of compensation.

Criminologist Rod Morgan from the University of Bath pointed out that fifty thousand people each year are sent to prison to await trial, and the numbers are increasing. Each of these people is innocent until proven guilty in court. One of them, commodity broker, Charles Tritt, had been held in Brixton Prison for a year and a half before a judge halted his fraud trial for lack of evidence, and even the impersonality of a satellite-linked telephone interview to his Canadian home could not hide the bitterness and barely suppressed fury Tritt felt about the British legal system.

'It cost me eighteen months of my life. Britain is not a free place, and I would liken it to Mexico or to Iran or to India or Uganda. The only difference is, those places let you know in advance . . . they say, "Mister, we're going to throw you in jail and keep you there for ever". There were times in Brixton when I thought – for Christ's sake, I'll never get out of here. Your system is very, very archiac. You're back in the 1700s, and I'm good and Goddam mad!'

Rod Morgan went on to explain why remand prisoners fare so badly.

'It's easier to exploit untried prisoners, because if you exploit long-term prisoners, or make conditions bad for them, they pull the walls down. They live there. It's their home, and they've got a vested interest in making sure the conditions are good. People who are untried are oriented to the outside. They're concerned about whether they're going to get convicted, whether they're going to get bail. And they're relatively easy to exploit. What this means in practice is that all the modern building in the system has now gone to sentenced prisoners, so untried prisoners are held in the oldest buildings, in the most over-crowded conditions, and have the fewest staff resources. And remember, these are the people who, according to the rhetoric of the English law, should benefit from the presumption of innocence until they are proven guilty by a court of law. Remember also: some of these people are never convicted.'

Cook rammed this home with a disturbing statistic. 'About 1,200 every year, in fact are acquitted. Iris Mills was one of them.'

Mills, accused of being involved in an anarchist conspiracy, told listeners how prison officers made her feel untrustworthy, even though she was only in prison on remand. They told her she could only use plastic knitting needles, not her preferred metal ones, 'in case I tried to stab somebody with them. I wrote to a friend that I felt very much in a Dr Jekyll and Mr Hyde situation, where I felt like Dr Jekyll and they treated me like Mr Hyde . . . It's terribly wrong that people should be kept in prison without any convictions against them when they're trying to prove themselves innocent of something. There are lots of people who are going to be in this situation, kept in custody and then acquitted, who have spent all that time in prison for no reason at all.'

Cook found out directly what it was like in a remand section by visiting Brixton Prison and interviewing two prisoners. One had been refused bail, the other could not raise it. The first, 'David', explained that he had been on remand for eleven months and that he thought the conditions were 'ridiculous.'

'You're locked up twenty-three hours a day, and, well, there's a lot of innocent people here waiting to go to court, and I think it's wrong to keep them that length of time without trial. People are living in conditions which should have been done away with at least fifty years ago.'

'How have you felt, waiting so long to get to court?' asked Cook.

'Terrible. It's just a thing you've got to accept. If you don't accept it you end up going crazy. And it's just ridiculous. I've had these clothes on for nearly two weeks, and I can't get any clean ones . . .'

This matter of clothes is one of the many dehumanising aspects of being in prison on remand. Remand prisoners are entitled to wear their own clothes rather than prison garb, but they are responsible for cleaning and maintenance. Those who cannot afford this expense usually end up wearing prison clothes.

Quite apart from illustrating how shockingly unfair our remand system can often be, *Checkpoint* underscored the personal tragedies and indignities. One wife found herself supplementing her husband's medication for epilepsy and a dangerous thrombosis by passing pills from her mouth to his during their visiting time because the prison doctors had decided to reduce his dosage by half. 'The fear when I did this was indescribable,' she said.

Under the circumstances it was perhaps surprising that Cook was allowed inside Brixton Prison in this way. In any event, governor Tony Pearson explained that he 'feels' for those who spend a considerable time in his care before being acquitted, and he agreed that, overall, Her Majesty's Prison Brixton is not a very pleasant place.

Sounds of the Thursday morning repeat of this episode had not finished reverberating before MP Arthur Lewis was on his feet in the House of Commons, furiously quoting *Checkpoint* and demanding a change in the remand system to redress the blatant unfairness. He and fellow MPs James Tinn, Bill Homewood and Lawrence Cunliffe tabled a Motion to the House:

'That this House is gravely concerned to note that for over twenty years innocent men and women have been incarcerated in British prisons for periods of between a few months and years, when they have not been found guilty of any crime for which they have been awaiting trial; deplores the fact that some five thousand persons are now in gaol, some for periods approaching two years, some locked up for twenty-three and a half hours per day, and are treated as convicted criminals; congratulate the British Broadcasting Corporation in broadcasting their *Checkpoint* programme on this subject on the third February 1983; requests the British Broadcasting Corporation to circulate a transcript of this programme to show how each and every honourable Member is personally responsible for this deplorable state of affairs, which is worse than is happening in the Soviet Union or any known country; and calls upon Her Majesty's Government to take immediate action to stop this disgraceful denial of fair play and decent treatment and to grant justice to thousands of Her Majesty's subjects.'

This was a classic programme: well structured and forcing home shock after shock with a deceptive mildness. 'We actually had a lot of co-operation from the Home Office,' recalled Cook, 'and I got the impression they were as fed up with the system as anyone.' It remains to be seen if this or any subsequent government will act to change the situation.

CHAPTER 11

Bureaucratic bungling

Nothing excites so much exasperation among the public as bungling by bureaucrats. In September 1977 *Checkpoint* examined the efficiency with which England's Commissioners for Local Administration (commonly called ombudsmen) were coping with local government and water authority bungles. The CLA's second annual report had just been published, which gave the team a chance to compare how the ombudsmen's performance had improved or otherwise since the scheme had begun. At that time *Checkpoint* had aired the case of Esther Neville from Weymouth. The outlook from her cottage and the light were blocked by the erection of another dwelling, even though she had been assured that no building would take place within sixty feet of her property. She told how she had suddenly seen that foundations were being built for a property no less than fifteen feet away. She contacted the local authority, and a planning officer visited her, bringing a plan for the building under erection.

'Oh dear,' he told her. 'This is terrible. This shouldn't have been allowed. We shall investigate.'

'Over the next few months, nothing happened – except that the offending building was nearly finished,' Cook reported. The council housing committee visited the site and resolved to take an enforcement action to stop the building. At a subsequent meeting they withdrew this order on the grounds that things were too far advanced. Mrs Neville asked a councillor to take her case to the local ombudsman, Dennis Harrison. He found that there had been 'maladministration by the council in relation to the delay in ascertaining the facts and dealing with the complaint and that the complainant had suffered injustice.'

So far, so good, but what happens when you reach a conclusion like this and the council disagrees, as in this case?

'Well,' said Harrison, 'it is for the council to consider the Commissioner's report, but the Act does say that if the Commissioner is not satisfied with the action that the authority has taken he can then issue a second report.'

'And if no action after that?' asked Cook.

'That is the end of it, as far as the Commissioner is concerned.'

So Mrs Neville got nowhere with the Weymouth and Portland Borough Council. In the intervening years many more people turned to the ombudsman. In 1973 Alan Severn from Yateley in Surrey moved to a semi-detached house in a pleasant cul-de-sac. The adjoining house came on the market and was quickly bought. A notice in the local paper informed him that planning permission had been sought to build a pair of semi-detached houses. He was horrified to arrive home one day to find that footings had been dug right up to his flank wall, despite the fact that the district council had passed plans for something else, somewhere else.

Severn advised the council that he wanted new plans submitted so that he could see what was actually being built, and it was obvious that the effect of the new building would be to turn his semi-detached house into one of a terraced row. The council allowed the work to continue on the grounds, said Severn, that otherwise the new buildings would have to be demolished, with compensation paid by the council or its members to the builder. Meanwhile the houses were being erected very quickly, and when the council failed to keep its promises to remedy the situation Severn took his case to the local ombudsman who sent round one of his inspectors.

'I was very impressed with his approach,' said Severn, after the inspector had spent a morning at the site and a considerable time interviewing the appropriate council officials. The ombudsman's report to Severn said: 'In my opinion injustice has been caused to you by maladministration (and) the authority are also required to inform me of the action they have taken or propose to take. They have been asked to do this as soon as possible.'

That was more than a year before the programme, but Severn had not been able to reach an agreeable solution, although he had been offered first £400 then £600 compensation by the council for the £2,300 drop in value of his house. As for his opinion of the ombudsman's inspector: 'The guy's heart is in the right place, but even with his aid and his findings I am still out of pocket, my house is no longer a semi, and his findings have not been acted upon. As far as I am concerned the ombudsman is just a toothless tiger.'

Not normally one to rub salt in this kind of wound, Cook

nevertheless reported that Severn's case had been given to *Checkpoint* by the Commissioner's office as an example of a success story. George Linney from Rotherham had more success with a building problem, although his problems had began with the nasty shock when a supposedly 'commendable' council housing scheme just over his back fence had turned into an architectural monstrosity. The ombudsman found once more that the local authority had been guilty of maladministration in that the housing committee had made a decision based on wrong information. His intervention obliged the council to reduce the height of two blocks of flats from three stories to two, but Linney still felt hemmed in and paid several hundred pounds to erect a fence to try and preserve a little privacy.

Meanwhile, Maurice Wheeler of Bracknell was taken aback when the councillor who lived next door sold part of his land for the construction of another bungalow 'cheek by jowl' with Wheeler's. This was done despite Wheeler's written objections (which the council said they had lost) and after a site planning meeting that the council had improperly convened. Only two out of thirteen members turned up, and most of them hadn't been informed that it was taking place. The council's planning officer read out his department's strong objections to the plans, and he recommended refusal. However, the two councillors reversed this recommendation and granted planning permission. Wheeler could get no satisfaction by contacting the council, so he took the matter to the ombudsman. It was found that there had indeed been maladministration and injustice, but, said Cook, Mr Wheeler was less than satisfied with the findings.

'. . . building was still going ahead, because the council were insisting that although they had admitted to doing things wrong everything was still perfectly legal. The only thing we're getting for our efforts is an apology.'

Anthony Target the council's chief executive confirmed that this was the case but felt that the local Commissioner's powers were 'quite adequate to ensure that justice is done to the citizen'. Liberal peer Lord Winstanley, a member of the Parliamentary Select Committee responsible for the creation of the ombudsman and local Commissioners, took a different view.

'I think the whole thing was rather oversold. I think a lot of us thought that once we'd got an ombudsman that will be the end of injustice, and of course nothing could be further from the actual case . . . The big weakness is that the ombudsmen have no teeth. They are required to see if maladministration has occurred, then they have to decide if injustice has arisen from this, and if so they can recommend a remedy. But they have no powers whatsoever to enforce that remedy.'

Although Lord Winstanley was opposed to the idea of any transference of power from elected councils to an appointed ombudsman, he opined that where an ombudsman recommends specific compensation there is a good case for making it mandatory upon the local authority to carry out that recommendation and pay the compensation. As for the volume of work handled by the Commissioners in the previous year and the success of this, the organisation's secretary Michael Hyde gave some figures.

'We completed investigations into 189 complaints. We also did detailed enquiries into 280-odd complaints. Of the 189 we investigated we found that something had gone wrong, in our judgement, in 107 cases, I estimate that of those 107 at the end of the day there will only be about six where there won't be a satisfactory outcome.'

Hyde agreed that what might be satisfaction for his organisation might not be for the complainant; in fact, the Act under which he and his colleagues work specifies that the person who has to be satisfied is the local ombudsman.

'The complainant will probably never be satisfied . . . he'll want the house next door knocked down . . . The Commissioner is the person that has to be satisfied, and I'm afraid that means that sometimes the complainant will not be entirely satisfied.'

Cook put it to Hyde that although quite a number of people have said the Commissioners have their hearts in the right place they also enquire as to the whereabouts of the teeth. Hyde accepted the idea that the Commissioners should be given more teeth, but felt that rather more time was needed to monitor what was, in England, a relatively new service.

'Our very existence is quite a deterrent . . . You have to judge whether the ombudsman should have teeth in the light of experience (and) perhaps it's a little early to judge.'

In May 1978 *Checkpoint* revealed in one programme how the Housing (Homeless Persons) Act of 1977 was being misused by local authorities to the detriment of the very people the Act was designed to help. A batch of letters followed, many from a group of people who felt that they were being misled badly over their family allowances. The worst hit seemed to be single parent families in which, for one reason or another, the parent is unable to work. 'They were relying,' said Cook, 'on an increase in Child Benefit promised by the then Chancellor, Mr Healey, at the end of his April budget.'

A recording of that proposal by Healey himself outlined this promise, which referred specifically to a 'major boost to child support for working families and those dependent on social security'.

Checkpoint broadcast just two cases to demonstrate the reality. First was Dona Lister from Warrington. Her husband deserted the family, and she went to the local Social Security office for advice and help. The first piece of advice she got was to start divorce proceedings as this would be a 'clean' way for them to handle her affairs. After a harrowing few months, during which her previously reasonable standard of living was miserably reduced, she was delighted with Mr Healey's news. Unhappily, she quickly discovered that because she was on Supplementary Benefit she was not entitled to any increase. Lister's misery came across in waves. Her finances were so tightly tailored each week that when her little boy had an accident she did not have the money to phone for an ambulance.

'It was one of those things where people laugh and say, well you must have had some money. I had none whatsoever. That's how badly off my family is, and I'm sure I speak for a hell of a lot more single parent families in the same situation. Whatever the Chancellor says we did not receive any increase, and the poor are still the poor.'

The next case concerned the Hall family from Whitten in Middlesex. Ted and Mary Hall were two old age pensioners who were looking after their grandchildren, Debbie aged eleven and Michael aged thirteen. They wrote to *Checkpoint* about a problem that Cook described as 'even more appalling in its origins'. In 1976 their daughter was killed by her husband who was convicted of murder and received a life sentence . . .

'Which left Debbie and Michael homeless,' said Cook. 'Grandpa Hall, who loves them both very much, took them in like a shot, dreading the thought of losing them to an institution.'

Ted Hall had a 'lower than average' pension and no capital, having retired early because of illness. The Department of Health and Social Security (DHSS) allowed him a child benefit of just under £15 to look after these two growing youngsters. This was not enough, and the Halls began spending most of their pensions on the children's necessities.

'So they were over-joyed when the Chancellor announced the

child benefit increases,' Cook said. 'Social Services Secretary David Ennals became something of a saviour for them. But not for long. The DHSS decided that they would gain from 'overlapping benefits', so the increased child benefits allotted to Mary Hall meant that an equal sum was taken off Ted Hall's pension.

There followed a disturbing recital by Ted Hall on the problems of bringing up his grandchildren under these circumstances. Could David Ennals bring up two children on £15 a week, he wondered? It's a vote catcher. He's taking it off one column and putting it on another, and you've got to tolerate it . . .

In order to make ends meet and ensure the children had all they needed Mr Hall practically gave up eating, relying on the occasional sandwich and Complan to keep his strength up. No meat, not even chicken.

'As long as they've got their bellies full, clean clothes and a good bed, I'm happy. It's a struggle, there's no doubt about that, yet if it comes to the test I'd carry on with the struggle because I never want to lose my two grandchildren. I want them with me.'

Are these two cases merely freaks, aberrations, or are they the tip of an iceberg, pondered Cook. David Holroyd, assistant general secretary of the British Association of Social Workers had an answer.

'It's no small problem, and it's the children who suffer. We have a quarter of a million one-parent families on Supplementary Benefit. There are one million such families in the country, plus people such as the Halls bringing up children another way . . . We've got the strange situation where the Government recognised the needs by providing a £2 addition to the child benefit to the first child of one-parent families, and now they're taking that benefit away.'

Holroyd gave a gloomy forecast: those on the lowest incomes of all would be pounds worse off next year, when in theory they need the greatest help of all.

Cook then interviewed the Minister for Social Security, Stanley Orme: Why should he appear to give a boost to child allowance on the one hand and take away supplementary benefits with the other? The Minister's reply perhaps gives a clue as to the reasons for confusion and unfairness at local DHSS level.

'The reason for this is quite simply that supplementary benefit is meant to bring people up and above the poverty level, and quite frankly we can't have overlapping benefits where, in effect, you're paying two benefits to the same person for the same thing,' he said. 'They are not actually worse off, but they would get 60p less than what they would (*sic*) if they got the supplementary plus child benefit, and this creates the discrepancy.'

Cook persevered through a number of questions and answers, with Orme expressing a great deal of concern for those unfortunates who fall outside the ninety-seven per cent of people receiving child benefits who, he claimed, would be better off in the future. As to the unfortunate three per cent . . .

'I think I ought to say that in a sense the government have created this difficulty themselves, by increasing the supplement.'

Cook presented him with the fact that by the following November a wage earner and tax payer would be about £4 a week better off with the government's new benefits, whereas the one-parent family would be getting about 65p, and others (like the Halls) would get nothing.

'Well let me explain to you,' said the Minister, 'that quite frankly if one does a lot for poverty in our society one area would be the husband and wife with a very small family, the husband on a low income and the wife not working, and we might find real poverty there, and child benefit is designed to help that specific situation, and we are concerned about incentives. Incentives for people to work and at the same time not in any way acting against the one-parent family or the mother who has great difficulty, and we've given special considerations to that group of people.'

Orme did not agree that the 'blanket coverage' of the benefits meant that the people who don't need financial help get it, while those that do don't, 'because the vast majority of people do need it . . . We don't think that the one-parent family has been disadvantaged'.

He accepted that problems remained and that he would 'do something' about this provided his actions did not violate the 'overlapping benefit'. Cook pointed out that many parents, faced with insufficient benefit, are tempted to put their children into care, at a cost of about £100 a week to the community.

'I can't see the majority of mothers doing that,' Orme said. 'And, all right, they want the benefits; we'll see they get the benefits to which they're entitled.'

The Halls received over £2,000 in unsolicited donations after the programme. The authorities did nothing.

On 24 October 1979 *Checkpoint* told the tale of two local authorities 'who hold some of their rate payers in mortal dread'. They were the North East Fife District Council and the Wakefield Metropolitan District Council. (See Case 14) Both councils were responsible for actions that excited considerable public protest over a long period. In the first example residents of Cellardyke, a small and well-kept fishing village, were faced with closing orders on their homes. In the second, some residents of Pontefract told how they were faced with a £30,000 bill from the council for making safe land at the bottom of their gardens. The Cellardyke story in particular caused a large number of people to write to *Checkpoint* about similar problems in which their homes were threatened.

On 21 May 1976 *Checkpoint* returned to the story of sewerage and of the many listeners who had septic tanks and got no drainage service out of the general rates they paid. Many people refused to pay, and, following a previous programme on the subject, one of them had the result of his actions elevated to legal precedent in the case of Daemon versus the South West Water Authority. The House of Lords laid down that rate payers who did not have mains sewerage should not have to pay for it. In addition, water authorities throughout the UK were faced with having to repay such charges, a sum amounting to over £60 million. This unexpected financial burden came at a time when the authorities had been told by the National Water Council to stop borrowing. The resulting confusion had many people who had hailed the Daemon victory as a triumph for justice and commonsense reaching for their handkerchiefs . . . and their chequebooks. Susan Hill from Lower Kingswood in Surrey, to take just one example, suddenly found herself saddled with the prospect of paying the local council over £600 a year to empty her cess pit.

At the heart of the problem was the fact that the water authorities had no legal obligation to empty a cess pit or a septic tank, but they had to accept delivery of the contents for subsequent disposal, once the pit or tank had been emptied by the council or by a private contractor. One of Susan Hill's fellow Reigate and Banstead ratepayers, Victor Bradley, outlined how the council had 'rubber stamped' an important amendment to the recommendations of the policy committee that led to a charge for emptying a cess pit or septic tank of £2.25 per thousand gallons of effluent. This worked out to be an average of £88 per year for the householders in his area. Another rate payer, John Woodman, felt that he could not trust the council to measure accurately the volume of effluent they might withdraw from his tank. How do they meter it, he wondered? Norma Hardy from Pembury in Kent explained how her family were cutting down the throughput of water with extremely unpleasant consequences. It was suggested by Bradley that to avoid the charges and the problems people would be tempted to break open their tanks to let the liquors drain into the soil.

Tim Whitely of the Thames Water Authority reacted firmly to such a suggestion: this would be '. . . an extremely anti-social action, and I can't condemn it too strongly. However, the charges for emptying pits and tanks were nothing to do with the water authorities,' although he commented that some of the figures quoted did seem enormous.

Denis Walker, chief executive of Reigate and Banstead Borough Council claimed that the council had indeed given considerable consideration 'over several weeks' to the matter of charges and how they might affect the people concerned. He absolutely refuted Victor Bradley's charge that the council had rubber stamped the vital costing amendment by acting in secrecy.

'The council acted with perfect propriety,' he said. 'According to standing orders, two days notice was given of the amendment.'

Unfortunately for the protestors, as mere members of the public they were not entitled to have any notice of such an amendment. Only councillors were so privileged. And as far as the reason for the amendment was concerned, Walker made it quite clear: 'The original proposal (without the amendment) would have left a deposit of approximately £20,000 chargeable to all rate payers. It was to recoup this amount that the additional charge per thousand gallons removed was introduced.'

Even after his several week-long considerations, Walker was not aware that any rate payer might be unable to pay such a levy. His justification for the extra charge was logical, if tortuous: 'We as an authority have not directly lost money. But the rateable occupier of premises not connected with mains drainage will receive a rebate equivalent to the amount that has been paid for the previous two years, and that would have been paid this year by way of Thames Water Authority precept, had not the Daemon case been successful.'

In other words, his council would be clawing back money paid to non-main-drainage rate payers by the water authority. He believed this was reasonable because otherwise the possessors of cess pits and septic tanks would receive a service 'free of charge' that was paid for by all rate payers. Neither his reasoning nor the charges were acceptable to the protesters, who promised to continue the good fight.

Looking back at the case, Cook commented wryly that this was an example of how bureaucrats can react to judgements they feel are against their interests.

'Their lack of logic or commonsense understanding is incredible.'

Problems with cars

Checkpoint receives many serious complaints connected with cars and motoring; unfortunately, because they are so common, the programme can only give space to the most extraordinary examples of chicanery and sheer gall. Cook, himself a keen motorist, points out the particular care needed in this field.

'Feelings run high if something goes wrong with your motor car,' he says. 'After all, you pay a great deal of money to buy a car and to run it. But there are many ways a motorist can seek redress if he believes a trader or garage proprietor has done something wrong. For instance, most reputable garages are members of the Motor Agents Association and agree to abide by a Code of Practice. Ultimately, this can lead to arbitration by a separate person, but most claims are settled well before this takes place. As far as we in *Checkpoint* are concerned, a complainant must prove that his problem is real and that he has taken all reasonable steps to sort things out for himself.'

An early programme demonstrates that 'reasonable' is a concept applied with a certain delicacy. Someone buying a cheap car from a local 'open site' dealer may not have the knowledge or the sophistication to move logically up the complaints ladder, but they're still entitled to a good deal, and if they have a good case that is representative of others against the same firm *Checkpoint* may be interested in reporting it.

The problems concerned a company called Stewart Motors, whose proprietor Sydney West sold nineteen-year-old Chris Watts a Triumph 2000, taking a Morris 1100 he'd previously sold to Watts in part exchange. The Triumph required a £300 deposit, but West agreed to accept £60. Happily Watts took his father for a spin, only to discover that the carburettors were badly worn, the exhaust was blown and the clutch was slipping. He took the car back to Stewart Motors, left it for two days and then tried it once more. At first it appeared to run well, but the faults soon returned. When Watts took it back to the dealer for the second time West refused to take it in. Watts insisted on leaving it there, but when he went back the following day to find out what had been done he was amazed to find his car with a 'For sale' notice in the windscreen at a price of £595. After a 'struggle' he got the car back, but it ran so badly that he could not use it.

'I didn't get a receipt for my £60, which was stupid,' he admitted with refreshing candour. 'In the end I lost my money, the 1100, and I've got nothing now, nothing at all.'

Ronald Tibbles, lonely after the death of his wife, and wishing to get away from it all, bought a VW minibus from the same dealer for £1200. After six hundred miles the engine blew up. The dealer's guarantee proved worthless, and he too ended up with no car and lost money. In the meantime, Stewart Motors changed its name to Flemming Motors, and Dudley Woods exchanged his Hillman Minx for a Morris Marina, with a balance of £600 to pay. Sidney West failed to give him the log book or MoT certificate, and after several weeks of delay and argument the car was mysteriously burned. Woods found that he could not claim on his insurance without the relevant documents which, for some reason, were still held by West. He too ended up without a car and losing money.

Eventually, Sidney West found himself facing the *Checkpoint* microphone in his office which, Cook recalls, had a shotgun hanging ominously on the wall behind the desk. West began by denying that he knew Woods, but admitted he sold the VW to Tibbles and that he had guaranteed it. Yet, said Cook, you are leaving him to pay the bill for a replacement engine. West claimed that VW did not honour their guarantee (which was not true, as this had expired), and therefore 'nor will we'.

'That doesn't seem terribly fair,' Cook observed, and 'What about Mr Watts?'

West remembered Watts. 'He could not have hire purchase on his own motor, and we, out of the goodness of our hearts, gave him our own personal hire purchase.'

'And when he found the car wasn't roadworthy you wouldn't fix it. He brought it back, and while he still had money tied up in the car you put it up for sale on your lot.'

'Impossible,' West exclaimed. 'Mr Watts has not told you the truth.'

'Are you saying that none of the people who have complained to us – and these are just three out of nine different complaints – are telling the truth, and that you're right all along?'

'Right,' said West, 'we are right all along.'

West refused to continue the interview. The *Checkpoint* team then verified that Tibble's engine was long out of the manufacturer's guarantee when West sold it under his own. And Chris

Watts's car had been resold, as he said. But what of Woods, of whom West had originally disclaimed all knowledge, and who had never received his vehicle's documentation? Cook took Woods back to the car lot to confront West in person. After issuing a torrent of abuse, West claimed that Woods had bought the car through Sterling Motor Company. When shown his own receipt, with the name Stewart Motors on it, he became decidedly rattled.

'What's your beef? Is it because you've not been paid by your own insurance company?'

'They won't pay me until I produce a log book and MoT certificate. I can't do that unless you give them to me,' said Woods.

'If the log book is lost, you can apply for a new one,' replied West.

And so it went on, with West denying he had anything to do with the matter, but contradicting himself frequently before finally terminating the interview with the memorable words, 'It's about time you got in your bloody Granada or whatever it is, and pissed off.' Cook told listeners that further enquiries on Woods's car had shown it was already the subject of another incompleted hire purchase deal when it was sold to him. West had arranged for another deal for Woods through Sterling Motors. The second finance company was the Hodge Group, and its managing director John Hodell looked into the matter. When he reported back to *Checkpoint* he said that he had arranged with Woods's solicitors to waive any outstanding balance owed by Woods and put him back on the same footing 'as if he had never bought the car'. In return, Woods agreed to waive his own rights to the proceeds of his claim for the fire damage to the car.

Cook asked Hodell how Woods had managed to get finance from the Hodge Group via a dealer (West) who had no connection with Hodge.

'The dealer through whom we believed Mr Woods was buying his car (Stewart Motors) is a dealer that we have dealt with for some time. We had no idea that we were, in fact, financing another motor trader . . . If it proved that there is some kind of accommodation between them (the two dealers), this would certainly offend the criteria we have in my company.'

This story is one of many examples that show how complicated things can become in the purchase of a motor car. During a subsequent follow-up in a compilation programme, Ron Tibbles described how he had pursued West through the courts, regardless of the intimidating treatment he received. As costs mounted he found that the bailiffs could not lay their hands on anything of West's that would help to repay him. Everything, it seemed was in his wife's name. Finally Tibbles, faced with a repair bill of over £600, arranged to have West brought before a Registrar to see if there were any assets as yet undiscovered.

'During the course of the proceedings,' Tibbles said, 'Mr West was pleading poverty, but he had a flash diamond ring on his finger. The barrister asked him if the ring belonged to him. "Yes sir," said West. "And what is the value of the ring?" "£2,000, sir . . ." Then two bailiffs were called in, and the ring was seized. West paid my money into court the same day and got his ring back, so he couldn't have been very hard up, could he?'

In January 1979 the team received complaints about a long established chain of garages called Seagull Autos Ltd. Before their investigations were finished they found themselves involved in a variety of associated activities as diverse as petrol stations, trade directories, finance and property, spread as far as the Isle of Man and the Channel Islands, but centred in West London (See Case 13). The story is a good example of how perfectly normal people, all of whom took appropriate steps to safeguard their investments, can be hoodwinked into losing their money. As usual, the meticulous research equipped Cook for an interesting denouement in which violence played its part.

Later in the year the programme investigated a nationwide motor car auction firm, the Victoria Carriage Company, with a second programme on 16 January 1980. Just before this second programme was broadcast I happened to be in the *Checkpoint* office when Cook took a phone call from a London evening newspaper's advertising department. They had discovered what *Checkpoint* was doing and asked Cook's advice as to whether they should publish an advertisement they had just received from Victoria Carriage. Cook confirmed that the company was the subject of the next programme but declined to comment on the content or to give the advice required. In any event, the advertisement did not appear, a trend that was later followed in a number of specialised motoring magazines in which the company had previously advertised.

Cook began the programme by asking, 'When is a car auction not a car auction?' He went on to describe Victoria Carriage as a big money, up-market sales firm based in a vast three-storey building in Buckingham Palace Road in London's Victoria. The firm operated with massive national advertising in the motoring press, organising monthly auctions claimed to be the biggest and the best in the business. At any one time the company might have over £500,000s worth of other people's cars on the showroom floors, with promises of quick sales and top prices keeping the sales premises well stocked and well attended. Yet over forty people told *Checkpoint* that they were dissatisfied. Ron Cartwright from Leeds and his son wanted to sell an immaculate 1950 MG TD. They made it clear to Victoria Carriage that the car was only to be entered in one auction, and they set a reserve price of £4,400. It was not sold, but they were told that they had received an overseas cheque as a deposit, so they were persuaded not to come and collect the car, as they had intended. A month later they were told that the cheque had bounced and that (without permission) the car had been auctioned for the reserve price. A cheque for £4,400, less commission of course, would be sent. Several weeks later they had not received the money, so they told *Checkpoint* about the matter.

So did Peter Harris from Malvern, who wanted to sell his totally restored Jaguar XK 150. He was told that bidding for the vehicle had not reached the reserve of £6,000 and that it had been privately sold by Victoria Carriage to a buyer in Sweden. This was a clear breach of his agreement. However, through his own endeavours he discovered the car's new owner, who was not in Sweden but in London, and that the price paid had been £8,000.

'I've been able to prove in several cases that cars have been sold for a great deal more than the reserve, which people have had to take legal action to get,' Harris said.

Cook reported that there were then at least seventeen legal actions in train against Victoria Carriage Company and that the firm was 'no more than a business name registered by a Mr Brian Muller, sometimes also known as Middler'. It was not a limited company, as once claimed, but there was an unrelated Victoria Carriage Company Limited operating elsewhere. It was backed by a private business called Victoria and Company, whose proprietor was also Muller. Muller's residential and business addresses were said to coincide at Victoria's rented premises, but didn't.

The day-to-day running of the business was in the hands of a 'very smooth' former police constable called Barry McLoughlan. He dealt with the sale of Brenda Gillott's red E-Type Jaguar. She set a reserve price of £4,500, agreed to a twelve-week consignment period and told him she did not include her cherished number plate, 528 COW. After being told several times that the car had not been sold, she learned from a friend who had gone to transfer the number plates that it had been, and, like so many other cars, for only the reserve price. Her husband traced the new owner and discovered that he had paid £5,500 to Victoria Carriage, not £4,500 as they had said. Not only did they have an extra £1,000, but the Gillot's were not even paid the £4,500. She telephoned McLoughlan about the incessant delays and pointed out that the agreement was to pay within thirty-five days.

'Any time *after* thirty-five days,' he said, so I told him this could mean up to two years, so he turned round and said, 'Yes, that's right.'

Paul Donovan told listeners about his much-loved Morgan, placed on consignment with Victoria Carriage on a reserve they persuaded him to lower, just one of the company's 'profit-making winkles', as Cook found out from a 'Deep Throat' from within the firm.

'The lower the reserve they persuade you to take, the more Victoria will pocket, because it has little relation to the price the car actually makes at auction . . . Very few cars are sold at auction. Bids are, as they say, "Bounced off the wall" to make things look good. What sellers think is their second string, the sale on consignment, is actually Victoria's first priority. The seller is left with his reserve price, regardless of what his car actually fetches.'

And there were many ploys used to protract the procedure and delay payment.

'The first buyer backed out . . . The cheque bounced . . . It's a foreign cheque, and there's difficulty clearing it . . . The car wasn't as described . . . The documents had disappeared . . . We had to send it to the garage . . .'

'You can keep it going for months,' Cook said, 'which is what they did to Paul Donovan.'

Donovan explained that the thirty-five day clause that had bothered Brenda Gillott actually said that payment would be made within a minimum of thirty-five days after completion of the sale.

'A minimum of thirty-five days, a maximum of infinity. It means absolutely nothing,' Donovan said in disgust.

Taxed by Cook with the complaints, McLoughlan tried to justify the methods used by the business. After denying that the company held onto money he said that they could not pay out straight away for two or three reasons.

'The car could be on hire purchase. The car could be stolen. And although we don't give any guarantees, the people that purchase the cars are obviously covered by the Trades Descriptions Act . . . We run our business the way we think best . . . If a person does request to see our sales invoice, providing the new purchaser does not mind and we've got his permission in writing, we will show them . . . It's made quite clear to people that we work two ways (selling by auction and privately) and we return their asking price (the reserve price), because obviously we couldn't survive on a commission basis . . . We've got nothing to hide whatsoever. There's no secrecy . . .'

Yet later he told Cook and Paul Donovan when they visited him at an auction that the prime mover, Brian Muller, lived in Munich and that he had no UK address.

'An outright lie,' Cook told listeners. 'Unless, of course, Bird's Hill Drive, Oxshott – where Mr Muller does live – has somehow become part of the Bundesrepublik.'

Cook called at the imposing £150,000 mansion, with its six-foot inner perimeter fence, and banged on the door. After a few minutes he heard the chains being removed on the inside. Muller opened the door and Cook began asking him questions about the firm and the complaints outlined above. The massive Mr Muller uttered not a word. Eventually he went back inside, and began arguing loudly with his German-born wife, Ulla.

'I have to thank her for emerging shaken but unhurt from what followed,' Cook reported. 'When the door opened again and Mr Muller charged out with fists clenched, Mrs Muller tried to restrain him. She leaped on his back and pulled his hair, shouting, "Don't, Brian, You'll give the game away!"'

The uncommunicative Mr Muller jostled and shoved Cook, while his wife tried to calm him down. She suggested that Cook leave, as he was 'trespassing' and that he should visit the company offices at Victoria if he had any questions. Even though Cook had tried several times without success to conduct a civilised interview with Muller at Victoria, he tried once more, but . . .

'They didn't want to know,' said Cook. 'Instead, *we* received several strange telephone calls and, from Mr McLoughlan, a telegram.'

This implied that the *Checkpoint* team had been involved in a burglary at the Buckingham Palace Road offices. The remedy was to read the telegram over the air, neatly defusing the squib, damp or otherwise.

The company subsequently went into liquidation, few creditors got anything, and the police began a wide-ranging fraud investigation which, at the time of writing had not been completed.

Some time after the programme Muller appeared unannounced at *Checkpoint*'s offices. 'All was fair in love and war', he said, but this time he wanted *Checkpoint's* help. The auction company appointed to dispose of Victoria's assets was doing him and the creditors down, he claimed. But before the programme could tackle that one, the second auction company had gone bust too.

However, *Checkpoint*'s biggest 'bust' in the automotive field involved a firm called Revolution Oil which dealt in extended warranties on used cars. The warranties were rarely honoured, though Revolution took twelve million pounds in premiums from the public. After the programme the whole company literally did a 'moonlight flit' from their exclusive London headquarters.

CHAPTER 12

Bankruptcies and liquidations

Checkpoint has dealt with hundreds of complaints involving companies that go into liquidation or that cease to trade for some reason. The creditors of such companies range from the Inland Revenue and HM Customs & Excise to the suppliers of goods and services and the customers who pay in advance for a service that is not provided. Although the law relating to the behaviour of companies and the way they can operate was changed early in 1981, many of the experts who have appeared on *Checkpoint* believe that the changes will provide little worthwhile protection, either from company directors who are merely stupid or from those who are downright dishonest.

On 17 September 1980, the programme explained how a company can cost its customers money and let them down in a way that is perfectly legal, and how it can run into debt, fail in its contracts and escape responsibility, all within the law, without having to explain why.

'Many companies,' said Cook, 'are catching on to how they can cease trading and do nothing more to wind up their affairs. This means that they may never have to face the awkward questions that go along with liquidation.'

The programme quoted the kind of letter arriving all too often through people's letter boxes: 'It is with regret that the directors have decided to cease trading in view of the general financial situation of the company which, over a period of time, has deteriorated. This is mainly due to the dramatic fall-off in business together with escalating costs and expenses. There are a number of unsecured creditors of the company, including yourselves, and the only real asset of the company is the leasehold office premises, which are fully charged to the Bank. The directors have taken professional advice on the situation and believe that in view of the lack of assets to distribute among creditors there is no point in calling a creditors' meeting.'

This undated and duplicated missive came from a company

called Glowbond Ltd that ran a car warranty company called Autocare, and it was sent to all creditors, including those whose claims had been agreed months previously. Anne Reagan, one of the complainants, lost £85.00. She told listeners that while she appreciated that there may well be nothing that can be done in such a case she was very annoyed to receive such a cursory dismissal of the matter. 'It occurs to me that it's a very convenient way of avoiding liabilities.'

Cook pointed out that many such victims do not know that a company's liabilities do not end when they 'cease to trade'. However, under the law a company was under no obligation to go into liquidation and have all its assets turned into cash for the benefit of creditors. It could simply cease to trade, and unless a creditor takes matters into his own hands, there the situation will rest. But if a creditor feels that it is worthwhile he can petition the courts for compulsory winding up of the company.

It is worth pointing out that there is a strict pecking order of creditors in a bankruptcy or liquidation case. The Official Receiver takes his fees first – often to the tune of several thousand pounds. Next come the preferential creditors including, as mentioned above, the Inland Revenue and the VATman. Firms with secured loans outstanding come next in the list, and these include banks and other financial institutions. At the bottom come all the people whose money ultimately makes the whole thing work: the customers. Time and time again *Checkpoint* receives complaints from people and firms – usually but not always small ones – who have paid for goods or services, only to find that as little as a week later the firm stops trading and that there is no redress.

Sometimes a firm refuses to go into liquidation. One such company, Gifthome Ltd, was run by Graham and Maureen Shaw who operated a gift shop in Blackpool. They wrote to all creditors on 17 November 1979, saying that the company had ceased trading owing to an inability to pay its debts. Cook interviewed a number of suppliers who were each owed about £500 by Gifthome, and solicitors were advising them not to bother chasing such an amount because the costs would exceed the sums involved. One complainant, Derek Gunn from London, wondered whether this had been an intentional plan of the Shaws to overcome the problem of anyone taking legal action immediately. In any case, Gunn said that he did not receive a promised statement of account; neither had there been an official liquidation. Yet Shaw was still in the business of trying to make money, as Gunn and another complainant, Arthur Glasson, discovered. One scheme was called The Millionaire Treble Chance System. Another would earn participants up to £406,900 in the next fifty days. A third promised people they could make £200 in one day. All three schemes involved sending money, of course. When they made contact with Shaw and reminded him about his debt to them, he told them to keep out of his private business affairs and mind their own business. Shaw refused to appear on the programme.

John Price, on the other hand, did appear, to try and explain why his various construction companies kept letting people down to the tune of several thousand pounds at a time, work being started and not finished on many of his company's jobs before it then ceased trading. The interview got off to a complicated start when Price gave a short run down of his businesses . . .

'Norjay Construction has ceased to work on these contracts because Norjay Construction was being financed by Norjay Developments Ltd. Norjay Developments had done construction work overseas for which it has not been paid . . .'

Price promised over the air to send one complainant a cheque for £500, and complained bitterly about the fact that a creditor had pushed the firm into involuntary liquidation 'in which nobody benefits'. When Cook confronted him with the fact that he had escaped his responsibility in no less than six companies in the recent past he claimed to have lost large sums personally and then produced another cry from the heart.

'Company laws in this country are such that on the one hand the wrong kind of person can abuse company privileges to trade into a bad position and do a flit (this is something which I've not done). On the other hand, the same law deprives the company of continued trading. The potential profit it can make has gone. The creditors lose everything, and this is madness.'

The problem is, suggested Cook, that people cannot truly tell whether it is madness to continue or madness to stop, unless they have 'more than just the word of the company director concerned'. And sometimes the problem is exacerbated when the company concerned offers what appears to be a way out of the mess they've got you into. He interviewed Alfred Tawn and Edwin Lobo who had both invested money with the Glayhill Group of Burgess Hill in Sussex, a group that once claimed to be the leaders in guaranteed stamp investment portfolios. Tawn was attracted by the idea of making a 'guaranteed' fifteen per cent on his investment of £1000 after a year, but when he had his stamps independently valued he was given an estimate of a mere £400 to £500.

Lobo invested two amounts of £10,000 at a promised rate of nineteen per cent per year over a five-year period, after which he would get his original £20,000 back. Well before he got any money he was told that his contract was terminated, and he received an unwanted settlement for the £20,000 in the form of stamps of doubtful value. Shortly after that he learned that a previous investment with Glayhill of £25,000 was in jeopardy, when the company offered to buy them back at this price under the original guarantee. Before this happened he received a letter from Glayhill Stamps (UK) Ltd saying that the company had ceased trading and could not buy back the stamps. However, they offered to put the stamps into an auction 'run by another part of their group . . . but after all that I'm not prepared to trust them.'

Checkpoint tracked down Glayhill's proprietor, Brian Blaber, who answered various questions initially but proved reluctant to be recorded for the programme. This was yet another case for the 'door stepping' technique, so Cook confronted Blaber, microphone in hand, only to receive a number of sharp and 'nasty' responses but no explanatory answers. At one stage Blaber tried to hit Cook and then threatened to bring in a colleague whose presence Cook 'might not enjoy'. Finally, Blaber decided to call the police. The officer arrived and spent a few moments trying to calm Blaber down. After that, there followed a delightful interchange between Cook and the policeman.

COOK: I'm here to ask some legitimate questions on behalf of . . .
BLABER (*shouting*): Not me, so get out!
POLICEMAN: Hang on. Come on. Calm down. You asked me to come here . . .
BLABER: Police Officer, will you get rid of this man. He's got in the office. . . .
POLICEMAN: Give me a chance.
COOK: I haven't been in the office. I stood at the doorstep.
POLICEMAN: If the gentleman does not wish to talk to you, and he's asked you to leave, will you kindly leave?
COOK: I will do so.
POLICEMAN (*who has recognised Cook*): I understand why you're here. I'm just asking you to leave.
COOK: Certainly.
POLICEMAN: Thank you very much.

Blaber later phoned the programme to say that in view of Cook's 'disgraceful, pig-ignorant behaviour' they'd be getting no explanatory statements from the company.

'But after all,' said Cook at the programme end, 'we'd only gone along to find out how directors, whose company had given investment guarantees that they couldn't keep, could simply cease trading and still end up with a stamp option business which was, in Mr Blaber's words "doing very well". So remember, if you get a letter saying that a firm has ceased to trade, don't just leave it at that.'

One week later came the broadcast that set this book into motion (see the Introduction). It dealt with personal bankruptcy, the other side of the coin presented the week before, in which ordinary people are forced into bankruptcy 'for debatable reasons' as Cook put it, and who seemed to have been needlessly punished in the process. Professor Roy Goode, director of the centre for commercial law studies at Queen Mary College, began by saying that bankruptcy law had been in need of a very substantial, fundamental overhaul for a considerable time. He explained that this was why the government some years ago set up the Insolvency Law Review Committee under the chairmanship of Britains's top company undertaker, Sir Kenneth Cork. His brief was to examine the whole range of insolvency law and procedure in personal bankruptcy and in relation to the liquidation of companies.

'That committee produced an interim report recommending a change in bankruptcy law. At the same time the government had produced a consultation document also devoted to the reform of bankruptcy, which moved in a diametrically opposite direction and seemed not to be concerned with anything other than a reduction in the number of civil servants.'

Having intrigued listeners with this assertion, the programme produced a number of harrowing cases, starting with the recapitulation of a story covered by the programme two years previously concerning Joy Keating, a state-enrolled nurse from Birmingham and a single parent with two children. In 1974 she decided to spend hard-won savings on the refurbishment of her small Victorian terraced house. The builder estimated £500, but when the job was finished he presented a bill for £800. She argued about this jump, and also told them that she was unhappy with several aspects of the work, including items that had not been done. The builder offered to drop £100, but she refused to accept this reduction, believing that if she sat back and ignored him he would have to return and put the matter right. Another reason for her inaction was that she was expecting a visit from the local authority's building inspector, and she was hoping to get his backing for her complaints. He did not turn up in time, and she was issued with a bankruptcy petition. She paid £40 to a solicitor to represent her in court, and he told her there was no need for her to enter the court. She sat outside, and when the case was over he told her he had got an adjournment but that she would have to pay half the claimed amount, £420, into court within seven days.

'He said, "Just send me the cheque. I'll do everything. I'll let you know what's happened." I sent the £420 off a few days before the hearing, because it took me that long to get it together. The solicitor now tells me that he did not go into court because he didn't receive the cheque . . . but he didn't ring me or tell me anything . . . The result of that was I was declared bankrupt.'

Cook elaborated on what followed when she was examined by the Official Receiver.

'More than a little confused, she was quizzed about her background, her job, her assets, which, counting her bank balance and building society account, came to a little over £1000 – well above her debts of £800. These assets were frozen by the Receiver who then dropped a bombshell. She was required by law to meet his costs, which even at that early stage had topped £300. She was stunned.'

'I got myself another solicitor,' Keating said, 'and they went to court to try and get the Receiving Order rescinded on the grounds that when it was made I had the necessary cash. But the Official Receiver objected, and it was put into the hands of the trustees. My costs have jumped to £700, and the Official Receiver wants £700. And although I have the money to pay my creditors, there's not enough to cover these legal costs. Now I've got to go to court because they're trying to get possession of my house to pay the Receiver his costs . . . I've got two kids. What the hell would I do with my children when they sell my house, for God's sake? And why should the Council house me . . . why should we be up-rooted, just to pay the Receiver his costs? I don't agree with those costs anyway. They're just downright ridiculous.'

'It certainly seemed that way,' said Cook, 'because after our intervention the Official Receiver cut his costs by £500 and stopped trying to gain possession of Joy's house. But no sooner were her problems with the Receiver at an end than problems of costs owing to her trustees in bankruptcy began. A generous listener sent her £400, but she couldn't borrow enough money to get out of trouble, because undischarged bankrupts can't get credit. So she struggled on for another two years.'

A year before this second broadcast she got an absolute discharge from her bankruptcy order, but the trustees were still trying to get their own possession order on her home to pay their costs which she had been disputing unsuccessfully. These had risen to an unbelievable £1500, almost twice her original debt.

'It isn't just big businesses going bankrupt,' she said bitterly, 'it's the ordinary everyday working man who's got his wife and family to keep, and circumstances make it so that he can't pay his bills, or he disputes a bill . . . And somebody can just take your property away from you . . . It's about time the government did something about this Bankruptcy Act.'

A more recent programme (on 23 February 1983) revealed that personal bankruptcies now run at some six thousand a year, and chose two particularly good examples of how bankruptcy law still often proves to be a sledge hammer to crack a nut. There was the case of the Nottinghamshire train driver made bankrupt while completely solvent, and the case of the solicitor whose discharge from bankruptcy had been considerably delayed by costly mistakes made by his trustee and by the inertia of the Department of Trade.

The train driver, Michael Riley, initially failed to meet a bill of £641 at a time when his proposed marriage broke up. In some distress, he 'let things slide', though more than able to cover his debts. His assets at that time exceeded £30,000. What he thought was an opportunity to explain his position, and to pay up, turned out to be his bankruptcy hearing.

'There was this chappy sitting behind a leather top desk, and he said, "Well what do you want?" The representative from the finance company said, "Mr Riley owes us £641." So the man at the desk said, "Have you got the cash?" and I said, "No," thinking he meant *with* me. He said, "Well we will make you bankrupt." So I said, "What are you talking about. How can one be bankrupt with assets of around £30,000?" He said, "You've not got the cash, henceforth you are bankrupt," and I was ordered out of the room.'

Riley was subsequently evicted from his home and now faces a total bill of around £9,000 in order to settle his debts, which now consist mainly of the enormous costs incurred by the bankruptcy procedure itself.

'The whole episode has now become quite fantastic,' he said. 'I just can't honestly see how I'm going to pay this lot off. It's absolutely terrible that all this should come about because of a £641 debt which I'd got covered in the first place. And then once the machinery had started it was impossible to stop it. It's just run over me like a steam roller. I thought I was quite a strong man, but my word this has broken me.'

The solicitor, a London-qualified Sri Lankan called Annett Asirwatham, showed how it is not only the ordinary working man who can get 'steam-rollered'. Asirwatham was temporarily unable to meet debts of around £2,000 because of delays in receiving monies due to him for the legal aid work in which he specialised.

'I should have thought that the Official Receiver or the appointed trustee should have assessed the situation properly the legal aid fees *would* come,' he said.

But no breathing space was allowed. 'As a result I had to go through five years of hell with everybody losing money except perhaps the trustee.'

Over those five years, Asirwatham's trustee made excessive claims for remuneration, mislaid key documents and operated without a properly constituted committee of inspection. All this considerably delayed his discharge, and was confirmed by the Ombudsman, who strongly criticised the Department of Trade for its inadequate supervision of the trustee. The Department of Trade, however, did not think the trustee had performed badly enough to call for his removal. The net result was that Asirwatham lost his home, his self-respect and that of his children, and tens of thousands of pounds. The Catch-22 for him was that as an undischarged bankrupt he was barred from earning his living from practising his profession as a solicitor, and therefore even less likely to be able to meet his debts.

'Thinking back, I must say that these five years were traumatic years, not only for myself but for my whole family. There's something fundamentally wrong with the whole system, and it's not appreciated that bankrupts also have rights and that they are not all villians.'

By the time this programme was broadcast the Cork Committee had published its full report (see Case 16 on company insolvencies), and Sir Kenneth himself had some harsh things to say about the current laws on personal bankruptcy.

'I think they're unbelievably severe and rigid, and the costs to the community, to the country and the individual estate are just ridiculous,' he said. 'We must find a simple way with dealing with simple but honest people who get themselves in a muddle and at the moment the way it's dealt with just does not do that.

'One of the problems is that once you start this juggernaut rolling the costs are absolutely enormous, and quite often somebody's actually ruined by the costs, when they might not have been – had they been given an opportunity to discharge the debt. But it's not the costs in big cases, it's in little cases because time of these officials is so expensive and therefore small cases and small people in the end are paying more to get out of the costs of bankruptcy than they actually owe to begin with. This is ridiculous. It's time we got civilised and stopped it. If we go on like this, we'll end up with a debtor's prison.'

'Like we used to have,' commented Cook. But 'How would the Cork procedure civilise things?'

'Under our system,' Cork explained, 'we have a debt arrangement order, and anybody in trouble goes down to the local court. He's not sold up. He pays something out of his future earnings, and provided he's decent and honest he gets through without all the officials, without the Official Receiver and without the whole panopoly of bankruptcy. This will be quicker, better for the creditors and better for the individual.'

So was the government taking any action on these or any of the other proposals made by Sir Kenneth's Committee?

'Well there are movements.' Cork said. 'They are taking the major items which are essential, but mostly for sorting out business and employment. There's no proposal at the moment to deal with the bankruptcy side. One must realise that this is a great piece of legislation, and before an election we're unlikely to get that through. But any government must realise that it is important for them to do the whole of it. People have said there are no votes in reviewing insolvency – but there are a hell of a lot of votes to be lost by not doing it.'

On 4 February 1981 *Checkpoint* presented a critique of the new Companies Act 1981 which made important changes in the law relating to companies and businesses. In particular, the Act changes what companies are obliged to tell the public about themselves. Pointing out that in its eight years of operation the programme had told hundreds of stories of companies and business people who take money from the public and give little or nothing in return, Cook pondered as to whether the Act will mean more or less protection for people dealing with companies and businesses. He turned to the matter of the Registry of Business Names, which the Act was to abolish. Previously, anyone trading in a name that is not their personal name must register that name and say who they are and where they live.

'Vital information for us, and for the public when things go wrong and someone takes off with your money,' said Cook. 'The new Act will scrap the registry and put a self-regulating system in its place.' The centre for this system was to be moved from London to Swansea. Cook explained how the registry had proved time and time again to lead to people; even though they could easily have given wrong information on the application forms, the fact is that many gave information that helped in the development of a story. Peter Harris of Tudor Stone Cladding gave an accommodation address, and the firm there in turn gave Cook a useful interview about Harris.

Brian Goldstein of Express Company Registrations gave a detailed account of how someone could buy off-the-shelf companies, at that time for about £100, with only £2 of issued share capital. He agreed that this was not much to pay for the purchase of 'all kinds of protection under law for what might be rather nefarious practices', as Cook put it. In fact, the Act could prove to be a 'con man's charter'.

Cook asked Professor Tony Boyle of Queen Mary College, London, what he thought of the Act, and Boyle's first criticism was 'the lax accounting requirements', in which small companies (that is, those with a turnover of less than £1.4 million) would need to file only an abridged balance sheet and not a profit and loss account or a directors' report. He saw the Act as providing encouragement for the small fringe of dishonest businessmen who hide behind the corporate forms and take advantage of limited liability. The task of pursuing those who run fly-by-night businesses would be more difficult. However, he welcomed the provision that extended the period of disqualification for directorship from five to fifteen years.

The final interview in this programme was with Reginald Eyres, Parliamentary Under Secretary for Trade. Cook asked him if an Act that was designed ostensibly to ease the administrative burdens on small businesses in particular might not also make it easier for a dishonest operator to conceal what he might be up to. Eyres did not feel that the original situation, with the

Registry of Business Names, was much of a help in this respect, and he put the view that consumers could improve matters for themselves if they took 'a rather more informed interest in noting with whom they are doing business and whom they would have to sue if they get in a dispute'. However, he agreed that with the current staff cuts in the civil service, and with the police and Trading Standards staff being very overworked, the government could not enforce the legislation on the country's business community. '. . . therefore I think it is right to put an emphasis on self-regulation and self-enforcement'. Cook argued that the system would not catch those who did not abide by it; as for the heavier penalties, what was the point in this if the government had fewer people to catch offenders? Eyre replied that the heavier penalties were intended as a deterrent that would make 'the bad element who might think of avoiding their responsibilities much more careful about what they do'. He rejected the view that the new legislation would make the 'engine of fraud' (as company law is often described) go faster. Neither did he think it would be a 'con man's charter', because he claimed that new efficiencies in his department meant that there would be a considerable tightening up of procedures.

'Are you saying that you will do us out of a job at *Checkpoint*,' Cook asked.

'No,' Eyres replied, 'because you deal with some of the frailties of human nature, and I'm afraid that they'll continue. But we are going to try with these alternative proposals to help people to get their rights.'

Since that broadcast there has been no noticeable diminution of complaints relating to company failures; indeed, if anything there has been an increase. Certainly, more businesses are prepared to take bigger legal risks in the face of inadequate regulation and often derisory penalties. 'In a time of recession,' Cook notes, 'when money is hard to make, the bigger the risk "sharp" businessmen are prepared to take.' Six weeks later *Checkpoint* commented on the seven thousand company failures in 1981, a fifty per cent increase over the previous year. The programme was to reveal a new kind of sharp operator: the liquidation specialist. In particular the rapid rise of the most notorious firm, called Chancery Lane Registrars Limited of London and Sheffield. In the past two years the three men behind the company had between them acted as liquidators in scores of liquidations involving millions of pounds.

Things began with a bang when the three men were named and

described: Maurice Sidney Caplan, with a criminal conviction for defrauding creditors; Stephen Willard Peplar, with a criminal conviction for defrauding five banks; and Paul Edward Davis, a solicitor with a criminal conviction for forgery. How proper is it, Cook asked, that such men could hold a position as liquidators, a position of 'the highest trust'? The short answer is that the law does not require a liquidator to hold any professional qualifications. And, not being a professional person such as an accountant, he can tout for business in a way that an accountant never could:

> Dear Sir
> Our records show that recently your company had a judgement debt registered, and consequently we are writing to you to enquire if we can be of assistance to you either now or in the future.
>
> We are a company specialising in deeds of arrangement with creditors, reconstructions and amalgamations, insolvency affairs and refinancing and recapitalisation of companies. Our services also include the introduction to financial sources. If we can be of any assistance to you, please do not hesitate to contact us.

The first piece of duplicity in this letter is that the 'records', far from belonging to Chancery Lane Registrars, are readily available in The London Gazette and Stubbs Gazette. The second was that the hint of new finance possibilities was all too often turned into an offer of pressure to liquidate the business concerned, which was how Chancery Lane Registrars made its money.

The touting for business was nationwide, through a network of associated companies and sub-agents working on commission, 'a corps of corporate body-snatchers, sending out yet more unsolicited letters,' as Cook described it. He also made the point that as the advertising was directed at the directors of companies that might be in trouble, these self-appointed liquidators might not be too concerned about the interests of creditors. As things turned out, even many of the directors who made contact with Chancery Lane Registrars found things not entirely to their advantage after the liquidation specialists had been at work.

The main ploy was to take a company showing signs of financial trouble, find some way of keeping up the appearance of normal trading, fend off the creditors and milk the company for all it was worth. One example quoted was that of Ralph Howe

Marketing Ltd, whose directors were running Howe International from the same premises at Poole in Dorset. Alan Berrett was one of the creditors of the former company. In April 1980 he was told by Howe that Ralph Howe Marketing was going into liquidation. Then Berrett was contacted by Chancery Lane Registrars and told of their forthcoming appointment as liquidators. Howe asked Berrett for his proxy vote at a creditors' meeting and, as the amount involved was not large, Berrett agreed.

'I wanted to help Mr Howe,' he said. 'On the other hand, I did write to Chancery Lane Registrars to offer my services on the committee of inspection, because I knew the business technically.'

To Berrett's surprise, no such committee was appointed, and the surprises continued. Howe's business carried on in the same premises under a different name, one of many examples of what is known in the *Checkpoint* office as the 'Change-the-name-and-do-the-same Game'. In Howe's case, according to Berrett, this meant that the many creditors of Ralph Howe Marketing (who were owed about £72,000 between them) were left 'to sing for their money'.

'Before Mr Caplan came along,' Berrett said, 'a friend of mine who was also a creditor served a winding-up petition on Ralph Howe Marketing, but after Mr Caplan became liquidator I understand that somebody turned up at my friend's solicitors and paid off the debt in cash, money that did not come from the original company. However, as the debt was paid the petition was withdrawn, and Mr Caplan continued as liquidator.'

The result of this was that Howe was able to continue trading with his new company, using the assets of the old company. To the outsider, everything appeared normal, with no sign of a liquidation.

'The situation stinks,' complained Berrett. 'It makes an ass and a mockery of the law.'

Not unnaturally, Ralph Howe felt that Caplan had done a good job, and he told Cook that Caplan was 'as straight as a die'. But things were even more complicated by the fact that Howe's new company was paying instalments to Caplan to buy back the assets of the old company. This followed a valuation of the assets by a man who was a director of a firm called London and Bedford Realisations Ltd, a company in which Chancery Lane Registrars had a fifty per cent stake. London and Bedford had handled many of the assets in Chancery Lane's liquidations, putting themselves in a position to make an extra hidden (and illegal) profit.

'As people have become aware of Chancery Lane Registrar's activities,' Cook reported, 'the techniques have been changed and refined. At one stage disgruntled creditors began going over their heads to the courts to ask for compulsory winding up and for other liquidators to be put in. Now the firm are seeking creditors' agreement to their appointment at the outset. This way they are able to stay one step ahead of the growing opposition.'

The convolutions of the three men running Chancery Lane Registrars were nothing short of amazing. One complainant told how they staged-managed a creditors' meeting by declaring that proxy votes against the appointment of Caplan as liquidator were invalid. The inside story of other shenanigans was told by Barry Calvert, who had worked for Chancery Lane Registrars. He was persuaded to act for the company in the Sheffield area. He believed he was there to help a company in trouble to be rescued if possible. Caplan and partners soon dispelled that notion: there's more money to be made in liquidations. The final straw for Calvert came when Caplan insisted on taking 'the lion's share' of the last £32 cash held by the wife of a small plumber who had gone bust.

'That was it, for me. I didn't want any part of that sort of business. I don't need to do that to earn a living.'

To set the record straight, Cook pointed out that Calvert himself was a former bankrupt who was then running his own business in competition with Chancery Lane Registrars. Calvert had admitted to *Checkpoint* that some of the liquidations he had handled had 'run into trouble'. In fact, he later fled the country, blaming *Checkpoint*, after substantial sums of money went missing from one of the companies over which he had been appointed liquidator.

The next step was an interview with Messrs Caplan, Peplar or Davies. At first none of them would make any comment. Then Caplan agreed to an interview, only to cancel it. He asked for a written outline of allegations. This was sent, but still no interview was forthcoming. When Cook visited the company offices, the police were called, and the trio remained incommunicado. This did not prevent Cook from broadcasting their unique qualifications to run a business based on insolvency . . .

'One dubious qualification is the high number of insolvencies in their collective business career. Even Mr Davies, at one time the liquidator of about fifty companies, has himself been a director of a liquidated company. And Mr Stephen Peplar has had a string of companies that couldn't pay their way. Amazingly, Mr Caplan is liquidating one of Mr Peplar's companies and one of Mr Davies's. Mr Davies is liquidating another of Mr Peplar's, but it's the record of Mr Caplan – or Hissing Sid, as he's known – that caps the lot.

'He was the director of at least nine companies compulsorily wound up before he spent ten years as a bankrupt. Later he went to jail for fraudulent trading. Mr Peplar, too, has been inside, for conspiring to defraud five banks. And Mr Davies, solicitor, has been heavily fined for uttering a forged document. And remember, it's these three men who are advising directors in trouble, acting as liquidators, and running the highly successful firm of Chancery Lane Registrars, whose affairs in the view of many are nothing short of a major scandal.'

In June 1982 the programme examined the business aspects of a report of the Insolvency Law Review Committee, chaired by Sir Kenneth Cork. (See Case 16) This was a fast response to the publication of the report, and it is a measure of *Checkpoint*'s standing that Cork and one of the government ministers responsible for this aspect of consumer affairs agreed to be interviewed at very short notice to explain some of the intricacies of the report and its possible effect on future legislation.

CHAPTER 13

Checkpoint 'compilations'

It has become tradition for *Checkpoint* to round off each season of editions with a programme devoted to summarising the highlights, giving listeners an opportunity to hear once more some of the sad, incredible, infuriating or perplexing stories of the previous few months. What follows is a typical example, broadcast on 17 June 1981. It began with the firm called Security Taskforce, 'Whose amazing antics you may find hard to believe,' as Cook put it.

An ex-employee of the firm called Tony Farrant described how his nightly round was supposed to cover thirty-four security check calls over a distance of a hundred and fifty miles. He was a driver for the company, covering an area from Portsmouth to Romford.

'No way could I ever get round all the places three or four times a night,' he said, referring to the contractual obligations. 'We used to go there once or twice and sign the book four times. During the day I used to do cash and transit runs in a Marina van that had no armour or protection of any kind.'

An ex-security guard for the company, Bob Thompson, told how one of his colleagues on the cash-in-transit run had been in prison for armed robbery, one of three employees with known criminal records at that time. A particularly dramatic story was told by a third ex-employee, Alan Roberts, on a bank run involving sums of up to £50,000 a call.

'First day, we're going to Birmingham, and although we've got a radio on board I find that once we pass Reading we've got no radio contact with any part of the firm. It would have been a dead cert for any criminal to have taken us, taken our uniforms and done the rest of the route. And they could have made a security pass, because the first time I went on that run I had to make my own up. I was given a plastic envelope and a bit of card with 'Security Taskforce' written on it. I was told by the company that when I got to Watford Gap service station there was a photo booth, that by paying 40p I could get two colour photos to cut in half and stick one in the envelope which I could seal up with my lighter, which is what I did. All right, so we had a crash helmet on, but I'm afraid if someone had stuck a shooter up my nose I'd have said, "OK, there's the keys, there's the cash. You take it, mate. I'm off!"'

The man behind Security Taskforce was Brian Anthony Wilson, and he was also instrumental in setting up an organisation called the National Union of Security and Allied Forces.

'It may come as no surprise,' Cook told listeners, 'to hear that this union seemed to have less to do with improving staff conditions than with infiltrating other firms with a view to pirating their business.'

After the original programme was broadcast, union activities dwindled to zero and Security Taskforce closed down, but Wilson remained working behind the scenes, seemingly involved in other companies in the security field.

The next case was described as a 'first' for *Checkpoint*. During its previous eight years of operation the team had dealt with many complaints involving solicitors, but in February 1981 came the tale of Marcus Jones, described by Cook as having two lives, that of a leading London tax barrister and, by contrast, that of a hotelier and property developer 'on a grand scale'. Jones first entered the hotel world in 1974 when he bought the Broadsands Links Hotel near Brixham through a company called Oceancrest Ltd. Before long the once-successful hotel was besieged with creditors, and Hazel Preston was left with the task of dealing with them. She told how people would come into the hotel demanding their money and that sometimes she would give them a cheque knowing that, because Jones's signature was not on it, it would not be honoured. Unfortunately she could never contact Jones to deal with such matters.

'On one occasion the gas was cut off,' she said. 'The guests were told it was a gas leak, but we all knew that the bill hadn't been paid. During all the financial problems, writs started to pour in . . . We had people ringing up and people knocking on the door, and no way could we contact Mr Marcus Jones who could help us out. We were not allowed to ring him at his London barrister's telephone number. Towards the end it got very hot, and he was not to be seen for the last two weeks when most of the staff didn't get any wages. Mind you, if he had come down I'm sure they would have lynched him.'

Before his Broadsands Links exercise, another company of

Still topical nineteenth-century cartoon by Daumier in which the evil Dr Macaire instructs his pupils in yet another new way of cheating the public, 'You set up a new company as cheaply as possible to take in as much money from the public as possible by advertising widely. You then syphon the money away, liquidate the company, and begin the process all over again.'

An apposite Punch *cartoon from the 1920s:*
SON *'I say, Father, here's a chance – an advertisement offering permanent employment to a young man willing to invest a hundred pounds. I wonder what the permanent employment is.'*
FATHER *'Trying to get the hundred pounds back.'*

Members of an earlier Checkpoint *team: this page, Andrew Jennings (left) and John Edwards (the current producer); opposite, John Stonborough (left) and David Perrin*

The Checkpoint *team planning a programme, from left to right: Dina Gold, Malcolm Stacey, Roger Cook, Tim Tate and Jon Danzig*

Editing tape in the small hours

Setting up the programme in the studio

Recording Checkpoint

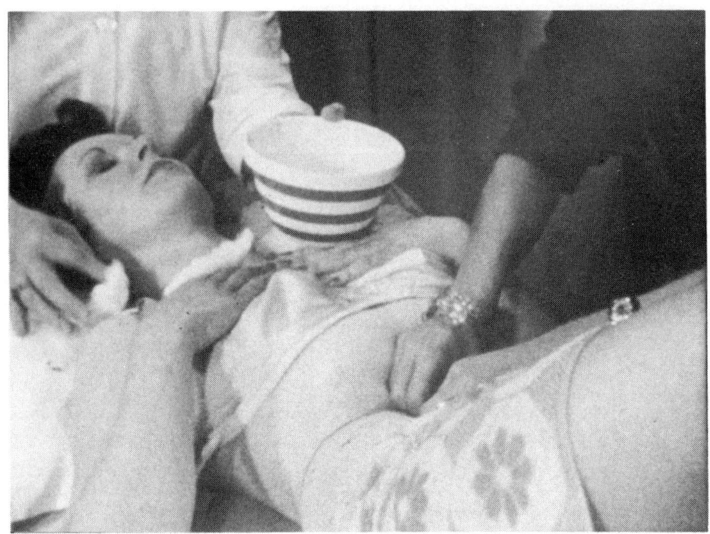

Psychic Surgeons, see Case No. 7. The moment of deception: The surgeon palms a balloon full of pig's blood and chicken giblets into the soft flesh of a hopeful patient's stomach to give the impression that his hands have 'entered her body' to remove a malignant growth

Opposite: A touch of violence involving an iron bar and three broken ribs for Roger Cook in the case of the fake ivory distributor

Only in the Express . . . the 14-stone star who risks life and limb chasing conmen and hucksters

VICTOR DAVIS

Checking up on the BBC's Checkpoint man

THE TAPED CRUSADER

CHUCKED OUT

And now a word from your unfriendly wrestler . . . Roger Cook offers the microphone and ends up at the bottom of a flight of stairs . . . his only thought was to give his audience the crash, bang, thud, as he made contact with each step.

INTREPID

PANTING

CAPTURED

DANGER, RADIO TEC AT WORK

Tenacity

'Ruthless'

Daily Mail Saturday February 3 1979

He's been beaten up, run down by a car, thrown downstairs by a wrestler—so what makes Radio's caped crusader keep coming back!

Cook's tour de force . . .

THE SUNDAY TIMES, NOVEMBER 19 1978

wounds of the Beeb's crusader

AUJOURD'HUI

GRANDE-BRETAGNE

Le justicier de la B.B.C. 4

Depuis bientôt sept ans, la radio britannique diffuse une émissi... de défense du consommateur différente des autres. Le responsa... un casse-cou de trente-six ans : Roger Cook.

Radio

Steve Race

Not enough cooks

32 The Weekly News, April 7, 1979

LISTENERS HEARD ROGER BEING THROWN DOWNSTAIRS

His job makes him five times more expensive to insure than a war correspondent

Discreet

On head

Cook is radio's No. 1

DAILY EXPRESS

Being punched in the mouth is all in a day's work for super sleuth Roger

Cook: "I get scared"

RADIO by Paul Ferris

Checkpoint strikes again

Checkpoint's *international news value is reflected in this selection of cuttings from the many stories published in newspapers and magazines* which Jones was a director, Janavale Ltd, acquired a hotel called The Globe at Newton Abbott. Peter Cantrell described how this good business was run into the ground.

'For two and a half years it went progressively downhill. I remember one Christmas, my cellarman and myself took all the available cases we'd got with empty bottles that had a deposit and with the cash we had to purchase stocks. We did this three times that Christmas, scuttling from hand to mouth. I suppose it's laughable now, but at the time it was very, very serious. *Fawlty Towers* (a popular TV comedy series about a hotel) has got nothing on this place at all.'

Cook reported that Janavale Ltd went to the wall owing more than £200,000. Oceancrest had already folded owing £500,000. 'But as Mary Davis of Broadsands Links recalls, that didn't stop Mr Jones.'

'While we were struggling, he was in the middle of making plans for new buildings, buying property, buying land all around. I know this because I did all his typing and saw a lot of letters that came to him. There was Mr Jones making all these grand plans, and yet off he goes and leaves us in the lurch. We were not paid for about three weeks, when out of the blue we're told the receiver is coming in. We've got to close. Seventeen staff out of a job, just like that!'

'But Mr Jones went on via yet another company to try to buy one of the hotels back,' said Cook. 'He then attempted a million pound property development deal on little more than £1,000 deposit. That project collapsed too, partly at the expense of the site owner and largely at the expense of the builder Marcus Jones had engaged. Mr Jones, whose use of legal action on his own behalf had become legendary, tried to get our programme stopped. He failed. As one of his victims said, he used his considerable legal knowledge very much to his own advantage.'

The next programme reviewed yet another aspect of the Companies Act 1981. As stated previously, many people viewed the introduction of the Act as being to their disadvantage because part of its effect would be to scrap the Registry of Business names at Companies House in London. Since 1916 proprietors of businesses had been obliged to register their names and addresses, who they are and where they can be found. In this way someone wishing to take legal action against a firm at least knew where they could begin. Cook pointed out that if such information was no longer available, this could only be done with great difficulty. Tom Smith MP, then the Labour Opposition spokesman for Trade and Industry, came into the studio 'to bring us up to date on the Bill's progress and to ponder why the Government still wants to scrap the Register despite howls of protest'.

'The real reason,' said Smith, 'is to cut the number of civil servants employed by the Department of Trade by sixty-five. But it's ludicrous in my opinion to put this forward as a justification, because the service can be made to pay for itself and for the salaries of those civil servants by the simple expedient of increasing the charges. At the moment it costs £1 to register a name and 25p for a search. That could be increased to make it £5 to register and £1 for a search. Everyone who's thought about the matter would be willing to pay these fees, and the Government would end up making a profit that would keep these civil servants in a useful job and continue an excellent service to the public.'

Smith described the difficulty the Conservative Government was having in trying to get the Bill through Parliament against opposition from the Consumers Association 'right through the whole range of business and commerce'. The House of Lords wasn't impressed with the Bill either, and many Conservative MPs rebelled 'and only got put back in by very energetic Whipping [parliamentary "Whips" ensure that party members vote in line with party policies] in the hereditary highways and byeways'.

According to Smith, the Government wanted the present system changed because it wasn't perfect, and he agreed that this was the case. Not everyone who trades under a business name takes the trouble to register it, and it is difficult to enforce this legal requirement. But a very large number of people do register, and Smith called for effective sanctions against those who did not. He agreed with the Government that someone trading will put his name and address on letters and other literature, but said that this should be complementary to a registration and not an alternative to it. He concluded that the new legislation would make it easier for people engaged in 'doubtful practices' to continue.

Next Cook looked back at one of two cases of alleged corruption in local authorities. In April 1981 the *Checkpoint* team had discovered an extraordinary story of council officers taking advantage of their position at other people's expense. The people concerned were generally elderly, living in what a property developer would call 'a desirable bijou cottage'. The area was

Surrey, and the local authority was Elmbridge. George and Millie Adams used to live there, in one of a row of such cottages near Thames Ditton. Millie began by explaining that her family had lived in the cottage since 1900, and the first news of impending changes came, innocently enough, when the landlord came to see them.

'We happened to see him coming across the Common,' she said, 'and he was speaking to a lady. He came in and explained to us that he had to sell the cottage in a block of four and that we'd be protected by the Rent Act. We found out later that the lady we saw on the Common was Miss Sally Bowden who bought the cottages.'

'That name, Sally Bowden, assumed great significance as our story unfolded,' said Cook. 'She was a Home Help organiser for Surrey County Council and was therefore in a position to know of elderly tenants who might be ready to move. Next on the scene came a Mr Stanley Baker, an Environmental Health Officer for Elmbridge Borough Council, whose job included the recommendation of Closing Orders which councils sometimes use to have run down properties brought up to scratch. After Miss Bowden had bought the properties and the Adamses at her request had done much work on the grounds, Mr Baker turned up and began to order them about.'

Millie Adams described their annoyance at this turn of events and how they wondered why Baker was involved, 'unless there was a connection between him and Miss Bowden'. Eventually Baker told the Adamses that it would cost many thousands of pounds to repair their cottage properly and that Miss Bowden couldn't afford it.

'He mentioned her by name,' said Millie, 'and by this time we felt as if we'd been set up. Then Mr Baker came along to tell us there was a Closing Order (on the cottage). Then we knew that our home was going to be taken away from us, which made us feel furious, absolutely furious. And very upset.'

The imposition of the Closing Order, which said that the cottages were unfit for human habitation, meant that they could be bought for an advantageous price and then, after the closing order had been lifted, sold with vacant possession at an enormous profit.

'We uncovered a dozen cases where Miss Bowden, Mr Baker or members of his family had taken or attempted to take that profit,' Cook reported. 'But a connection between the ostensibly happily-married Mr Baker and Miss Bowden had never been established. Not until one afternoon when we called on Miss Bowden's imposing new residence at Ripley in Surrey. There the couple were, arm in arm in the garden.'

As Cook went down the drive to meet them, Mr Baker set off to fetch a wheel barrow and Miss Bowden began weeding. There followed an example of those recorded conversations for which the programme has become famous.

COOK: Good afternoon. Are you Miss Bowden?
BOWDEN: I am.
COOK: My name's Roger Cook from the BBC *Checkpoint* programme, and I'm here to record an interview with you and Mr Baker, whose motor car is over there, about the way houses have been acquired by you and how a part played by Mr Baker seems to have. . . .
BOWDEN: Well, actually I'm on holiday at the moment. So I . . . I'm on holiday . . . So I'm not prepared to say anything at all.
COOK: That is Mr Baker's car?
BOWDEN: Oh yes. He's down there.
COOK: Good. Let's have a word with him, too. Mr Baker! My name's Cook from the BBC *Checkpoint* programme. I'm recording an interview now about the way houses have been acquired following Closing Orders being put on by you and how houses have been acquired very cheaply. . . .
BAKER: I suggest you put your complaints in writing to the Council.
COOK: You're the person who ought to be answering the questions.
BAKER: No. You do as I say. You put it in writing.
BOWDEN: Come on. We've got some gardening to do.
BAKER: Off you go.

For the next few minutes they both ignored questions about whether they were in a position to gain and exploit knowledge about such obviously profitable property and about Mr Baker's professional connection with property in which his family had interests. Eventually they turned their backs on Cook and set off for Bowden's house.

BAKER: You clear off.
COOK: How was this place paid for? Was it paid for out of the profits from your house dealings?
BOWDEN: Mind . . . I think they're the sort of people who'd put their feet in the door.

At this point Cook had the door slammed in his face.

Following that programme both Baker and Bowden were suspended from their jobs and Scotland Yard fraud squad mounted an inquiry into the matter. Baker was subsequently dismissed for 'Gross misconduct'.

The round-up finished with three more stories, the first about the fringe banking empire called Barnet Christie that collapsed in 1978 owing over £4 million in fixed deposits made mainly by elderly people. A large part of the deposits were taken in the Channel Island of Guernsey by one Barnet Christie company for two years after it had lost the right to do so. Following the programme one of the key company men was given a suspended jail sentence and fined twenty-five thousand pounds, and the one-time chairman was charged on the island with conspiracy. (See Case 12)

Then came the case of the Enfield-based mortgage company, Accrohurst Ltd, that took a great deal of money from desperate would-be house purchasers but delivered few of the promises.

'Three of the principals beat me up during the course of our enquiries,' recalled Cook, 'but I am now able to report that John James O'Brien and his cohorts were convicted of conspiracy to defraud and are now serving sentences ranging from twelve months to three years.'

Finally came the case of the families Randall and Sumner (see Case 2) in which Cook was swilled with the contents of a chamber pot and subjected to a degree of violence to the accompaniment of some explicit four letter words.

'My tape recorder was literally torn to pieces, while the two families danced about saying that an "incompetent and insignificant" programme like *Checkpoint* wasn't going to affect them. But it did. Their business has ceased and, following a police investigation, they were charged with conspiring to defraud newspapers and the public by mail order advertisements. Stanley Randall was acquitted, but his wife was jailed for eighteen months. Barbara Sumner got three years, and Gordon Sumner, the brains behind the operation, will be a guest of Her Majesty for five years.'

CHAPTER 14

'You come across some very odd things'

Every now and again *Checkpoint* deals with a story that stands out as being particularly strange or bizarre.

'You come across some very odd things in this programme,' said Cook, 'and one of them concerned a programme we did in October 1976. Until then, I'd always thought that words like feudalism, serf and vassal belonged to the Middle Ages. Then I visited an estate near Aviemore in Scotland and talked to Sandy Lindsay, a former Battle of Britain fighter pilot who lived under the thumb of a feudal superior. And archaic though it sounds, feudal superior is still the correct term to use if you are, as he was, a feuar living on a feu.'

Lindsay reeled off a list of just a few of the conditions imposed upon people who buy property in one of Scotland's many feudal estates, some of which are as large as Sussex county in England.

1. One dwelling only to be permitted on the feu for use as a private residence by one family only. No other buildings allowed on the feu without the consent of the feudal superiors. Plans of all buildings to be approved by the superior prior to their being submitted for planning application to the local authority.

2. The feuar to relieve the superiors of all expenses by the local authority in respect of pavements, roadways, drains etc. and of all expenses in connection with legal documents and fees.

3. The superiors shall have the right of pre-emption, and it shall not be in the power of the feuar to sell the feu without first offering it to the superior.

4. Quality and quantity of water supply is not guaranteed, and no steam engine or noxious substances shall be permitted on the feu.

Of course, most of the conditions are never fully spelled out on paper, so when George Patterson sold part of his property for improvements he was faced with an unexpected bill from his feudal superior for £600. That was the 'fee' for letting the deal go through. Patterson objected to paying the money, but put the blame not on the superiors, who are 'only people, after all', but on the system. 'It's high time the law was changed,' he said indignantly, thinking of the oil and minerals that might lie under his land but belong to his superior.

'Speaking as a vassal,' said Sandy Lindsay, 'there is no other place in the Free World where people not only call themselves your superior but in actual fact are legally superior.'

Church of Scotland minister Jim Benson had publicly condemned this system from his pulpit. He called it inequitable. 'I want to see the system removed, whereby some people are in a position of being superior to another, when in the eyes of God men are equal.'

Except, interpolated Cook, if you happen to be living on a Highland feu, like Chris Fraser, Aviemore's former sub-postmaster. He used to live in rented property on a feu. He decided to buy the property so he could build up a business to pass on to his family. The seller consulted the feudal superiors who assured him that they wouldn't be interested in the deal. Fraser then bought the property.

'I was immediately notified by the agents of the estate that they were exercising their right of pre-emption,' he said. 'They were taking the property off me at the price I had paid for it, I had been planning the move for years, and in twenty-four hours it had all gone. It lost me thousands of pounds.'

Sandy Lindsay told listeners about a former War Memorial in Aviemore, built as a public hall by local people. The twenty-five year lease ended, and the hall became the property of the landowner, without any compensation.

'Our hall is now a supermarket and laundrette,' complained Lindsay, 'but at least the old soldiers can get their shirts washed, which is more than most people can say about a War Memorial.'

Needless to say, *Checkpoint* sought an interview with those responsible. Much of the property in question was owned by the Strathspey Estate which in turn was the concern of Lord Seifield. At first they were invited to telephone him to arrange an interview but, as in other cases, this arrangement was not honoured. No one else on the estate would talk, either, but another local laird, John Grant did agree to volunteer his views on feudalism. He had previously repossessed a village school, playing field and tennis courts.

Grant said that his control meant that no one could develop a site improperly, and he claimed that as he took local views into account there was simply no problem. He saw nothing wrong in, for example, taking over the War Memorial when its lease ran out. In a rather convoluted argument he blamed the modern system of taxation on what had happened to some of his own properties.

'Twenty-five years ago, if I had been a landowner I would have felt it important to provide a piece of land for the church and for a school and for a playground for the children, and in this particular case a tennis court was given. The school was provided on the system of the feu and so was the manse and a playing field. It was the right system then. Nowadays things have changed enormously, and we have capital taxation. There isn't the same money in owning land, and everyone must pay for what they get. I think this is perfectly fair.'

Grant admitted that he would like to see 'the planners' gradually assume more responsibility for controls that are now written into feus . . . 'But there are definite situations in which planners for one reason or another, are unable to exercise control, whereas I am able to do so.'

Asked by Cook if he thought he was the right man for that kind of responsibility, Grant replied, 'I don't think there's anyone else actually capable of doing it; therefore it's on my plate, and I'm afraid that, like conducting this interview, I just have to take it on and accept it as part of life.'

'A sort of divine blight of kings,' joked Cook, before seeking advice from Michael Lorimer, legal consultant to the Scottish Landowners Confederation. After nine hundred years, shouldn't something as archaic as feudalism be pensioned off?

'No,' said Lorimer. 'There have been two Acts reforming the feudal system, one in 1970 and another in 1974. This first was important because it allows any feuar to apply to a Lands Tribunal to have any feuing conditions varied, and I think that feuars should make more use of this.'

Cook questioned the apparent reasonableness of this by suggesting that feuars might not wish to incur the wrath of their superiors by taking such action over, say, the payment of a large fee for the 'privilege' of building an extension on their own property. Not to mention the rights of pre-emption!

The feuars should take legal advice, stressed Lorimer, but he agreed that there was room for considerable reform, the Acts of 1970 and 1974 having taken things 'a long way down the road' in this respect. But Sandy Lindsay was not so sanguine.

'It's a great secret society that we're all under as far as land is concerned,' he said. 'The Seifield estate, for example . . . it's about the size of some of the countries in the United Nations, and I'm surprised they don't actually ask for a vote in that organisation.'

The case known as the Nottingham Swarm attracted the attention of the national Press, after Jean Joynes and her husband had described on *Checkpoint* how part of their house was demolished by masonry bees. Hordes of the winged monsters appeared over a period of weeks in daily and unceasing shifts to drill little holes into the kitchen walls, causing £1500 damage and laying an estimated 60,000 eggs. All proprietary pesticides sprayed on the walls were promptly gobbled up by the bees. But the Joynes were to face more problems, this time over the house insurance, and *Checkpoint* investigated. . . .

'We didn't worry too much,' explained Mrs Joynes, 'because the house was insured, although the council didn't give us any choice as to the company. So for fifteen years we paid our premiums, then when this happened I rang up and asked for a claim form. Before we could send it in we had a letter telling us they would not accept liability . . .'

The policy did not cover 'damage by insects', so Mrs Joynes tried to get the council to put some pressure on the insurance company. After all, she thought, this would be in the council's own interests. She told the council she was prepared to give the keys to the house back, so they could rehouse her. And that, she said, was when her troubles *really* started. First they threatened that if she did so they would not rehouse her because she would have made herself homeless in order to get another house. Then the Joyneses found to their horror that the council intended taking legal action against them unless they got a builder in to repair the damage. The council sent their inspector to examine the property, and he came to the conclusion that the bees had got into the walls because the Joyneses had allowed the pointing to fall into disrepair. They in turn called in a local builder, Norman Green, to examine their house. While he had a sneaking admiration for the bees, said Cook, Mr Green didn't think much of the man from the council.

'It's marvellous what a colony of bees can do . . . the force they can use in pushing out this brickwork,' he said. 'In my opinion the council inspector didn't make a thorough examination of the brickwork on the fore of the house . . . You can see for yourself, the house has been repointed and the pointing was in good condition.'

Green came to the conclusion that the back of the house would have to be rebuilt, and the council offered the Joynses a loan. As Mr Joynes was out of work they couldn't have met the repayments, so they refused this remedy. Meanwhile, bricks kept dropping out of the walls, insect specialists arrived to dig amongst the debris, and neighbours discovered bee-holes in their newly-painted walls. Cook interviewed the Rushcliffe Borough Council's chief executive, David Ashford. He explained that the council's view was that the Joynses had got themselves into a difficult position. The council no longer harboured thoughts of taking them to court; on the contrary, they were sympathetic and wanted to help. After a discussion as to the responsibilities and the means involved it became clear that the insurance company was the focus of the problem. Cook's interview with the claims manager of the Municipal Mutual company, Francis Bailey, did two things. It alerted us all to the fact that our insurance policies are strictly limited to certain specified events. And it gave rise to one of the funniest interchanges to be heard on the programme . . .

COOK: Why did your company accept fifteen years of premiums from Mrs Joynes in respect of structural damage and then turn her down the moment she tried to claim for just that?
BAILEY: Because the policy covers perils which are specified in that document, and quite clearly there is no cover against damage by bees. The insurance is against fire, explosion, lightning, aircraft . . . all sorts of things like that . . . but nothing which could cover damage by insects.
COOK: Most people would think when the person giving them a mortgage says they must take out an insurance policy and specifies with them that they were getting proper structural cover for anything that might happen.
BAILEY: No. They're not including cover for *anything* that might happen. It's only cover for damage that's specified in their document. There's a peril (*sic*) in the policy which insures against impact by vehicles or animals. We would cover damage to the building if an elephant or rhinoceros came into contact with the building, but we certainly couldn't give it for bees nibbling away at the mortar. We would be creating a dangerous precedent if we started to give cover of this kind, because we would then have problems with people claiming for woodworm, dry rot, deathwatch beetle and all other insects that are likely to be encountered. So while the policy does not *exclude* damage by these

Gary Hopkins and Jill May from Swindon, about to be married, thought the hotel sounded just the romantic place for their holiday together. After being dunned for an extra £12 on top of the £72 each they were paying for the week, they went up to their room.

'Sheets round the windows,' said Gary. 'The walls were stone, the floor was stone. No carpets. Cobwebs, dirt, dog's muck round the doors and leaves on the floors . . . Like the Black Hole of Calcutta, to be honest.'

They tried unsuccessfully to find another hotel, but finally stayed for half their allotted week before leaving. 'It was even worse for John Wittingham and family from Epsom,' said Cook, 'if you can believe that's possible.' After a duly inauspicious beginning (during which he was beguiled for five minutes into thinking what a fantastic character the place had), the Wittinghams tried eating a meal. The result of that imprudence was a physical row with the manager.

'I went to the governor and explained we were leaving,' he said. 'He said, "Well you'll have to pay for the room." I told him No, and he said, "Well I want £30 off you." To stop a scene I offered half, £15. His character completely changed. Talk about a Jekyll and Hyde. He just went for me, snatched my wallet, pushed me on my side, tore across the lawn . . . I chased him. He took some money and threw the rest on the grass, told me to leave my car and boat as this was his property and told me to get the hell out of it.'

With complaints from dozens of customers through no less than four different authorities being ignored by the hotel management, Cook called to see if he could meet any of the people whose names had appeared throughout the proceedings . . . Grantham, Grimes, Smith, Purse . . . His first encounter was with a man working on the engine of a Volkswagen van in the courtyard. He had never heard of Grimes or Grantham, he said, and was 'not allowed' to say who the proprietor was. A second man appeared and contributed even less to the conversation. Cook went into the village and ascertained that the elder of the two men he had just met was known as Charles Smith and that Charles had a brother called Alan.

Back at the hotel the two men once again put up a smoke screen, and Cook left 'with some understanding of how frustrated and angry' the hotel customers become. Back in London some more digging revealed that the hotel did have a connection there. Cook made contact with a man who called himself Alan (remember the brother?) *Wilkinson*. He agreed to accompany Cook back to the hotel where they met a young lady. Cook asked if she was Lynne Purse. She flatly denied this, and she and 'Wilkinson' hurriedly left the hotel together in a car.

So, who does set and police hotel standards, pondered Cook?

'The nearest we've got is the voluntary registration scheme, set up in 1974 by the English Tourist Board and the other national boards who are currently considering the Bevis Report on compulsory registration,' he reported.

Tony Pavely administered the scheme in England, and Cook asked him to whom should people complain about a hotel, Trading Standards, Environmental Health, Licencing Authorities, the police, the Fire Department . . .? Pavely admitted that life would be much easier with one central gathering point for such complaints, but suggested that compulsory registration ran the risk of being 'a pretty Draconian sort of measure', even though other countries did operate such a scheme. Pavely favoured a 'more positive' approach.

'If there are delinquents in the business, I think the Tourist Board would be more concerned with encouraging them and helping them to improve their standards, rather than going in with a big axe. But cases do occur from time to time where you're dealing with people who are not open to that kind of persuasion. The question arises, does one shrug one's shoulders or is there a case for bringing in sterner measures for the protection of the public – and the interests of good hoteliers as well?'

Cook answered this question with one of his own: 'I know the trade doesn't like the idea of a statutory registration scheme, and I don't think the Minister does either, so what are the chances of the Bevis Report discussions that are now under way?'

'I wouldn't give too much of a chance for statutory registration at the present time. Having said that, powers for such a scheme do lie in the 1969 Development of Tourism Act, and they can be activated at any time by an Order in Council, if the government so wishes.'

And until they are, concluded Cook, 'Care' is the watchword when selecting a hotel for your holiday. Go there by personal recommendation or through a reputable guide book, and if the hotel of your choice wants a whopping cash deposit, give it a miss. As for the filial proprietors of the hotel, they fell out and took each other to court. The hotel is now closed.

The growth in the number of language schools in the 1960s and

1970s has provided a new industry in Britain and other countries. London and many university towns and cities provide a centre of attraction both for British people wanting to learn French, German and other languages and for students from overseas wanting to learn academic and conversational English. On 13 August 1980 *Checkpoint* examined one of the dozens of language schools that have mushroomed on the south coast and in particular, one in Kent, the Thanet School of English in Ramsgate. This was operated by Robert Lawrence 'Salam' Blackmore. His main aim was 'to help students learn as much as possible in the shortest period of time' by concentrating more on what they were worst at doing.

According to a number of students and teachers interviewed, this laudable objective was not always realised. One Swiss student who paid more than £1,750 through her Credit Suisse account to the school found her 'advanced class' both disappointing and depressing. Things began well enough, but week by week they worsened.

'Every day was really hell to go there, and I worked properly . . . I only got a few weeks happiness and good teaching, and all the rest of the time was worry and stress. I feel I have been cheated very badly.'

Hers was not an isolated case by any means. One teacher recollected a group of twenty-seven Algerians who walked out in disgust at the poor level of teaching.

'Mr Blackmore treated them like a bunch of silly children. They certainly didn't get the course they were expecting.'

Another five interviewees drove the points home. Unqualified teachers, a lack of facilities, erratic behaviour by Blackmore, unscheduled closure during term time and strange recruitment techniques were highlighted. Cook finally interviewed Blackmore, who began with implausible excuses for some of the allegations and ended by losing control completely. He claimed that if the two teachers he had left in charge during an extended visit to Switzerland had followed his instructions there would have been no difficulties. But, pointed out Cook, there was no money for them to follow the instructions with.

'That's false,' said Blackmore, although he added, 'It's true that several cheques bounced.'

He attempted to lay the blame for this on a member of his staff, then had to respond to a series of questions about Value Added Tax. He had been charging VAT, but some people had the feeling he was not registered at that time.

'We've been registered for the whole of the year,' Blackmore stated.

'Yet according to the facts as we've been able to check them,' Cook replied, 'you're not currently registered for VAT.'

Blackmore tried once more to lay the blame for any apparent discrepancy at someone else's door, Cook's and the VATman's.

'I'm sorry to say that your skill as an investigative reporter has let you down again, so seriously that I wonder that you ought not to reconsider your profession. We are registered with the VAT authorities . . . The matter is not in dispute.'

'The local office seems to think it is,' Cook said.

'That is because their left hand doesn't know what the right hand is doing.'

Blackmore's reaction to the idea that the Algerian students should be cross, not only because the course was unsatisfactory, but because their paying authority, Insed, had been refused a refund: 'They're lying'.

At the end of the interview Blackmore was asked why he had found it necessary to advertise for 'attractive young ladies and models' to help recruit students. At that, Cook recalled, he went right over the top. The following interview shows how *Checkpoint* handles such a situation, with inserts linked for the listeners to cover the tactical problem that the recording tape ran out at a crucial time.

BLACKMORE: I expect that if *you'd* been running the school you'd have advertised for all the cripples and perverts and Quasimodos, and you'd have sent them out to try to attract people. Perhaps your school would have been even more successful than mine.

COOK: (*to listeners*) During a change of recording tapes, and having already described researcher David Perrin as 'an impertinent little sod' he went on to describe me as 'an unprincipled cheat and a long-time practitioner of trickery and chicanery . . .'

BLACKMORE: I have to choose between two thoughts: either you're a cynical liar or you're totally incompetent at your job.

COOK: (*to listeners*) Nevertheless he felt sufficiently threatened to have his wife take some flash photographs of us which he said he'd pass to 'special friends'. He also said he would run us through his secret files.

BLACKMORE: Flash isn't working. Sorry.

COOK: You suggested during that little break while we changed tapes that we are trying to 'stick you' with anything we could find and that it wasn't going to work. Now you say you'll run the same process on us. Is that correct?'

BLACKMORE: Let me put it this way. I think you're part of a group of Communist agents and that your job is, by fair means or foul, to incriminate me because I'm a well known anti-Communist.

COOK: You're joking, of course.

BLACKMORE: Not at all. I'm deadly serious.

COOK: But it always seems that someone else is at fault. The students who complained have got it wrong somewhere . . . we've got it wrong because, according to you, we're Communists . . . It does suggest a slight degree, to say the least, of paranoia, doesn't it?

BLACKMORE: Perhaps you're right. I don't know.

The school is now closed, and at the time of writing Blackmore was threatening legal action against the BBC for 'libellous statements made on tape but *not* broadcast.' Eccentric to the last, commented Cook.

A personal view of *Checkpoint*

One question frequently asked of Roger Cook is: 'What is it *like* to do a *Checkpoint* programme?' His first response is to say that there is no such thing as a typical programme, but that all the stories covered have a number of things in common. In particular, each one must provide a challenge, something that stands out and demands one hundred per cent attention.

'They must also be *new*', he says, 'We don't like to cover stories already covered elsewhere, unless we can take them a good deal further. If some of the stories you've heard on the air or read in this book seem familiar, that could be because they've been followed by newspapers or other programmes. So the first challenge is to find something both new and worthwhile, and that usually means starting from scratch. It also means careful consideration of how – or indeed *if* a particular story should be approached. I realise it is possible to make a case of sorts against some of the programmes we do. That's what the courts are for. It is also possible to argue against the concept of the programme as a whole. I sometimes do it myself. However we do our level best to ensure we are not found wanting on the grounds of fact or fairness. Taste is another matter.

'Much of what we do ought to be described as "routine enquiries",' he says. 'We can't press the Go button on a story until we are sure it *is* a story. By that I mean that all the evidence is true, that all documents and witnesses support what our complainants are saying. Sometimes we have to discover what they should, in fact, be saying: in a complicated case complainants are often unsure exactly what has happened to them, and that, of course, is a key ingredient of a successful "con".'

Another regular problem is that complainants have to be persuaded to 'go public' and to explain in their own voices how they have suffered. The challenge, says Cook, might well lie in digging out the final case history that dovetails the others together to reveal some kind of pattern, the *modus operandum* of a villain, or a widespread social problem, or an example of bureaucratic insensitivity or foolishness.

'Sometimes we get the excitement of an extra, unlooked-for bonus, the revelation that comes after burning the midnight oil in the office or talking with dozens of people on location . . . Finding that one person who says: Hey, you should talk with Jack What's' is Name. I think he got caught twice.'

Such a surprise contact may lead to more information on the villain's past or provide an insight to future ventures. Sometimes it gives clues as to company names that can be followed up with company searches and interviews with other directors and associates.

'Many a bean has been spilled by a disaffected colleague who realises that public exposure may not do him much good . . . The *Checkpoint* equivalent of Turning Queen's Evidence! Mind you, one has to be very careful here: a number of miscreants have tried to shift the blame in an exercise like this. Attempts to wine and dine to persuade us to drop all or part of a story are not unknown. Less civilised efforts have involved threatening phone calls, sabotage to motor vehicles, and in one instance a curt message that arrived through my front window attached to a brick.'

Interviews with *Checkpoint* villains have their own kind of excitement, but paradoxically Cook finds a proper face-to-face interview more exciting than a doorstep confrontation. Sitting down with all the evidence and choosing when to fire it off to achieve the best and most enlightening effect he compares to a game of chess. The resulting admissions or circumlocutions are extremely worthwhile, even though a slammed door or a string of abuse hurled across the doorstep can also be very revealing.

If it proves impossible to arrange a formal interview with a villain, despite all efforts, working out the best time and place to mount a tape-recorded ambush can present many difficulties.

'One has to try and get inside the mind of the accused and figure out which way he'll jump,' says Cook. 'It can be very frustrating when he fails to turn up, despite your best information. Was that information wrong, or has he been tipped off? How many more hours will have to be spent at some out-of-the way location in a cold car with only a Thermos flask and a tape recorder for company? Will we strike lucky before our broadcasting deadline? Fortunately, we usually do.

'Doorstep confrontations, while usually difficult and sometimes painful are, happily, seldom prolonged affairs. The hardest part is not screwing up the courage. I don't think much about that. The most difficult problem is marshalling what questions I'll have to put to a possibly violent man in such a way as to extract revealing replies.'

The reason that these events come off in radio terms is that Cook remains as low key and polite as circumstances will allow and leaves the pyrotechnics to the villain. He has discovered over the years that this approach tends to show the villain in his true colours. And as far as facing fists is concerned, Cook admits that if he *knew* he was in for a punch-up he would think twice about going. But even after ten years he is never sure what will happen at any particular time.

Rarely does someone complain or 'confess all'. But Cook remembers the amazing candour of Royston du Maurier who ran a substantial mail order fashion house which had disappointed customers to the tune of several hundred thousand pounds. Asked why he had not met his commitments, while at the same time continuing to spend other people's money, he replied: 'Well I suppose it's because they keep sending it in'!

'Sometimes people with unenviable reputations "come quietly", while more than one modestly propositioned pin-striped businessman has lost his cool in a big way,' he says.

A number of doorstep stories are described in this book, but Cook's favourite involves a man with a reputation for violence that was backed up by a conviction for Grievous Bodily Harm. The team had taken an interest in him, on and off, for a couple of years. They had made tentative approaches on several story lines, but found nothing concrete. Eventually they pinned it all together and finally it was doorstep time.

'The big day dawned,' said Cook, 'and with a certain trepidation I knocked on the door. Suddenly there he was, six foot four of potential aggro standing there with a broad grin . . .'

'Hello, guv'ner. Took your bloody time getting here, didn't you?'

'He gave me a very good interview,' recalled Cook. 'It produced results for many of the people who had lost money at his hands. And that's what *Checkpoint* is all about. Results.

'Of course success in our endeavours is always relative and never certain, no matter how hard we all work. Many's the villain who's sunk without trace, but many's the villain who's lived to cheat another day – and sometimes to feature on another programme.'

CHAPTER 15

The driving tension

Alan Rogers has been Head of Current Affairs Magazine Programmes (CAMP) since *Checkpoint* began. He, like the programme's producer, is a link in the chain stretching between those that make programmes and the senior hierarchy of the BBC. At the time of writing, Rogers reports directly to the Managing Director of Radio, Dick Francis. Understandably, he has clear recollections of *Checkpoint*'s early days.

'I remember the sense of excitement on the day of the first transmission, when I went down to the studio to meet Walter Wallich and Roger. I listened to the tape, and I thought, that's really marvellous broadcasting, but we can't get away with it. Yet it was all true, all substantiable, and it went out. And right from that point it's been a programme that's excited me. Initially I went to the final studio recording as often as I could. Just like the lawyer who went along, so did I, because although the team had researched and double checked the story there might always have been a chance that they became so involved they might be partial, although they're terribly good at not being partial. So I went along to ensure that the language was fair, that kind of thing. Once or twice I felt they went over the top and we'd discuss things and Roger would stamp out in a temper, but in the end we worked things out . . . And all the time the programme was breaking new ground.'

Preoccupation with legal matters has been another of the BBC's main concerns about *Checkpoint*, and Rogers has emphatic views of the part played by BBC lawyers over the years.

'We've had an amazing set of lawyers on the programme. Tony Jennings started with *Checkpoint*, and he is now top legal man in the BBC . . . After Tony, Don Christopher handled it, before moving to be legal advisor to Equity and now with Channel 4. Since 1977, we have had Rhory Robertson, a fiercely determined professional with a strong moral conscience . . . Altogether, a most unusual set of lawyers . . . they're very impressive as a team. It's very seldom you can ask a question that they don't have an immediate answer to.

'On this particular tack, wherever I go, inside or outside the BBC, people are always asking about *Checkpoint*. It's one of the programmes in my department that people always want to know about. And they always ask, what's the latest writ?

'Over the years there have been one or two very hairy programmes, where I felt we had to get some more supporting evidence before we put them out. That's the kind of thing that the team are doing at the last minute anyway, double-checking. But there was a programme about a shipping swindle where our thoroughly researched documentation was, to an extent, contradicted by a voluminous pile of legal papers, all in Greek! We pulled it out of the schedule, and the team worked right through the night and produced another edition in twenty-four hours.

'In the case of Chief Nzeribe in 1982 we held off for a week because his solicitors said he was out of the country and wasn't available to answer the questions. We said we'd wait until the following week when he was due back, to give him a chance to answer. In such a case the most important factor is not our own timescale but the need to be fair to all sides . . . to give the person concerned time to see what they need, to look up their own arguments . . . You can't run the risk of damning someone's career or business just because you have a deadline to meet and they haven't had a chance to get themselves together.'

As everyone involved with the programme has stressed, the fairness aspect has been significant right from the start.

'This is why we keep the whole of the tape of anyone accused of some kind of dodgy practice. We can prove we have edited the tape fairly. We also used to tell people how long they had on the air, so they could try and talk to that length, to marshall their arguments for the time available, although this proved not so easy to achieve in the later and more complex stories.

'Another problem is when a firm has ten dissatisfied clients and a thousand satisfied ones. How do you approach that? How much weight should you put on the thousand satisfied ones . . . should you mention this, or should you take it for granted that in their business they do give satisfaction most of the time? We developed the view that if the people concerned want to say this themselves, this is all part of letting them defend themselves against accusation in a fair kind of way.'

As for the position of *Checkpoint* in the general field of investigative journalism, Rogers turns to the years before the programme was conceived. He feels that *Checkpoint* is very much a child of its time.

'The consumer movement was new and exciting in the 1960s, but the movement needed more teeth, to be sharper, to have more strength. *Checkpoint* arose from that general feeling, from the ethos that although people had been told of their rights they were still getting a bad deal. We needed to take things a stage further and have a go at people and organisations who were screwing them. In my opinion, the programme led the field in developing the fight of the small man against bureaucracy and big business.

'It certainly set new standards for investigative journalism in the BBC. There have been other investigative programmes over the years, but no one has done it with such a regular strike rate and at such a level of cleanness. Since *Checkpoint* began it has been successfully challenged only three times. Twice we settled out of court and in another case concerning a fringe theatre and acting school we were criticised by the Broadcasting Complaints Commission. As far as this BCC case was concerned, I thought there had been a very odd weighing of the evidence, to be honest. There were oddities in the procedure that the Commission has since put right, but also they were taking the word of the complainant against three or four witnesses on our side . . . It seemed very odd . . .

'When you consider that over the ten years we've named the best part of a thousand villains, and we've been right on all bar two or three of those . . . that's an amazing record to keep up, and this has been recognised around the Corporation . . . The reaction around broadcasting is, how the hell d'you do it, how d'you keep it up, the sheer broadcasting standards of interest and excitement?'

Rogers is very involved with the reactions of listeners to the programmes in his department and liaises frequently with the head of broadcasting research, Peter Meneer. Until 1982 audience reactions to programmes were tested by teams of researchers literally in the streets. Each day about two thousand people would be asked a range of questions on their listening habits and preferences for both TV and BBC radio programmes on the previous day. Such a relatively small sample is valid in market research terms if it is continued over several months or years. Now there is a new system. Audiences for both BBC and ITV television are measured through a system of metered TV sets. Radio research is carried out through a thousand interviews in listeners' homes each day. This gives accurate audience figures for all programmes. In addition the BBC has what it calls the 'GE' factor. About five thousand audience members volunteer to be on a special panel for a year to report on what they consider to be worth hearing, and what is not. The system gives an average audience for any one *Checkpoint* programme at around one million. Bearing in mind that each week there will be considerable gains and losses in individual listeners, the total audience in any year is probably two or three million. Perhaps more importantly, *Checkpoint's* 'GE' rating is consistently very high, as is Roger Cook's own personal rating as a radio presenter. Such information is used in a variety of ways. At Establishment level, it helps programme planners to assess a programme's viability. On the other hand, the programme team are left in no doubt as to the nationwide impact their stories will have. Whether or not such understanding feeds any egos, it certainly imbues them with increased caution as to the merits of a story and the care they must take to ensure that all the high criteria of standards are achieved.

Alan Rogers sees another aspect of this high profile: 'As far as the listener is concerned, the programme is seen as being very brave and standing up for them with businesses and bureaucracies etc. It's a process that has always involved a lot of tension within the team. They're consistently arguing about the programme's true purpose, which is simply one aspect of their total commitment to the programme. In my view *Checkpoint* would not have developed without the tension . . . you have the team all working flat out in their respective roles and everyone developing self-confidence. . . . So if anyone goes in there to argue a point with Roger and the team they must be prepared to slug it out, because they're dealing with a group of committed and very able people.'

Rogers says he has never discerned lack of support for *Checkpoint* at any time among senior BBC people, except over the matter of Roger Cook's insurance (a matter that has caused Cook himself no little concern).

'Because of what he does he is a very hard man to insure,' says Rogers, 'and he felt the BBC should cover him. But it's not easy, looking at his record of injury, which he suffered as a result of doing the programme, of course. His colleagues have often been a great help, especially when he injured his back in the early days, but insurance brokers do tend to duck back when they realise the kind of thing they're dealing with.'

Alan Rogers sums up his view about *Checkpoint* succinctly: 'For the BBC to do its job it needs *Checkpoint* as well as all the other kinds of programmes prepared by journalists . . . a programme that can take on anybody, get under the skin of individuals or organisations . . . examine apparent abuses . . . give people a chance to defend themselves. *Checkpoint* is an absolutely essential part of public service broadcasting.'

'Sons of *Checkpoint*'

In November 1975 Roger Cook submitted an idea to the BBC for a programme he called '*Son of Checkpoint*'. Titles for new programmes are not easy to create, and this was meant to be a working title for a new kind of programme, developed from the lessons learned by the *Checkpoint* team and aimed at a different audience. The document concerned gives a good insight into the issues Cook felt were important at that time, and to the way he viewed existing programmes on television.

'The idea,' he wrote, 'would be to give listeners involved in some of the wider issues *Checkpoint* has discussed (and some of those we haven't covered because they were outside our brief) direct access to Radio 4 in a new and hopefully stimulating way. Those involved in a particular problem would be given the opportunity to say whatever they wanted to say about it, on location in their own environment. This ought to help overcome the glassy-eyed unnaturalness of people given similar opportunities on late night television.

'Another key difference from that format ought to be that the complainants should be given professional help with the assembly and presentation of their material. It's no use giving people air time in which to bore everyone else. That could well result in access to nothing!'

Cook emphasised the need to select topical issues, and not rely on whoever was next in the queue. He listed subjects with the kind of problems raised by the Hunterston nuclear and industrial complex, covered by *Checkpoint* on 4 April 1974, tied cottages and race relations. The programme would present problems 'on a human scale'. They may stem from the actions of pressure groups or from the efforts of the production team pulling together similar strands of the same story from various parts of the country. He envisaged a regular monthly, hour-long programme as being within the then existing capabilities of the *Checkpoint* team. In particular, he suggested that the programme should be repeated on the air 'to ensure that (it) didn't run into *Checkpoint*'s original problem of having a relatively small catchment area. (Radio 4 audiences are, for example, smaller than Radio 2 audiences, particularly at the times at which *Checkpoint* and its repeats are broadcast.)

One result of this initiative was the production of the *Time for Action* series, in which two reporters each took a side on a major current issue. They took this issue to people representing the two sides, giving the right of reply to those who were responsible for the subject in question. Cook presented and reported, with Nick Ross (who later went to work with *Man Alive* and then with Breakfast television) taking the second microphone and Ritchie Cogan producing the programmes with great care and technical skill. Research was by Sharon Banoff and Maggie Redfern, both of whom had worked on *Checkpoint*. A typical story was the conflict between the traditional fisherman and the brash new offshore oilmen in Peterhead, Scotland.

Cook later found himself presenting another *Checkpoint* derivative in *Cause for Concern*, a twenty-minute insert once a fortnight in BBC's *Nationwide* programme. The producers on this were Ken Vass, David Darlow and Mike Robinson. Most of the stories were supplied by the *Checkpoint* team, and many of the programmes were joint productions with *Checkpoint*. 'This was a very successful symbiosis,' recalls Cook, quoting such highlights as the case of the so-called psychic surgeons. He also reported a number of stories on the television programme *Newsnight*, a notable one concerning the Brighton manufacturer of fake ivory Japanese miniatures. The latter story resulted in one of Cook's most violent confrontations, seen by millions of television viewers, in which several of his ribs were broken under the administrations of an iron bar.

Perhaps the best example of a *Checkpoint* spin-off involving Cook and senior producer Ritchie Cogan was *Reel Evidence*, the pun being intentional but not too easy to spot as a radio listener. In this series the production team was joined by John Smithson (now with *World in Action*), and several of the programmes were presented by Bill Breckon. These were complete forty-five minute documentary programmes, covering a wide and international basket of stories. The 'Belfast Dream' of John De Lorean was incisively criticised many years before the rest of the media got hold of the fiasco. The 'Whistle Blowers' dealt with official secrecy and those who 'blew the whistle'. Then there was the remarkable case entitled 'The Spy who caught a Cold', concerning Maltese-born Stanley Adams.

Adams worked as a senior executive of the Swiss pharmaceutical company Hoffman La Roche. There he observed a number of irregularities and was faced with the problem of either keeping his mouth shut or reporting the company to the authorities, which in this case was the European Economic Commission. He chose the latter course, and entered a nightmare world of deceit, delay, pressure, arrest and financial disaster, inspired by his opponents. His wife, told by the police that she would never see her husband again, committed suicide, leaving two small children. Adams was released, and began the fight to build up his own business and bring up his family. But the pressures continued, and his various business ventures were brought to ruin. The impact of this programme was stunning. Listeners found it well-nigh impossible that such things could happen, and it must be said that the reputation of Cook and the BBC itself were necessary to transmute the incredible into the sadly believable. Unsolicited gifts amounting to thousands of pounds poured into Broadcasting House, giving Adams a well needed (and many think a well deserved) boost. However, at the time of writing, his troubles, it seems, are by no means over.

Perhaps most amazing of all was the case of the music promoter, Don Arden, the self-styled 'Al Capone of Pop' which concluded a programme that graphically described how pop stars are often deprived of the bulk of their earnings. Arden had managed or otherwise handled such pop notables as the Electric Light Orchestra, Lyndsey De Paul and the Small Faces. Many of his clients had substantial complaints: Lyndsey De Paul, for example, had to pay for a UK concert venue out of her own pocket, when she thought the arrangement was that Arden should pay. At one stage, she said, with her career almost ruined, she was close to suicide. I was with Cook for several days in Los Angeles during the run-up to this programme. Unknown to me, Arden was also there, and Cook kept vanishing to make phone calls, trying to arrange an interview with him. In the light of the threats that followed, I remain grateful that we left that sun-drenched city in one piece.

As the programme developed, all kinds of disturbing rumours began circulating about Arden's business contacts, not to mention the methods he used to keep his clients under his thumb. And then contact was made by phone between Arden and Cook. It resulted in one of the most astonishing interviews ever heard on British radio, let alone the BBC. After being duly appraised that Cook was recording him for broadcast, Arden totally 'blew it', as the saying goes. Carefully Cook presented the allegations. Arden practically ignored them, and began a menacing build up of invective, including such gems as: 'Mr Cook, I could take you with one arm stuffed up my arse!' and 'Roger Cook, you can go fuck yourself!' Suddenly those rumours of young guitarists with broken arms seemed less fanciful. Here, one felt, was a man who considered himself above the niceties of normal business procedures.

Unintimidated by threatened law suits, the BBC promptly opened the story up by broadcasting this edition of *Reel Evidence* to the multi-million devotees of Radio One, Arden grabbed a handful of writs and showered them at all and sundry. Lyndsey De Paul's participation in the programme resulted in a writ in Los Angeles for seven million dollars (Arden lost), and Arden is on record as saying he would take Cook for twelve million dollars. No action has been taken on those writs since 1979.

A number of programmes have developed that clearly owe a great deal to *Checkpoint*. *Watchdog* with Hugh Sculley has taken over the *Cause for Concern* slot on *Nationwide*. Outside the BBC, Capital Radio has begun *PDQ* (Pretty Damn Quick), presented by John Stonborough who cut his radio teeth as a *Checkpoint* researcher and reporter. The popular television drama *Shoestring*, about a questing radio reporter and his programme, was inspired by and initially modelled on *Checkpoint*.

Channel 4 has *For What It's Worth*, featuring *Private Eye* columnist Penny Junor. In the *Daily Mirror* dated 16 November 1982 this programme was described as 'a hard-hitting consumer programme, tracking down swindlers, much on the lines of Roger Cook's *Checkpoint* on BBC Radio 4'. Penny Junor, who had told the Mirror that she wanted a 'minder' to protect her from all the villains she felt likely to meet in her work, presented her own view of Cook:

'Roger's face isn't known by the crooks, so they don't know who he is when he arrives on the scene. It's quite different for me, because everybody recognises me.'

Maybe so, but how recognisable would she feel in the basement of a hotel in Reykjavic, a motel in California's Highway 1 or even the book department of Selfridges, I wonder. I have been with Cook in these and other unlikely places when he has been recognised by people. Many of them ask for an autograph. Cook always seems genuinely embarrassed by this kind of thing, although he admits to having been rather piqued by the small boy outside a BBC function who deciphered his signature, then tore it up in disgust because he had wanted to nab Tony Blackburn. Such Cookish pique never lasts long, and he now delights in telling the story against himself. He sees being sent up, as he was in a recent edition of *Not The Nine O'Clock News*, as every bit as much of an accolade as being described in College of Law examination papers as 'the last resort' when the system has failed.

Penny Junor's comment, given no doubt in good faith, shows a fundamental misunderstanding of Cook's kind of well-researched investigative journalism. To start with, any 'crook' he interviews has been contacted, often several times, to arrange the meeting. A 'doorstepping' interview is only undertaken if such efforts fail. So all the crooks concerned know that they are likely to be confronted by Cook before he turns up. Whether they recognise his face or not is irrelevant: they have certainly learned how to hit it over the years. And even if, after all the preparation, they deny that such attempts were made by *Checkpoint*, Cook's first few words always clarify the issue.

'I'm Roger Cook from the BBC *Checkpoint* programme, and I'm here to record an interview with you *now* about. . . . There are questions that must be answered!'

Others are now using these or similar words. No one else does so with the same preparation or authority.

CASE 1
Complaints against Peter and Richard Newton

Broadcast date: 31 August 1978
Researchers: David Perrin and Sharon Banoff

Introduced as 'a classic example of the kind of Checkpoint story that sprouts from a little acorn', this edition dealt with the business empire of Peter and Richard Newton, father and son, and the investigation began with a complaint by Dennis Woodman whose family owned storage space in Lymington, Hampshire. According to Woodman, Richard Newton, who owned a company called Camargue Motors, contacted him because he wanted to store his collection of Jaguar cars. Newton paid one month's rent in advance in August 1976 and another in September. In October, nothing was paid, and eventually Woodman issued the first of five summonses. The Court Bailiff who called on the Newtons was told that Camargue Motors had no assets. Most people might have given up at this stage, but Woodman carried on the fight.

'I did some company searches and found that the Newton family were involved with at least twenty different companies, from Scotland all the way down to Lymington. I also found that they had entered into contracts with other people through their many other companies, and acquired goods and services which they apparently had no intention of paying for, leading to disastrous results for the people concerned.'

Woodman contacted the *Checkpoint* team, and they discovered that the Newtons were involved with at least thirty different companies, ranging from a smart restaurant called The Slipway in Lymington, through a number of boating companies, to property and building firms and what purported to be finance houses.

Another of the Newtons' victims was Charles Smith, at that time Deputy Mayor of Lymington, who owned a small hotel in the town. He told *Checkpoint* that over a period of eighteen months his hotel catered for many guests and staff of companies associated with the Newtons, and that he had endless difficulty in getting paid.

'Cheques were presented to my bank, and they were returned to me marked 're-present'. I did so, and they were returned with the same mark. Eventually I phoned my bank manager and asked him how long could this go on for. He told me that they could do it for years, as long as the cheque was not marked "referred to drawer".'

Smith took the matter to the County Court, and when he arrived there he found 'at least three people' waiting to see the Registrar to issue writs against the same company. It took him eighteen months of trouble and expense finally to get his £800, and he commented that he knew of many other hotels in the area who were owed even larger sums who never managed to receive payment.

Other debtors interviewed in the programme included a builder, Alan Patten, who was owed five and a half thousand pounds, and a printer, John Baker, who did work for a number of Newton companies. This included the preparation of company letterheads, which revealed yet more business names and yet more victims. The sum finally owed to Baker was £3,000, and at one stage his wife Beryl took a hand in trying to get the Newtons to pay up.

'I felt the only thing to do was to go round to his house which was across the river and very affluent,' she said, and told Peter Newton: 'I am not leaving until you pay some of the money you owe us . . .'

'Eventually Richard Newton got his shotgun from the cupboard with the hope of intimidating me and getting me to leave. I didn't leave. I waited, and the police arrived. They explained it was a private house and that I would have to leave. So I left without any money.'

The Bakers did manage to get some of their money after a period, but not before the printing business was ruined.

Other companies that fell into the Newtons' net included a number of boating firms and a company called Air Bearings of Gosport, who made hovercraft under the direction of Julian Cook, who admitted to *Checkpoint* that he was much more of a boffin than a businessman. He explained what happened when Peter Newton moved in.

'We were looking for backing, and Newton certainly seemed to be a very impressive figure. He brought parties of Arabs to us in helicopters, and we gave them demonstrations. He was so smooth. He had this fantastic way of saying "It's all going to be marvellous, boys . . . We have this big deal lined up in the Middle East, and how much money do you want to develop this thing?"'

Newton suggested that the firm took on twenty men to proceed with the construction of more hovercraft, promising a grand future with large injections of capital to revitalise the company.

'But, of course, nothing ever happened,' said Julian Cook,

'and we reached the situation where Newton actually removed a £15,000 hovercraft in our absence. Our directors walked out, because they were owed three months salary. I ended up with no pay, no expenses, nothing. When Newton suddenly discovered that he couldn't run the company without our expertise he sacked the twenty men, and we were forced to put the company into liquidation. Had we not been led up the garden path by Newton, we would have found other backers and would probably still be in business today. It not only destroyed my livelihood, but that of a number of people who were involved in the project.'

Checkpoint discovered that Air Bearings was not the only company to have been 'led up the garden path' by the Newtons. One finance house had a judgement of £30,000 against Peter Newton over his house, a judgement that couldn't be enforced because the property had been transferred to his wife's name. Many UK banks were involved; Barclay's, for example were owed £89,000 and had to resort to bankruptcy proceedings. Travel agents, architects, engineers, quantity surveyors and other professional people had been badly bitten, to the total tune of several hundreds of thousands of pounds.

The *Checkpoint* team traced down another Newton company, a finance company in Liechtenstein, that allegedly owned £2.5 million to the Abu Dhabi branch of a Bangladeshi bank. Understandably, the bank's chief executive was reluctant to discuss the case on the air.

At the end of this particular investigation Cook managed to track down the elusive Peter Newton, who was running his octopus empire from a Portacabin situated in the approach to Brockenhurst Station, near Lymington. There followed an interchange that would have been rejected as unrealistic if a television drama writer had penned it in a script.

Scene: The approach to Brockenhurst Station. A golden Rolls Royce outside a Portacabin. Roger Cook and builder Alan Patten arrive. Cook knocks on the door. A man opens it.

COOK: Are you Mr Peter Newton?

NEWTON: No. My name is Fred.

COOK: You are Fred?

NEWTON: Yes.

COOK: I am from the BBC *Checkpoint* programme, and my name is Roger Cook.

NEWTON: I am not Mr Newton.

COOK: You are not? That's funny, because someone over there

says you are.
NEWTON: No. He has gone home at the moment . . .
(*The telephone rings*)
NEWTON: (*On the phone*) Hello . . . Tom? Yes. It's Peter. Yes . . . OK. I will have a chat with you now. Hold on a tick . . . (*to Cook*) Excuse me a moment.
COOK: You are Mr Newton, then.
NEWTON: No.
(*Newton slams the door, and Patten confirms to Cook that this is indeed Newton senior. Cook manages to get him to the door again and confronts him with the names of several of his debtors, facts and about his companies and about judgements against him. None of the questions are answered. Newton slams the door again, then by coincidence his son Richard drives up. Cook asks him about the companies. Newton snr opens the door again.*)
NEWTON SNR: It sounds very childish. Don't listen. It is absolute nonsense. Don't listen. It is just stupidity.
COOK: What about Rickmain? (*One of the Newton's three main operating companies*)
(*Newton jnr steps forward threateningly*)
NEWTON SNR: Please Richard, don't. It is only just childish nonsense.
COOK: It is not childish nonsense. It is deadly serious. You have cost people a lot of money.
NEWTON SNR: Rubbish.
COOK: Have you nothing to say?
NEWTON JNR: I could say something very good if you put that off. I don't like talking to machines.
(*After fending off more questions both Newtons go inside the Portacabin, then the son, Richard comes out to address some words to Alan Patten, delivered, Cook recalls, 'with a steely glare'*)
NEWTON JNR: Believe me, this sort of thing . . .
PATTEN: The Bailiff of Southampton Sheriff Court would love to know where you are.
NEWTON JNR: This sort of thing . . .
PATTEN: Yes, we know what you are going to say, Richard.
NEWTON JNR: Believe me, if anything happens to my father as a result of people like you, believe me, you will have to answer for it.
COOK: That is a threat, is it?
NEWTON JNR: You want to learn the English language.
COOK: You are aware that there are a number of complaints. Are you saying that they are without justification?

NEWTON JNR: Not at all, no, but I don't like this sort of thing, believe me. I was trying to sort things out quickly, and this sort of thing goes on. I don't like it, and, believe me, I sincerely hope you are totally legitimate in this, because I take a dim view of this, as well. It is all very well smiling, and I am sure that it is very clever, but some people work very hard to try and sort this type of thing out.
COOK: All the people who are legitimately owed money will be paid, will they?
NEWTON JNR: You have had your fun and games now. You have got lots to write about, but make sure it is accurate, because it had better be accurate.
COOK: And that is a threat?
NEWTON JNR: No it is not a threat, just people should be accurate, and you are threatening me with this thing (*The microphone*) shoved in my face. That is a threat.
COOK: No, it is not a threat.
NEWTON JNR: Of course it is a threat.
COOK: It is an opportunity to answer the case which is being put up against you.
NEWTON JNR: Of course it is a threat. (*He slams the door*)

Circumlocution, *non sequiteurs* and accusations of unfairness combine with a threatening manner in many of the *Checkpoint* 'confrontations' with people accused of malpractice. But the point about this kind of interview is that it is designed purely and simply, as Cook told Newton, to give an opportunity for one of the sides to give their point of view on an issue that has been thoroughly researched before the meeting takes place.

'During the course of this particular story,' said Cook, 'it became obvious to us that Newton Senior thought that somehow he was above the rest of us, that laws, rules, regulations etc didn't concern him. He thought himself above the law, and he would march into companies and take them over with such aplomb, or bullying, that people used to let him. He had cards saying he was the Managing Director of this or that company when he had absolutely nothing to do with them. One public trust company is still trying to recover about £1 million which they believe Newton Senior siphoned away. He had managed to avoid any suspicion – until the programme was broadcast.

'We now understand that he is in self-imposed exile in Nepal, which has no extradition treaty with this country, although his dealings in the UK seem to have stopped.'

CASE 2
Complaints against the families Sumner and Randal

Broadcast on 28 March 1979

Researchers: David Perrin and Debbie Fleming

The programme first told the story of a young man from Edinburgh, Scott Ferguson, who saw an advertisement of the firm Interlink Planning and Promotions of Southport for jobs in Canada. He sent off the coupon and received an application form and a request for £3, and as it seemed to be from a genuine employment agency he duly completed the form and parted with his money. Nothing happened, so he started enquiring and asking for a response. After five months he was sent a useless list of addresses, and then he discovered that the newspaper in which he had seen the advertisement had not been paid for the space.

'I realised then it had been a con,' he said. 'I was very annoyed about the £3, but not annoyed enough to go to the police, and I doubt whether anyone else would have bothered. So they carried on making money, and that would be the secret of their success: the fact that the individual sums involved were so small nobody would really complain about it.' The sums may have been small, but as Cook subsequently explained the operations were conducted on a massive scale.

Two of the victims, Steven Westerland and his fiancée, were so excited at the prospects offered in one of the advertisements that they didn't bother to write their reply but leapt into their car and drove from Leeds to the company's Southport address. They arrived early in the morning to find a dilapidated shop with a few maps pinned to the walls inside. By nine o'clock no one had shown up, and they asked a neighbour what time people arrived to start work. They were told that no one ever stayed very long at the shop. What they had yet to learn was that this was just a mailing address for the Sumners and Randals. However, that morning one of the people running the business turned up.

'He was wearing Wellington boots and a scruffy old overcoat,' said Westerland. 'He said he's got the builders in, and I thought it was a bit funny, because if you've got the builders in you don't usually dress as a builder yourself.'

After being handed a bunch of leaflets, plus a comment that he would have to send off about £80 for a flight on a Laker Skytrain, Westerland and his fiancée set off back to Leeds, realising that the offer of good jobs in the USA was not what it seemed.

'We came to the conclusion that they were con merchants,' he said flatly. So all they lost was a night's sleep and the price of the petrol for the round trip.

During the programme, Cook pointed out that the company claimed to be able to arrange a Canadian passport, visa and citizenship for £3 or £5, but this kind of thing had to be done in person through the Canadian High Commission. They also claimed to be able to do the same thing for the United States of America, and that their clients would need no work permits, which again was untrue. They claimed that all monies paid for air fares went to Laker Airways with whom they had a 'special arrangement'. Not true, said Cook, who went on to detail other 'profitable but unpublicised' interests of the two families, including the Summit Hair and Scalp clinic in Southport. This attracted the attention of Mary Jones from Caernarvon who spotted the company's advertisement in the *Caernarvon and Denbigh Herald*, sent off her £10 for a three month course of medication and received nothing in return except one of her own letters of enquiry marked 'Unoccupied – gone away' on the envelope.

Mary Jones and many more people who received no medication for their £10 were, according to Cook, the lucky ones. Those who did end up with a bottle found that it contained strong industrial detergent.

Another project operated by the Sumners was the recruitment of agents, allegedly to sell costume jewellery, operated from that address in Southport at which Steven Westerland had been disappointed by Interlink Planning and Promotions. The Checkpoint team received complaints about this from as far afield as Fiji, Gibraltar and Grenada in the West Indies. The advertising manager of the newspaper *Torchlight and Speaker* in Grenada, George Pilgrim, explained how he was caught out.

'We received an advertisement in November 1978 from the Cannibar Jewellery Supplies for male and female agents who could earn up to £100 a week in their spare time,' he said. 'The cost of this advertisement was £60. We have not heard from Cannibar Jewellery since. Further, someone who had answered the advertisement came in complaining that she had sent money to the people and got no reply.'

The lady was one of many people caught out by Cannibar, and if respondents had not lost their £10 agent's recruitment fee to this company they might have lost it to B. S. Business Enterprises, another Sumner company in the same dubious line of business.

'George Pilgrim didn't fall for that one,' Cook told the *Checkpoint* audience, 'but he did fall for yet another Sumner company operating from another address and using different names and different advertising: Gould's English Football Forecast. This offered chances to win a fortune on the football pools, and the space in the Grenada newspaper cost £150 – another sum that was not paid – leaving George Pilgrim a total of several hundred pounds down and many disgruntled readers.'

Meanwhile, after Steven Westerland's adventure in Southport with Interlink Planning and Promotions, that company seemed quietly to pass away. But it was to reappear at another Southport address as Granville Travel Publications, offering better paying jobs for students and seniors from 'ordinary' schools, for teachers and nurses, retired people and families, together with opportunities for summer jobs in European and other countries.

Newspapers that had blacklisted Interlink Planning and Promotions for misleading and unpaid-for advertisements subsequently accepted those from Granville Travel Publications, and thousands more victims sent off their £5 for useless information. By this time *Checkpoint*'s enquiries had not yet uncovered the whereabouts of the families Sumner and Randal, except for a misleading note left at one address by the Randals that said they had gone to live in Australia. In fact, the two families were living together in a small village outside Penrith in Cumbria. Cook tracked them to this new address, only to be caught by a heavy fall of snow that kept him isolated in a nearby village. By the time he could continue his journey the Sumners and Randals had once more changed their address and disappeared again, following Mr Sumner's arrest and release on bail on a charge of theft.

Yet another forwarding address, this one in Carlisle, proved to be empty, although the premises were sporting a new company name, Transarch Research and Marketing. Searches through Court records proved fruitless, despite the fact that Mr Sumner and Mr Randal had been convicted the previous month in Carlisle for obtaining money by deception. Eventually they were traced to a luxury rented house in an estate in a village called Rockcliffe.

'By this time,' said Cook, 'we had amassed a considerable amount of information on the way these people operated, changing companies and addresses like the rest of us change socks. We also met a Post Office man who told us that he had seen how they dealt with the large volume of mail that arrived in bags at the many phoney business addresses they used. All they did was to open the envelopes, take out the money, and throw the letters away.'

At Rockcliffe, Cook had one of those confrontations that ended in considerable pain. The recording was drastically cut to minimise the language, and he had to seek permission from the Managing Director of Radio to broadcast rude words.

'I'm not in favour of broadcasting rude words,' Cook said, 'but if we'd taken them all out, there would have been next to nothing left of the interview, and I argued that I didn't go all that way and subjected to the violence just to have the whole lot edited and discarded. The purpose of *Checkpoint* is to report first hand, where possible. It would have been a silly ending to say, Well they didn't have any answers and they hit me, Goodnight!

'I don't like the confrontations, but when that is all you have you broadcast it.'

(*Sound of Cook knocking on the Sumners' door.*)
COOK: Mr Randal?
RANDAL: Yeh.
COOK: Could I speak to you and to Mr Sumner please, about your business activities and about firms like Interlink and Randal Travel Publications?
RANDAL: No.
COOK: My name is Roger Cook from the BBC *Checkpoint* programme, and I have come to interview you. There are many things that you ought to talk to us about. Would you like to call Mr Sumner, please. We know he's in. There are many, many dissatisfied customers of the business ventures you tried to mount all over the world. Have you nothing to say. (*A woman appears.*) Ah, you are Mrs Sumner?
MRS SUMNER: Who are you?
COOK: My name is Cook, from the BBC *Checkpoint* programme.
MRS SUMNER: Fuck off, or you'll get swilled.
COOK: I beg your pardon? . . . An explanation is due . . .
(*A chamber pot is emptied over Cook from an upstairs window.*)
MRS SUMNER: Fuck off!

The recording ended seconds later when Mr Randal and Mr Sumner charged out of the house and tore the microphone from its lead. Cook was elbowed and jostled, while Mrs Sumner and Mr Randal ripped open his recorder in an effort to tear out the tape. After the chamber pot incident, recalled Cook, he felt an uncontrollable desire to clean himself up, thereby becoming the first reporter to his knowledge that has gone through a car wash on foot! That was the end of that particular *Checkpoint* investigation, but police enquiries were to continue, leading to the arrest of both families. Mrs Randall was sent to prison for eighteen months, Barbara Sumner for three years and her husband Gordon for five years.

CASE 3
Complaints against Raymond Hill

Broadcast on 16 March 1978
(Joint production with BBC Nationwide*)*
Researcher: Julia McLaren

The kind of man and activities that the team were looking into in this story was graphically described by the first complainant, Lou Lewis, a former night club manager. He was involved in a fracas in 1976 outside a club in Strood that was owned by Hill and 'protected' by doormen specially imported from London.

'There was a major incident outside the club entrance,' he said, 'one of the worst I've ever seen. Two or three youths who had previously been banned tried to gain entry, and the doorman went in rather strong and violently. I attended to find several men seriously injured – and I'm not talking about minor cuts and bruises. I'm talking about fractured skulls, broken bones, deep cuts and abrasions. I pushed one of the doormen away and was seriously injured. I received a fractured skull in two places, a broken nose and a cut above the eye.'

Lewis spent the night in a coma in the Medway Accident Centre, the fourth visit to the hospital in three months after brushes with the London doormen. He phoned Raymond Hill to ask that the men concerned should be removed, and was himself dismissed. In January 1977 he took his case for unfair dismissal to the Industrial Tribunal at Chelsea. The case was undefended, and he was awarded £1,300. At the time of the broadcast, more than a year later, he had not been paid, and neither had any of the club's suppliers or directors, the latter group claiming losses of £21,000 and staging a ten-day sit-in, to no avail.

After the initial *Checkpoint* programme, the BBC received dozens of phone calls concerning Hill, one of the first being an anonymous warning to 'Lay off Ray Hill!'. The subsequent investigation revealed a chain of liquidated companies that owed hundreds of thousands of pounds to all kinds of individuals and companies for goods and services ranging from luxury carpets, curtains and wall coverings to interior design, architecture and building work.

A young designer, Chris Henahan, was a typical victim, lured into Hill's net with promises of good things to come.

'We were a very young company when I first met Ray Hill,' said Henahan. 'He offered us four very large projects. One was worth about a quarter of a million pounds in contract value, and we agreed to do this at a cheap rate, because we needed the work, and we were very young and enthusiastic. When the time came to present the final invoice for about £1,300, I was never able to get hold of him. I spent many hours sitting in his office. I telephoned him. I called at the office again. I banged on the door. And eventually – nothing! Which, I guess, was a major factor in us ceasing business.'

Henahan and Partners lost almost everything, and their business was in ruins, a plight typical of scores of people caught up in the Hill Empire of businesses that sprang up, amassed huge debts, folded up when the creditors pressed and sprang up again under other names, a sequence of events that, incredibly, was perfectly legal under British law.

It is due largely to *Checkpoint* that this process has received enough publicity to prompt changes in the law, but not before Hill and an associate called David Zachin capitalised on yet another perfectly legal operation. This concerned the largest of Hill's ten companies that owed a quarter of a million pounds to creditors who were clamouring for payment. Zachin invested £200 in this company and so became what is called a debenture holder. For that trifling amount he acquired a kind of mortgage over the company's assets, and this enabled him to call in his own Receiver. The significance of this was explained on the programme by solicitor Michael Cooke.

'This is the sort of devious tactic that many companies are increasingly using to avoid or delay payment of their debts,' he said. 'When a Receiver is appointed, there are a number of results. Firstly, when the County Court Bailiff or the High Court Sheriff come along to execute on the goods (of the company), they're told that a Receiver has been appointed and that he has got a charge on all the goods, so there is no way they can levy execution. Secondly, once a Receiver is appointed, every letter that leaves the company must state that this is the case.

'Now, most people when they see that think, "Oh well, the company's up the spout, it hasn't got any assets, and it isn't worth pursuing." Alternatively, they aren't able to tell the difference between a Receiver under a debenture (as in Hill's case) and the Official Receiver, who is appointed Liquidator by the Courts when a company is wound up for any reason.

'The Official Receiver is there to look after the interests of all the creditors, so the average creditor will think that his interests were being looked after. But in fact, the Receiver under debenture is only looking after the interests of the person who put him in.'

Michael Cooke pointed out that in such a case the Receiver can be used not to protect the debenture holder but to protect the company from its creditors.

'The only way for the poor creditor, in Law, to get round this is for him to present a Petition for the compulsory winding-up of the company. But that's a very expensive procedure, and it often involves costs out of all proportion to the amount involved.'

The results of this kind of chicanery are typified by the experience of one of over sixty hapless creditors of Hill's club in Strood, Alan Stanley, who was commissioned to install a disco system. His working conditions were 'impossible', as various items of equipment he needed from other suppliers were not delivered by the club's opening date.

'I had to instruct solicitors for my money, in the end,' he said. 'I obtained judgement in the High Court for over two thousand pounds. The legal costs have been just over two thousand pounds, and I haven't seen a penny of it from anybody.'

Meanwhile, Lou Lewis, Hill's former club manager, received a visit from two men who said that they had been offered a hundred pounds each to forcibly shut him up, and at about the same time Roger Cook's car was involved in an act of vandalism.

'It might have been unconnected with the case, but it was covered in paint stripper in a BBC car park, after we had been warned to "lay off" and when no other car was touched,' he said wryly.

A number of attempts were made to interview Hill, all of which were fended off by his business associates. One appointment was made and broken, and on one occasion Cook managed to unearth Hill for a few seconds of negative reaction at one of his two homes. There followed more requests on the phone and in writing to interview him, all without success. In the end the team had to resort to the 'door-stepping' technique.

'When we eventually found him we had to stake the place out

in an unmarked van with a film crew. We had been told by a "deep throat" in the business what his movements were, and we did know he was in the building, because we'd seen him go in. So we waited for him to come out for his usual morning stroll down to the shops, and he didn't show up. The crew was sitting there until three o'clock in the afternoon, all desirous of paying very urgent calls of nature! Then at last Hill appeared with his accountant and co-director Nat Vasani, and we all piled out of the van. There followed an extraordinary sight of this man in a vicuna overcoat, crocodile shoes and so on, sprinting up the street to avoid us. Eventually we got close to him, but got no sensible answers at all . . .'

COOK: Mr Hill, my name is Roger Cook from the BBC, and I've come to talk to you about your activities with various companies which seem to owe an awful lot of money.
HILL: Do they?
COOK: They certainly do owe a lot of money. The suggestion is that it's been several hundred thousand pounds. Mr Vasani has been involved as well.

(*There is an inaudible comment from Hill to Vasani, who leaves and gets in his car.*)

COOK: Wintshower (*one of Hill's companies*) went down owing a hundred and seventy thousand pounds.
HILL: I have just written a letter, asking you to spell out in detail what your requirements are.
COOK: But you don't keep appointments. We've made them before, and you haven't kept them.
HILL: Get my letter, and reply to me, and then perhaps we can meet on agreed terms of reference with what you want to know.
COOK: We don't know that we will even get your letter. You don't keep appointments . . .

(*Hill clambers into his accountant's car and vanishes up the street.*)

'We never received a letter,' Cook recalled, 'but we did demonstrate dramatically how vulnerable people are to unscrupulous yet perfectly legal behaviour.'

Cook recalled two incidents vividly that occurred during the course of this programme. The first was yet another attack on his car, which had been wired with an incendiary device so that it caught fire while he was driving it (the car was badly damaged, but he was unhurt). The second followed the film crew's six hour wait outside Hill's HQ. As one of the crew leaped out to take up the chase, the strain on his bladder proved too much, and he was forced to retire in some confusion as his colleagues sprinted down the road after Hill. After the programme, Hill adopted a much lower profile. At the time of writing, official investigations were continuing into his multifarious activities.

CASE 4
Complaints against the Hetmanski brothers

Programme date: 27 August 1980
Researcher: Andrew Jennings

Cook introduced this edition as 'The continuing saga of the brothers Hetmanski – Kings of the cowboy plumbers', proprietors of the Ever-ready company and other plumbing services all over London and the Home Counties. The advertisement for Ever-ready promised: 'Ever-ready (24 hour Plumbing Services) Ltd. Always ready. A blocked sink or drain? A burst pipe, maybe? Perhaps problems with your central heating system? Just a loo that doesn't work? Ring for fast, effective relief to any plumbing or heating problem, and you'll know why London call us Ever-ready. If we can't do it, no one can!'

The first complainant was Valerie Wilde who responded to this advertisement in London's Yellow Pages directory, because the roof of her house and garage and the roofs of two of her neighbours needed urgent attention. But when she phoned them, she was told that Ever-ready had been taken over by City-wide, who did the same kind of work. The company sent a man over, and he completed the work in three days at a total charge of £600.

'Everything was fine for three days,' said Valerie Wilde, 'until it rained. And then the rain came in exactly as before.'

Understandably annoyed, she phoned the company and was told that a man would come as soon as the weather improved. When the weather did improve, no one came, so she phoned again, to be told not to be so impatient. When she phoned again she was disconnected. A third call elicited the information that all complaints had to be sent in writing to an address in Hertfordshire. She wrote several times, but received no reply. More phone calls to City-wide.

Finally a girl took one of her calls and transferred her to a man 'whose voice sounded very familiar'. She explained her problem, and he told her that City-wide had gone into liquidation. The company was now called Ever-ready, and they were trading from the same premises. He advised her to write to the liquidator at the same address in Hertfordshire. But, of course, Valerie recalled that Ever-ready was the name of the original trading company, and when she checked on their telephone she found herself speaking to the same girl, who put her through to the same man, who gave her the same response. Later, she was told that both firms had ceased trading, although this was not the case.

Her comment: 'Between us, my neighbours and I have spent £600, and the firm seems to have gone out of their way to cover their tracks, so that we can't get them to put the work right.'

Other complaints poured into the *Checkpoint* office: gross over-charging, rudeness and appalling workmanship, and even complaints from plumbers who had found themselves in a particularly unsavoury kind of trap. One, who worked for the Hetmanskis for about a year, thought he had started a good, straight, highly-paid job. He was to be sent on a job, do the work and be paid thirty-four per cent of what he charged the customer, and from that sum the firm would stop thirty-four per cent tax. So if a job came to £200, he ended up getting about £40.

'This sounds all very well,' said the plumber, 'until they start sending you on tap washers for £10, and then you realise that you're not going to earn much money.'

But when he pointed this out to the firm they told him he was working the wrong way. The right way was: 'You go there, and if it is a tap washer you say, well, it needs a new washer, but the tap's had it, so you put a new tap in. Then you charge them £50.'

According to this plumber, the firm's favourite swindle concerned boilers.

'Anyone who rings up about a boiler, whether it's a gas valve or pump problem, you go there, take all the parts off the boiler, and tell the customer that you're taking it back to the office for repair. Then you go and do another job and a few hours later phone the first customer. You tell him that the boiler is repaired and that the bill comes to £200 or £300.'

Surprisingly, nine out of ten customers accepted this story without question. If they didn't, they were told that a great deal of work had been done on the boiler, for which there was a charge of £120, and if they wanted to come to the office to collect the parts they could have them back – as long as they brought the cash.

He and other plumbers later discovered that they had been cheated out of money by the Hetmanskis; typically, over £1,000 having been deducted from their earnings for tax payments not passed on to the Inland Revenue. And other deductions from their pay were so massive that they found themselves doing 'some pretty dastardly deals'. A simple air lock in the pipes would be turned into an operation for removing a blocked section of pipe and replacing it with a new one.

'A ten-minute job would end up as a day's work,' said a second plumber. 'I did another job where I charged £560 to put two ten-gallon plastic tanks in the roof, which cost £4 each, and about twenty feet of copper tube. The cost of the materials came to about £30 at the most, with four hours work. The joke was, the customer was so pleased he even gave me a drink.'

One of the Hetmanskis' customers told how a leaking bathroom turned into a nerve-wracking problem that led to their getting a Court judgement for £215 against the firm for the return of money paid for work that was improperly done. At the time of the programme, this had not been paid. As the team discovered, as far as the Hetmanskis were concerned Court judgements were for ignoring!

If the Hetmanskis came across a customer who was less likely to complain than most, such as a foreigner, they went in really hard. A diplomat from El Salvador returned to his London home to find that his hot water cistern had failed. By this time the Hetmanskis were operating under another company name, Destaton Plumbers.

When the plumber arrived he told the customer's wife that she was faced with a major job that would take about four days and cost some £400. When she asked what an alternative would be, the Hetmanski man said that a replacement boiler would cost £1,000. She agreed to have the repair work done, but instead of the four days, the work took only three hours, and the plumber demanded payment in full, a sum that totalled £429. At first she objected to this, but the plumber put her under considerable pressure, and in the end she gave him a post-dated cheque.

Her husband returned home, and on being told the story began liaising with the firm to accept an independent and reduced sum of £130. After a certain amount of toing and froing, in which he found himself pointing out to the Destaton's financial director that there was no Value Added Tax registration number on the firm's invoice, he managed to persuade the company to accept his offer.

A Japanese student paid £169 for a Hetmanski repair to a leaking bathroom, only to find, as many had done before, that the problem remained. After a round of complaints that led nowhere, she called another plumbing company who completed the work successfully at a cost of less than £20.

But, 'foreigners weren't the half of it!', according to another disillusioned ex-Hetmanski workman.

'What really got up my nose is the way they treated older citizens, with total disrespect. They used the term "old grunters", especially if they had plenty of money and lived in nicer parts of London.'

'Prime targets for Ever-ready's way of working, a little bit slower, more gullible . . . a prime "suspect" to take as much money as possible from!' listeners were told.

One victim was seventy-seven-year-old Kathleen Beattie, half-paralysed as the result of a stroke. Her waste disposal unit broke down, so she looked in Yellow Pages and called Ever-ready Plumbing Services. Their man solved the problem in about five minutes and presented her with a bill for £56. She queried this, but was told it was a standard charge, so she paid the full amount.

The *Checkpoint* team contacted the Institute of Plumbers, the trade organisation of the plumbing industry, who were also concerned about the 'depredations of the Cowboys', and the Institute agreed to co-operate in a project aimed at finding out exactly how the Hetmanskis set about their business. They borrowed a flat and rigged the toilet cistern to over-flow by replacing the ball valve with one that leaked. The replacement cost 60p. The time it took was two minutes. They hid their microphones and contacted the firm, and eventually two plumbers arrived. Their price for the work: £25.

'Mind you,' revealed Cook, 'one Cabinet Minister paid Destaton £57.50 for the same job! In our case they used secondhand parts instead of the new ones they claimed to have used, and presented a bill with yet another name on it – Alice Plumbing.'

Determined to interview the Hetmanskis, Cook waited on the doorstep of their Brixton office . . . 'almost as impregnable as KGB headquarters'. There followed a totally one-sided interview with Leon. Cook persisted in his questions, with such interjections as 'Why did you find it necessary to hit me . . .? Leave the microphone alone.' Leon was then joined by brother Stanley and office manager Mike Saunders, and they set about Cook with a length of building timber and a cosh, causing severe bruising, lacerations and cracked ribs. They also offered to take him down an alley behind their offices to 'sort him out properly'.

After two *Checkpoint* exposés the two brothers concerned set up yet another plumbing business, but Cook was told that the Inland Revenue was interested in their activities, to the tune of £250,000 in unpaid tax. They are currently still operating in and around the London area, though on a much reduced scale.

CASE 5
Complaints against Sean Mallin

Broadcast on 3 September 1980
Researcher: John Stonborough

This edition covered a number of complaints against Sean Mallin, a Belfast man operating in the guise of a builder. The first complainant to tell her story was Kathleen McEvoy. She contacted Mallin after seeing his advertisement in the *Irish News*, with a view to having her home extensively renovated. He quoted £5,750, and she applied for a grant. The Housing Executive allotted her £3,750, which meant that she had to borrow the balance. Mallin then agreed to start work and asked for £1,000 cash, which she gave him.

'. . . and then another thousand, then another thousand. But I didn't know that a lady up the street was doing the same thing . . . Inside five and a half weeks, Mr Mallin had received from me £6,100, and he says, "Your work'll be finished in two weeks". That was the end of July. Three weeks before Christmas I was without a back wall. There were no floors in. No hot water. Toilet wasn't working then. And at that time I had a boy very seriously ill.'

Despite urgent telephone calls and a harrowing personal visit to his luxurious home, Mallin and his men did not come back to Mrs McEvoy's home to finish the work, and she was forced to spend the winter of 1979 sharing one tiny room with her husband and seven children, with total debts approaching £9,000.

Mallin played the same trick on one of Mrs McEvoy's neighbours, Lilly McGuinness, who had been impressed at the 'quick and efficient' way his men had started work. She finished up paying him £5,000 and having no back to the house, no toilet, no windows.

'We went to the police, and everywhere,' said a distraught Mrs McGuinness, 'and nobody seemed able to help us.'

Further down the street, Rose Curly was faced with a similar problem. Her family savings of £2,000 were the first to go, followed hotly by several more thousands borrowed from the bank against the promise of a grant.

'It was fast approaching Christmas when the workers stopped coming. I was expecting a fourth baby, and I was going to have to spend Christmas with no back wall or toilet. No drains or sewers. There was a hose in the back yard for water, but it was very dangerous, because the rats were coming at night. Christmas wasn't very nice . . . It was very sad . . . heartbreaking . . .'

Another of Mallin's enterprises involved the restaurant business. He opened the Hilltop Restaurant in 1974 in Hannahstown, and that burned down in suspicious circumstances in 1975. About twenty creditors, who were owed around £40,000, believed they would be paid out of the insurance, but the premises were underinsured and the bank had a prior claim. Mallin offered one creditor, John Kelly, a share in another restaurant venture that Mallin said would more than recoup his missing £2,000. This began a confusing sequence of events that began with Kelly realising that Mallin was 'a cowboy' and advising his own partner to have nothing to do with him. The partner did not take Kelly's advice and agreed to go into the restaurant business with Mallin on the promise that Mallin would build a £40,000 bungalow on the partner's land for £20,000. Kelly ended up running the restaurant, the Crossroads in Anne Street. This was not in a very healthy shape, and things were not made any easier when Mallin borrowed a van and a car from the partners that he promptly sold, giving them cheques totalling £700 that were not honoured.

'It was all a fiasco,' said Kelly. 'I closed the place up, and I was in Dublin. He (Mallin) arrived at my house and threatened my wife that he was going to shoot me in the knees if I didn't open the place again.'

Kelly took the precaution of visiting some Republican clubs in Belfast and informing those who cared to listen what Mallin was doing: 'Threatening to harm the staff in the restaurant'. Kelly's debts, many of which were incurred in his name by Mallin, totalled £17,000.

'I took advice on the possibility of issuing a writ against this fellow . . . but I'd already discovered there were more writs against him than sheets of paper in a toilet. It'd be just a sheer waste of time.'

The *Checkpoint* team traced twenty-two writs against Mallin, of which less than half had produced any results. Eight of them totalled over £14,000, to banks, builders and various merchants. Most of these were unenforceable. Many were incurred by Mallin using other people's names, which further confused the issue. Cook entered into a string of negotiations to interview Mallin about these and his other enterprises, negotiations that were convoluted and protracted. One meeting with Mallin's wife resulted in abusive phone calls to the *Checkpoint* office and the threat of a telegram (never sent) to the BBC's Director General. Mallin then agreed to meet Cook, provided there was no tape recorder. He protested his good faith and made a series of claims, one of which was that he had a degree in Civil Engineering from Queen's University, Belfast.

'The University have no record of a Sean Mallin with a degree of any kind since 1849,' Cook reported.

Subsequent efforts to record an interview resulted in a terse, one-way conversation on the telephone with Mallin, who refused to identify himself or answer questions. However, it was made plain that any broadcast would have 'dire consequences'. Efforts were also made to have complainants withdraw from the programme, either by threats or offers of money. Work on the story was not made any easier, recalled Cook, by unwanted offers of 'protection' from Republican elements who did not like Mallin 'cheating his own' and who thought that publicity would be more effective in stopping him than 'knee-capping', which had been tried before on two occasions.

'So Sean Mallin continues to answer to no one,' Cook said at the end of this edition. But, 'what he's been up to is now public. One wonders why he hasn't been caught up with before. Has he taken advantage of the Troubles, which have pushed the police hard and made people frightened to talk? Or is it the legal system he seems to have played and won? Whatever it is, something's wrong.'

After the programme Mallin laid low for two years, then began the same old game again, with more false promises, false addresses, false names, threats, judgements and bounced cheques. This time officialdom has begun to move against him, and detailed investigations have been set in motion.

CASE 6
Complaints against Janet Pitman

Broadcast on 20 February 1980
Researcher: John Stonborough

This edition introduced Janet Pitman to the listeners at the beginning. 'We go beyond the fringe of fringe medicine,' Cook said, 'to the wondrous world of Janet Pitman, performer of miracles and practitioner of what she claims is Tomorrow's Medicine: diagnoses by dowsing and cure by controlled dieting'. Pitman began by saying her work involved a new science of molecular nutrition and a measurement of bodily imbalances that can be repaired by a very up-to-date training in nutritional science. Diagnosis is a hundred per cent accurate, 'more accurate than any physical method of diagnosis'. She produced a pendulum and described how its motion revealed that the subject was 'deficient in magnesium'.

As dowsers know, a subject does not have to be present during the dowsing operation, and Pitman swung her device over letters and samples of hair sent by hundreds of hopeful people each year, from all over the world. Cook saw one for which Pitman had diagnosed a bad case of multiple sclerosis. 'But, not to worry,' he said. 'Her diet sheets, now at an initial £10 and then £5 every few weeks thereafter, actually do work miracles'.

'There is nothing, no disease incurable,' claimed Pitman. 'I have discovered how to restore our system of natural immunity, which is the lymphatic system, and I can now remedy kidney disease, which is being researched at enormous expense ... multiple sclerosis ... muscular dystrophy ... Huntingdon's Chorea ... now cancer. This is no problem at all!'

From hammer toes to homosexuality, Mrs Pitman claimed she could 'cure' them all, after thirty-five years of Somerset-based research. Such claims may sound unlikely to many people, but those desperate to find relief from suffering, those who have tried all other paths to health found her claims irresistible. The first of these introduced on the programme was Marjory Price from Gwent in Wales. For many years she had been suffering from acute sinusitis, and she wrote to Pitman after seeing a letter from her in a newspaper. Pitman wrote back asking for a fee of £7.50 which Price sent to her. Back came a letter, with no mention of sinusitis.

'She told me I had nephritis,' said Price, 'and that I wasn't to take any drugs. But I was taking (a drug) for angina. She said that

I didn't have angina, but that I had got Huntingdon's Chorea, and that was causing the chest spasms.'

This 'news' not unnaturally upset Price, who learned that the disease was hereditary. One of her daughters-in-law was expecting a baby, and the entire Price family began to feel concerned with Mrs Price's situation. Pitman explained to her that thousands of people are suffering from Huntingdon's Chorea that doctors have not diagnosed.

'... which seemed a little bit far-fetched, and, you know, I thought, well, perhaps there's some truth in it,' Price told listeners, putting in a few troubled words the classic dilemma of those who sincerely wish to learn the truth and are presented with the deliberations of an expert, self-professed or otherwise. Pitman's 'expertise' extended to the formulation of a curative diet for her new patient: water, but no tea, coffee, flour, bread, fish, dairy products, sugar, salt, and certainly no drugs. Apart from the continuing expense of dealing with Pitman, Price complained that as time went on Pitman would 'bring in something else ... I began to think I was just a walking nightmare of diseases'. In fact, in four months, Pitman told her she was suffering from Huntingdon's Chorea, nephritis, cancer, an underactive thyroid and fifty-one gall stones. 'Once the seed of doubt has been planted in one's mind, one can imagine all sorts of things wrong. You can feel really ill, and yet there isn't anything wrong at all.'

Jim Rivett from Norwich was another patient, whose hair samples produced a dramatic response. He was told he had a seventeen per cent chance of inheriting Huntingdon's Chorea. At first he was very worried, as there was a high incidence of this disease in his area, but on reflection he realised that what he'd been told was probably wrong.

'I'd been fortunate to have a slight knowledge of genetics, but I can imagine that, without that knowledge, what I'd been told would have been very distressing. I'm a healthy young man, but I can well imagine that someone who's ill or old, given this added burden, would find themselves so frightened that they would be unable to do anything about it.' A description that fitted the unhappy Marjory Price only too well.

Pitman's activities attracted the interest of a Norfolk doctor who specialised in Huntingdon's Chorea, Adrian Carro. He pointed out that the disease is always inherited, never 'developed' and that it is not a dietary problem.

'It's a pretty nasty disease ... incurable ... so telling anyone that they have it when they do not . . . is a disaster,' he said.

Carro put Pitman to the test by sending ten hair specimens from people who definitely did not suffer from Huntingdon's Chorea. Five of the ten were told they had 'varying degrees' of the disease. Not only was this untrue, but, according to Dr Carro, 'It is not possible to have a "degree" . . . you either have it or you do not have it'.

Dr Carro dismissed Pitman as a fraud, and Cook decided to send off a sample of his own hair. Even though a recent check-up had pronounced him A-1, Pitman informed him he was suffering from malnutrition, advanced cellular breakdown and cancer of the larynx. His 'cure' was basically to eat three pounds of grapes each day. On what, he speculated, are such frightening pronouncements based? Pitman had no recognised qualifications of any kind, but had on occasion used the names of qualified people to lend credence to her claims, one of whom described her as 'a potentially unsafe, totally unreliable, scaremongering menace'.

As for her methods, claims and diets, Cook sought the advice of Noel Dilly, Professor of Anatomy at St George's Hospital Medical School in London and a long-time student of 'fringe' medicine. Professor Dilly pointed out that while orthodox medicine doesn't claim to have all the answers to all the diseases, and, while there may be some value in fringe medicine, 'this women certainly has none of the answers. What she is doing is the classic thing to do in fringe medicine – to play on fears and to choose diseases where the natural history is for the disease to come and to go, whatever you do to it . . . then claim, when it goes, it's her treatment and, when it comes back, it's you abusing her treatment'. He also told listeners that the 'new science' of Pitman wasn't new, but had been put forward in a book published in 1912 and written by a man who died in 1955 trying to cure a 'perfectly treatable case of jaundice' with one of his own fasts.

Professor Dilly did not belittle all so-called fringe medical practices, but he did point out the dangers involved when some proponents go to extremes, inventing deficiencies that do not exist or giving them on a misleading scale, and relying on a tiny amount of fact to seduce the gullible.

'They can do a tremendous amount of harm, because . . . they will often say that orthodox medicine must be stopped before their treatment will work. Sometimes this can be very dangerous. If you are a diabetic, maintained on insulin, and you stop your insulin, you will die.'

Such fringe practitioners are dangerous, because they are very persuasive, and they are persuasive because anyone who is ill wants to get better. As for Cook's diet of grapes, the professor dismissed it as 'lethal' and described as 'rubbish' Pitman's claims that Cook was deficient as she described on her chart . . . 'I've got even worse news for you; some of these deficiencies mean you're now dead!'

It was at this stage that Cook visited Janet Pitman, who was living in a large, beautifully-furnished modern house on a 110-acre farm in the Somerset village of Charlton Mackrell. In the lengthy interview that followed, it was apparent that Pitman was either a consumate actress or genuinely sincere in the belief of her own powers. In any case, she gave explanations for most of the problems with which Cook confronted her. She claimed to be able to diagnose diseases 'long before you get the symptoms'; which explained, at least to her satisfaction, why Marjory Price's doctors did not agree that Mrs Price was suffering from Huntingdon's Chorea and cancer.

'You see, people come to me usually when they're disillusioned with their medical advisers, as the doctor simply hasn't the means to detect disease in the early condition, as I have.'

The doctors, Pitman claimed, were absolutely wrong, but rather put her own foot in it when she told how one of her patients had 'rushed off' for an X-ray after being told by Pitman that her cancer was 'moving to the advanced stage' in her gall bladder.

'She . . . got an X-ray, and it showed nothing. Well it doesn't, you see, show on X-ray until it's very advanced.'

It is difficult to believe that an X-ray could miss a cancer that was 'moving to the advanced stage'. Nevertheless, Pitman continued her explanations. Her diet for repairing magnesium deficiency had cured 'scores and scores of people' whom she had diagnosed as having Huntingdon's Chorea, and she stuck to this even after Cook pointed out the fact that if her 'patients' did not have the disease in the first place, as the doctors had said, she couldn't lose anything by claiming she had cured it.

'I have a patient now with about five weeks to live, no more. He's a very busy man, and he says, "Oh, I feel all right. I can't bother with your (treatment), and I don't feel ill." But if he's going to wait for symptoms, then it's too late.'

When asked by Cook to clarify this statement, Pitman agreed that what she meant to say was that the man would die if he took no notice of her treatment, as would many other patients. She claimed that people in twenty-six countries had accepted her reasoning and had therefore been rescued from certain death. She refused to name any, because that would be medically unethical, and she again denied that if someone had not got the disease she attributed to him it is all too easy to claim a cure. There then followed this interchange:

COOK: Do I look healthy to you?
PITMAN: Yes, but looks are nothing to go by.
COOK: . . . because some hair samples were sent to you from me, and you wrote back saying I had cancer of the larynx.
PITMAN: Well, I can't tell you anything about that unless I look at my files.
COOK: I've had a complete medical check-up, and they say there's nothing wrong with me, and yet you say I have cancer of the larynx. That's a very worrying thing, isn't it?
PITMAN: Well, it's probably too early to be diagnosed by physical means, you see. I mean, this happens all the time.
COOK: There are those who would suggest that you had ulterior motives, and the reason for keeping people on the hook, for frightening them, was that they keep writing to you, sending you money.
PITMAN: Oh dear no. I'm an absolute sucker for sob-stories. I'm always writing to people . . . because I'm a Virgo. The Virgo motto is 'I serve'. Oh dear me no! I've done far more work for nothing.

The programme gave the last word to Professor Dilly: people such as Janet Pitman ought to be stopped, but in a free society like ours he wasn't sure how this could be done.

'I personally believe that education on this sort of programme is an effective way of dealing with these people. I think to honour them with the power of the law is to elevate them far above their crank, fringe powers. We must, however, expose them for the stupidity they propound, and try to protect those people who, out of a sheer fear that modern orthodox medicine doesn't have all the answers, go to the fringe. When someone is desperate (they) cling at straws.'

Mrs Pitman no longer publicises her 'powers' – and, happily, the man to whom she gave five weeks to live was, some years later, very much alive.

CASE 7
Complaints against David and Helen Elizaldes

Broadcast on 23 May 1979
(Joint production with BBC television Nationwide*)*
Researcher: Mike Robinson

Psychic surgery – miracle or fraud? That was the simple question posed to listeners about the activities of David and Helen Elizaldes, two so-called psychic surgeons based in Australia, who visited Britain and toured the country from the Spiritualist National Union's headquarters at Stanstead Hall in Essex. David was a Philippino and his wife a Cypriot. The first person interviewed was Kate Moira, an ex-nurse, who had brought her little daughter Sharon for treatment, hoping for the medically impossible. Sharon had suffered for eight years from a spinal tumour. Doctors had taken away six inches of her spine in an attempt to cure her, but she was paralysed. Her mother was hoping that even if the Elizaldes couldn't make Sharon walk they might be able to take away her pain. She herself wanted psychic surgery. She had 'tummy pains' and had already spent over £200 in osteopath fees for treatments for her slipped disc.

David Elizaldes explained to Cook that he had discovered his healing gift while he was a boy. He was able, he claimed, to open a person's body with his bare hands and remove whatever malignancy is affecting the patient. Although the blood flows freely, no scars were left because the opening of the body did not involve any cutting, just 'a parting of the cells'.

After long negotiations and finally with the full co-operation of the Spiritualist National Union and its leader, Gordon Higginson, Cook recorded a number of activities at Stanstead, including a moving attempt by a twenty-three-year-old boy suffering from cerebral palsy to walk from his wheelchair, aided, in fact, by his friend. The boy 'was lifted painfully from his wheelchair and literally dragged a few paces forward . . . His will-power was obviously far stronger than his wasted legs'. Yet he retained complete faith in the efficacy of his treatment.

Next, Cook attended the operation on Kate Moira, performed against the background of 'mysterious oriental music' on a couch. Kate's stomach was kneaded vigorously by Helen Elizaldes, while David Elizaldes began pushing wet swabs between his wife's fingers. 'Bits of matter' appeared to be removed from the bloody stomach area, then it was all over, with a swab down and instructions for Kate not to wash the operation site for twenty-four hours.

Gordon Higginson told Cook how impressed he was with the Elizaldes and their work, and how the Union had provided everything for the operations and kept a watch on the proceedings to ensure there was no hanky-panky . . .

'They never left the sanctuary,' he said, 'after seeing probably seventy-five patients in the morning and seventy-five in the afternoon. It was just impossible for them to be fraudulent, it was just impossible.'

Cook wondered why the two surgeons always went into the body through the stomach, when they claimed to be able to remove malignancies from anywhere, and was told they could 'magnetise' toxic material to the stomach area with their hands.

Commenting on the not insubstantial sums of money earned by the Elizaldes, Cook said, 'Of course, if the Elizaldes really do have a remarkable gift, then there's absolutely no reason why they shouldn't make a living out of it. But are they genuine? Or can it all be hocus-pocus, aided and abetted by desperate people who want to be convinced that miracles really can happen?'

Phillip Towner, an ex-member of a Spiritualist Church, then told how the Elizaldes had claimed to have removed kidney stones that had plagued him for twenty-five years. Against his will, his fellow church members proclaimed a miracle, but a year later the stones were still there, X-rays revealing them to be in exactly the same position as before. A fraud! he exclaimed. This sort of thing must stop!

Fraud, or a genuine mistake by the Elizaldes? Cook interviewed American illusionist James Randi who watched the team's film of the operation and then said that the 'surgeons' were nothing more than fellow magicians, and not very good ones. Randi took listeners through the operation sequence and explained what was happening . . . 'Take a look at that hand . . . he's got something in his hand . . . That's the look of the conjurer . . . Definitely something large concealed in the right hand . . .'

Randi then performed a 'messy' operation on Cook to show exactly how it can be done. The body is annointed with oil and massaged vigorously. Then the second member of the operating team steps forward to 'introduce what the conjurers call "load".' This is perhaps a child's balloon or merely a little paper cup (containing) chicken blood, guts and little bits of chicken liver, sometimes human blood . . . I call it the process of Digging For Gold, and believe me there's a lot of gold to be dug for in this business . . . It's an excellent conjurer's illusion . . . There is, of course, a small benefit to be had from the process, as many people with psychosomatic ills go away believing they've been cured. The great danger is that regular medical help is not sought and that the patient can then go away and simply die, as has happened in many cases in the past. And dead people don't do very much complaining.'

Cook examined an operation carried out under the cameras on George Higginson's ulcerated leg by the Elizaldes. Unknown to the surgeons, two of the team members had managed to obtain one of the blood clots said to have been removed from Higginson's body. This clot, together with some of Higginson's apparently blood-stained clothing, was sent to Dr Patrick Lincoln of the Department of Forensic Medicine at the London Hospital Medical School. He explained the tests that were carried out on these specimens and on a fresh blood sample given by Higginson. The clot came from a pig, and the blood stains were Group B, whereas Higginson's blood was Group A. Neither the clot nor the blood on the pants could have originated from Higginson. Cook also referred to another operation, in which the patient had discovered that the stains on clothing apparently caused by his blood during the operation were also pig's blood. In addition he explained how the 'cured' kidney stones were still in place, their X-rays matching exactly those taken of the stones a year previously.

Confronted with these facts, Higginson showed that he, at least, was utterly sincere in his belief of the Elizaldes's powers, while the Elizaldes stoutly professed their honesty through several minutes of Cook at his most persistent.

COOK: But the tests were done by one of the world's leading forensic laboratories. Would it surprise you . . . that it couldn't have been anything other than pig's blood?
HIGGINSON: Well, that I wouldn't believe!
COOK: So either they've got it wrong, and we don't think they have because they are experts in the field, or you are a pig, which you're plainly not.
HIGGINSON: No, they've got it wrong.
COOK: (*to Mrs Elizaldes*) What would your reaction be, then?
MRS ELIZALDES: Well, I would think that's very strange, although I've heard that . . . the structure of the blood does change. But . . . I'm surprised by that, all the same.
HIGGINSON: Yes, I'd be very surprised by that.

COOK: You're saying that one of the world's leading forensic laboratories has got it wrong?
HIGGINSON: Yes, I am.

COOK: Have you had any independent, closely medically-controlled observation?
HIGGINSON: No . . . I am convinced. I don't need to test.
COOK: Mr Higginson, nobody doubts that you're a very sincere man, but could it be that you just don't want to believe that something isn't quite what it seems?
HIGGINSON: No, of course not. I have been too near these people. I know they are genuine . . .
COOK: (*to the Elizaldes*) You can put your hands on your hearts, both of you, and say that you're not actually misleading anyone?
MRS ELIZALDES: (*hand on heart*) We're not actually misleading anyone.
HIGGINSON: Of course they're not! It's absolute nonsense for anyone to even think about it.

'So,' said Cook at the end of the edition, 'despite all the scientific and other evidence to the contrary, the leaders of the Spiritualist National Union are sticking to their guns. Perhaps what they should do is admit that they've been taken in by a couple of unscrupulous confidence tricksters and cancel the tour the Elizaldes are due to start soon. That way they'd be prevented from making a mockery of the spiritualists and a tragedy of their victims.'

Shortly after the broadcast the tour was cancelled, and the Elizaldes face police prosecution should they ever return to Britain.

CASE 8
Complaints against Dennis Kendall

Broadcast on 3 December 1980
(Joint production with BBC-TV Newsnight*)*
Researcher: Mike Robinson

For this edition, *Checkpoint* travelled to California to interview Dennis Kendall, former MP for Grantham in Lincolnshire, to ask him about his claims for a treatment for arthritis, a treatment that involved the injection into the patient of a substance called dimethyl sulphoxide, DMSO, a powerful industrial solvent.

Kendall, then in his late seventies, enthused over 'this wonderful drug' and told Cook he had started selling the treatment in the UK (where there are about six and a half million sufferers of the disease) to 'give them the benefit of what's been happening in the United States, Mexico and other countries', where many thousands of 'cures' were claimed.

Arthritis is a painful and crippling disease, and in the UK nearly a quarter of the average doctor's time is spent in its treatment. Everyone, said Cook, is looking for a cure, including Sandra Harrison who, in her late twenties, was frightened of facing a miserable and immobile old age. After being told about Kendall's treatment she accepted an 'invitation' to attend his clinic in Cricklewood, north London, where, at a cost of £350, she spent three days undergoing a course of treatment during which DMSO was dripped into a vein for one and a half hours a day.

'I didn't feel any different after the treatment,' she said. 'My arthritis was as bad as it had ever been, but during the treatment I felt very ill indeed – and for some days after having the treatment. I went home extremely disappointed and very upset about the whole thing.'

Cook visited the clinic and was allowed to record the conversation between the doctor in attendance, Dr Lawrence Knott, and a patient. (Kendall himself is not a doctor, and according to UK legislation the treatment must be conducted under qualified medical supervision.) Knott told Cook that some patients had been on 'most of the current cures for arthritis' and said that DMSO produced an eighty per cent claimed success rate in America and that the clinic's findings would 'probably agree with that'.

Cook introduced Audrey Webb from Leicester who had suffered from arthritis for thirteen years, one of a number of former patients who wasn't happy with this statistic. She became ill on the third day of the treatment and passed blood in her urine. Following Kendall's treatment she couldn't move for two months and spent the following six months in a wheelchair.

'The treatment's dreadful . . . I wouldn't wish it on my worst enemy.'

Next came an elderly married couple from Weston-super-Mare, John and Francis Bagley, who were told at the clinic that they had arthritic knees. After one course of treatment each, after which the pain in their knees diminished but returned, they both paid for a second course. After the second day at the clinic they both became ill with vomiting, and Mrs Bagley became unconscious. She was taken to the Royal Free Hospital, where the diagnosis was that her kidneys were now in bad shape and that she had suffered a slight stroke. Mr Bagley was told she'd almost died and had required a complete blood transfusion. He collapsed a few hours later, and they were both hospitalised for a week. After a thorough examination, which was published in the *Lancet*, it was discovered that Mr Bagley did not have arthritic knees in the first place.

After hearing from Mrs Bagley that DMSO had 'upset' their previously excellent general health, Cook talked again with Dr Knott, who was paid to administer the substance in Kendall's clinic. Cook pondered whether the Department of Health and Social Security should allow the use of DMSO. Knott explained that its use was covered by legislation (Section 9 of the Medical Act) . . . 'Which means that it doesn't need a licence for clinical trial. It can be used immediately for treatment purposes. It doesn't need investigation as regards clinical efficiency and adverse effects. But what Section 9 states is that a doctor must take responsibility for its actions. Now, I'm quite happy to do that, because, having gone over the work that was done in the States, Mexico . . . Tel Aviv and in Denmark . . . I'm happy to administer the drug'.

Knott claimed that, in America at least, the trials on DMSO were proper clinical trials and that DMSO had been used in 'probably hundreds of thousands of cases since 1965, without one single long-term adverse effect'.

Cook pointed out that this was not true, and neither were the claims for thousands of cures in Mexico, many of which turned out to be no more than improvements in mobility brought about by other drugs such as steroids. As for the American claims, the American Arthritis Association said: 'DMSO has not been adequately tested and is very possibly dangerous. Many arthritis sufferers are being exploited daily by sensationalist testimonies, unscrupulous promoters and unsafe products'. The US Food and Drug Administration made the point: 'DMSO is not approved for any use save one rare bladder complaint. The evaluation studies so far are of such poor quality as to be useless, and there is no evidence that DMSO alters the course of any disease or is in any sense a miracle drug'.

These views appeared to be shared by the UK Department of Health and Social Security: 'Makers must prove a drug is safe and effective by applying for a licence under the Medicines Act.

This has not been done for DMSO, which is not licenced or approved or likely to be so for intravenous use. (Kendall's) brochure is therefore misleading'.

Cook interviewed one of the UK's leading researchers into arthritis, Dr Edward Huskisson, consultant rheumatologist at St Bartholomew's Hospital in London, who emphasised that DMSO had not been adequately tested for the treatment of arthritis and that the medical profession did not know enough about its side effects and long-term toxicity. So, asked Cook, how can it be sold so effectively to the patient? He interviewed Derek Needs, a chronic arthritis sufferer for sixteen years, for a possible clue.

Needs said that he never took anything 'at face value', and he decided to see a patient who had already taken Kendall's treatment in order to see what the results were. After such a meeting he was 'pretty convinced that the treatment was OK'. He had his treatment, and for the following week felt marvellous. While he was at home, Kendall telephoned him to see how he felt, and, on learning that Needs was 'great . . . got rid of my arthritis after sixteen years', Kendall offered him £20 for every patient Needs sent to the clinic.

'After I put the phone down,' said Needs, 'my suspicions were that this is not quite right. I wondered if the people who had recommended it to me had received payment . . . But after another week, and I was feeling really ill, I thought I'd been done. I'd been led up the garden path.'

Dr Huskisson told Cook that he and his team at St Bartholomew's were prepared to test any possible remedy for arthritis. He pointed out the prime need to test a product fully, in such a way that they could show, in a way that was acceptable to other people, that the drug works and what its advantages and disadvantages are . . . to make the information available throughout the world.

'I think it would be quite wrong for me to disappear into Harley Street and give this treatment to people for money. That would be business, not medicine.'

And business, continued Cook, is what Mr Kendall had spent much of his life promoting. First was a night club in Shanghai. During the Second World War he ran a company that made 20mm cannon for the Spitfire aeroplane, and it was alleged that he had actually held up production of much needed war supplies until his terms were met. At the time, the Parliamentary Public Accounts Committee reported: 'An investigation into the actual cost (of the cannons) made after formal refusal to give full access to accounts and records disclosed that prices hitherto demanded and paid to (Kendall's) company had been altogether excessive . . . A reduction of profits on war contracts of £1,700,000 is recommended'.

Undaunted by this episode, and having previously been elected Grantham's Member of Parliament, Kendall turned his attention to the manufacture of a £100 people's car, claiming that he would employ twenty thousand people and make a hundred thousand cars a year. Finance was collected, orders taken and brochures issued, but two prototypes were all that were ever produced, and the company went into liquidation in 1946, owing nearly £500,000. In the court case that followed, the judge said of Kendall: 'He has shown a crass incompetence and carelessness of the welfare of the affairs of his company that would be hard to equal'.

The indomitable Kendall was rather more successful with a plan to produce a three-wheeled tractor, and subsequently he left the UK to live in California in 'a dream home, with a kidney-shaped swimming pool and an organ that wouldn't have disgraced a cinema'. He faced up to Cook's questioning with total aplomb.

KENDALL: I would like to see DMSO used for other ailments besides arthritis because it has that potential, in the treatment of Parkinson's disease, mental conditions and tumours. I believe there's a great future for DMSO.

COOK: But it's a very controversial drug, and there are those who say that not enough studies have been done on what you're using it for. For example, we've spoken with the FDA, the American Arthritis Association and to arthritis specialists in the UK, and to the DHSS. They say that DMSO is not approved of in the way you're using it. It hasn't been scientifically tested. There's no evidence that it permanently alters the course of any disease whatsoever, but it's possibly dangerous and it produces unwanted side effects. To make any kind of claims is, to say the least, misleading.

KENDALL: Well, of course, that is untrue. They certainly have not approved the way we're using it, but they have not ever shown that it is not effective in the treatment of arthritis.

COOK: But nobody's shown that it is! There's been no scientific testing . . .

KENDALL: Well, yes, but that's easily explainable. To do a scientific test following the demands of the FDA, you need a double blind study, and you cannot do that with DMSO because of its obnoxious smell.

COOK: So the only evidence . . . is anecdotal, the stories people tell?

KENDALL: That is true.

COOK: And you say there are no side effects?

KENDALL: There are some very gentle side effects, because every drug has side effects.

COOK: What about the Bagleys, though? Mrs Bagley, at least, was said to be 'touch and go' whether she lived after the treatment.

KENDALL: No. I remember the Bagley case very well. They came and had the treatment, both the Bagleys. Some months later Mrs Bagley talked to me, because we always follow up our patients. She said she had a pain in her knees. I said, come to London, and we'll give you another treatment. What she hadn't said when she came to us was that she had taken other drugs the night before.

COOK: She says she didn't, and her doctor confirmed that.

KENDALL: I don't care what her doctor said, but the blood test showed she had.

COOK: Are you saying it's the Bagley's fault that they had trouble after the DMSO treatment?

KENDALL: Oh, definitely.

COOK: If DMSO is so good, why do you have to pay for testimonials? Why did you offer £20 to Derek Needs?

KENDALL: . . . I don't remember Derek Needs, but it is perfectly true that I have given £20 to those who have been to us . . . if they would telephone people whom they knew had arthritis. I felt they were entitled to receive something for doing it.

COOK: Rather undermines the value of the testimonials, though, doesn't it, if they are paid for?

KENDALL: Not at all, because the people that come to us are not paid when they come to us.

COOK: And you plan to continue the use of DMSO?

KENDALL: Oh definitely, definitely. It's a splendid, wonderful drug that does the job of work it's supposed to.

And there the programme left it, with Cook questioning his statement: 'But, does it? Don't say you haven't been warned.'

After the programme the DHSS reinforced that warning by announcing that they did not support the use of DMSO under

Section 9 of the Medicines Act; as had been implied by Dr Kendall and his colleagues. Further, they said no licence would now be granted, or was likely to be granted for the medical use of DMSO.

CASE 9
Complaints against Cambridgeshire Area Health Authority

Broadcast on 11 February 1981
Researcher: Andrew Jennings

Cook set the scene for this edition by introducing 'yet another dispute over heart transplantation' and describing the now famous Papworth Hospital in Cambridge, 'the last hope for a select and carefully selected few of Britain's quarter-million sufferers from chronic heart disease'. At the time of this programme, surgeons at Papworth had completed sixteen heart transplants, and the central point raised in *Checkpoint* was: Is this high technology, high-cost hope for the few prejudicing the chances of the many by using up scarce medical resources?

Apart from any moral considerations about transplants, *Checkpoint* had come across considerable unease within and without the Papworth walls, with allegations of funds being 'siphoned off' and promises of money from a charity broken. Several leading consultants refused to have anything to do with the programme, and Cook's first interviewee was Kenneth Robinson, who had been Minister for Health eight years previously, when the first British heart transplants had taken place.

Robinson explained that he and his colleagues were aware of the problems involved in funding such high-cost, high-technology work, and it wasn't just the money.

'One of the things we learned,' he said, 'was that the National Heart Hospital, because of the post-operative conditions required for the patient, stopped all admissions of other cases for several days . . . We were beginning to worry, because there were patients for fairly routine heart operations, who certainly could have been helped, whose lives might have been saved, being denied admission or delayed because of this one, dramatic surgical operation. That didn't seem to me to be a particularly sensible use of limited resources.'

None of the early transplant patients survived, and a halt was called to the programme. It was generally agreed that if Britain were to resume, this should only be after a great deal of discussion and consultation between all interested parties about the best use of resources. Cook made the point that such open discussion did not seem to have taken place before the current programme of heart transplant operations at Papworth. In fact, the first the local residents and even local doctors knew about it was as a result of a news broadcast that reported how 'Britain's latest heart transplant patient . . . a forty-four-year-old heating engineer' was said to be 'doing well' at Papworth. Charles McHugh was Britain's fifth such patient and the first after a break in the operations that had lasted over five years. In the previous case the patient died after four hours, and, according to the news bulletin, the Health Authorities discouraged transplants on the grounds of poor results and high costs . . . 'But last year, after improvements in survival rates, that policy was relaxed.'

Sadly, Mr McHugh survived only seventeen days after his operation, but by that time the media had got hold of the story and the publicity juggernaut began to roll. A national programme of operations was started, paid for out of local funds. No one in East Anglia benefited directly from it. Dr Derek Cracknell, Chairman of the Cambridgeshire Area Family Practitioners Committee, referred on the programme to 'this unfortunate snowball effect' and stressed that the Area Health Authority should not deprive any existing group from receiving care by diverting resources ineffectively.

'If, as we see in cardiac transplantation, the development of these services goes ahead willy-nilly, without control and without the allocation of proper resources, then there must be a restriction on the existing services,' he said.

It was not difficult for the *Checkpoint* team to find cases of medical hardship in the area. Cook visited a unit for disturbed adolescents, run by Dr Kay McLoughlin, with bedrooms that had fitments in tatters and an asphalt floor.

'It's a slum,' said Dr McLoughlin flatly, 'and it's typical of the conditions that the kids have to live in and that we have to work in. . . . We have no money . . . We'd like to know, for example, what happened to the £50,000 that was given to the District for mental health last year. It seems to have completely disappeared.'

The doctor listed examples of how funds were 'siphoned off' from much-needed medical programmes to pay for the transplants: medicine for old people, child health and child psychiatry. Seventy-seven-year-old Dorothy Anderson from

Cambridge had been expecting a surgical end to pain in her left hip and gave a harrowing description of her disappointment when she arrived for admission at Papworth.

'I went to the hospital at quarter past nine in the morning, and I was there until six. Then they came in and said, "I'm sorry, but there isn't a bed." . . . I get home at ten past six, very exhausted, very depressed . . . I can't walk. I'm like a nutmeg grater. My bones are scraping. You see, the hip joint is completely worn out . . . I mean I could scream. I do scream. But what can I do? It's the transplants that I think are awful, because the ratio isn't all that good in Papworth. I think the money could be (better) spent. If your heart goes, that's that. Mine's only a bone worn out. Once I've had my operation and my hip replaced I shall be a new woman again.'

Taking the understandable emotion out of it, Dr McLoughlin made the point that such operations were more cost-effective than heart transplants. He commented on 'headline-grabbing medicine' and said that anyone who knew anything about accounting could see that the cost figures 'put out' about heart transplants were 'fictitious', a case for the Crown Commissioners.

Waiting lists were in a shambles, too, at the hospital, according to certain consultants. And Dr Cracknell commented on the enormous sums of money spent by the Regional Health Authority in 'maintaining Papworth in its existing state' which would 'probably have not occurred if it had not been for the cardiac transplant programme'. He said that the situation had been likened to a hi-jacking, where there are limited funds available and one particular segment takes the lion's share.

'It is unfortunate,' he said, 'that the public debate with respect to this sort of advance in technology is marred because of the absence of the comments of the consultants within the unit itself, both those in favour and those against the procedure.'

Cook discovered that neither those for nor those against were, in fact, willing to give interviews, but those against gave him a number of unattributable points to ponder. 'You'd have to be a bloody fool not to see funds being diverted,' was a typical comment, together with accusations that the heart transplant programme had got in the way of 'less glamorous' surgery by monopolising facilities, that the money for it was not coming, as promised, from public donations and that there was much concern about the probity of a major fund-raising organisation. This was the National Heart Research Fund.

The first two operations had, in fact, been paid for by the Health Authority. The next six were assisted by a £50,000 grant from the NHRF, and the man behind this, Robert Sharp, had promised much more, a two-pronged fund-raising scheme that would make heart research and transplants independent of public funds, with Papworth as its spearhead. Sharp proudly told Cook that he had helped to organise a separate transplant fund with a planned £250,000 target.

'This promise,' Cook reported, 'was apparently the spur that kept the programme rolling, but the promise wasn't kept. Of the £1,250,000 actually collected by the fund, nearly one million went into the pockets of Sharp and three other fund officials. They were all subsequently gaoled for fraud.

The problems with money for the transplant programme, and the fact that no proper debate had preceded it, were taken up by two members of the Area Health Authority, Roberta Cannon and Janet Jones, who were among those concerned about the situation. In particular, they felt that a long-awaited report had done little to clear up the various disturbing matters.

'The report completely fudges the issue,' complained Mrs Cannon. 'It is designed, I believe, to blind the members of the Authority with science – if one can describe it as science – and that is very typical of reports that appear before the Area Health Authority.'

Her colleague Mrs Jones put forward the view that the heart transplant programme had not been paid for by charities but with 'hidden monies which have come out of our own stretched resources . . . The whole National Health Service is in trouble financially, and we in Cambridge are £1.5 million overspent. Every department is having to cut back, but this programme seems to be sacrosanct, and I really don't understand it'.

Cook, in a kindred spirit of non-comprehension, sought out and interviewed Pauline Burnett, chairman of the Area Health Authority to see if she could throw some light on the subject. Her qualification for doing so was highlighted by Cook in his recorded link: 'The first that members of her Authority had heard about the recommencement of transplantation was on the news, after she'd given personal approval for the first two operations. So, how much public discussion had there been?'

Mrs Burnett said that there had been considerable consultation between the medical staff of the Cambridge District, the Area Medical Officer, herself and the 'Department'. This culminated in a paper by a senior surgeon that stated he was ready to comply with the conditions laid down by the Transplant Advisory Panel. However, she admitted that there had been no discussion within the Area Health Authority about whether or not the first operation should or could take place . . .

'But the members were warned that it was likely to take place,' she said. 'And then there was discussion after the first operation. Two operations took place, but we did not embark on a programme.'

Taxed by Cook on this point, Mrs Burnett emphasised that a programme did not get under way until the Authority had taken the decision that it should do so. She also denied that any promises for funding (for £250,000) had been made to the Authority by the National Heart Research Fund; thus, there had been no financial spur to the transplant programme. The waiting lists she dismissed as being part of a bottleneck that had always been present at the hospital. When Cook put the point that people felt that resources were being siphoned off other projects to keep the transplants going, Mrs Burnett denied that this was the case.

The interview was interrupted a number of times by the comments of two officials who sat with Mrs Burnett 'to make sure that we got it right,' as Cook put it. One interruption came after this exchange.

BURNETT: The spending on the transplant programmes cannot be cut, because the money that we've had so far has not been our money. It's been charitable money, or money from the Department of Health and Social Security. We have not spent our money.

COOK: But there is additional cost, is there not, in doing transplants . . .?

BURNETT: That is met by the money we are given.

COOK: What is the true cost of a transplant?

BURNETT: The additional true costs of a transplant have been in the region of twelve . . . or will be in the region of twelve thousand pounds.

COOK: But what is the total true cost of the transplant?

BURNETT: Twelve thousand pounds.

COOK: No, that's the additional cost. What's the total true cost, surgeons' time, everything?

BURNETT: We don't bring the surgeon's time into this because he would be there anyway.

COOK: But if he was there, he might be doing simpler operations, operations which could benefit more people.

BURNETT: I think that's unlikely, but the actual cost of his time has not been included.
COOK: So people may have a legitimate worry that the surgeon's time, for example, is being channelled into transplants when he could be doing something else?
BURNETT: Mostly, he does these transplants at night, in his free time.
COOK: Does he sleep?
BURNETT: Occasionally.

Eventually, said Cook, they got back to the interview after another break during which Mrs Burnett vehemently denied that the hospital was being hi-jacked or that routine operations were being rushed through to make the statistics look better. Mrs Burnett said that only a very small proportion of the cardiac unit's work was concerned with transplants, and she claimed that there were spin-off benefits from the programme because the team was learning so much about the working of the human heart. Morale was high too, she claimed, and Papworth was doing a good job for all patients. As for reports of disharmony, there had been, she said, one or two doctors who disliked the programme and had been casting aspersions at it. Any muddles about the 'fudging' of accounts or the mystery of funding were caused by the media. No local money was being used for the transplant operations. All additional costs were being met by a 'very generous donation from a local philanthropist who has given us the actual costs of eight transplant programmes per year for the next two years'.

COOK: He's given you the extra money, but you don't really know what the true cost of a transplant is.
BURNETT: He's given us whatever it costs over and above an ordinary operation to do the operation.
COOK: So, you're saying that the people we've spoken to, very well-informed people both inside Papworth and out, and certainly people with experience of health care in the local area, these people don't understand what you've been doing? They have completely unjustified fears?
BURNETT: Absolutely! They're completely unjustified fears.

And, said Cook in his tail-piece, we'll leave listeners to judge whether they really are or not.

CASE 10
Complaints against the Department of Trade and Industry

Broadcast on 29 April 1977
(Joint production with BBC TV Nationwide*)*
Researcher: Julia McLaren

The case was introduced as: 'The inappropriate safety regulations that inshore fishermen said would put more than half of them out of business'. Stan French had been a fisherman all his adult life, and by 1972 he had saved enough money to buy his own vessel. This was a forty-nine feet long trawler named *Our Adriatic*, based at Brixham in Devon. At the time of the programme French faced a £400 fine every time he cast off, because new Department of Trade and Industry regulations, originally designed for deep sea trawlers, had resulted in *Our Adriatic* being classified as 'Unstable and therefore unseaworthy'. This was despite the fact that the boat had an unblemished safety record over a quarter of a century of operation and despite the fact that French had taken her out just two weeks before the programme to rescue another trawler that had got into difficulties.

There was no way that he could get the boat through the test without rebuilding her from the keel up, and as he had already mortgaged his house to pay for her, that was out of the question. Cook began by asking him if he had confidence in the boat.

'It came over from Belgium in Force eleven gales, and there was no trouble then, and I don't see why there should be any trouble now,' he said, 'apart from the odd occasion when you may have engine trouble or you foul the screw with the trawl lines. But that can happen to any fishing boat. I have a lot of confidence in her, but I wouldn't have if I had to do what the Department of Industry wanted me to, even if this was possible. I don't think the boat would be safe.'

French said that he felt that the Government just didn't care what happened to fishermen in his position as a result of the new regulations. His boat was worth between £60,000–100,000 if it was 'seaworthy' but zero as things stood. Bankruptcy was staring him right between the eyes, and he was angry and confused.

'If you had a boat made to their requirements you'd never be able to stand up in her. They want a boat with stability, but that doesn't mean seaworthy. The boat I've got now is what's required for my use and is a good sea boat. This regulation was brought out for deep sea trawlers. They're a stupid lot of . . . well the word's a bit too strong to use.'

Cook next interviewed one of French's strongest allies, surprisingly the very official whose responsibilities included the policing of the regulations that were threatening French's livelihood, Chief Fisheries Officer Barry Warden. The interview took place at sea on the Devon Fisheries patrol boat *Miriam Ford* just after Warden had checked *Our Adriatic*.

'It has failed the Department of Trade and Industry test,' said Warden, 'but in the opinion of the Devon Sea Fisheries District Committee this is an extremely stable boat, and this man had been put out of a livelihood through rules and regulations which are completely inflexible. This boat and a number of other inshore fishing boats are being blanketed by regulations which were designed for deep water vessels.'

Cook asked just what was meant by 'stable' and 'unstable'. Warden's next statement proved to be a devastating indictment of those regulations.

'Well, you're on the *Miriam Ford*,' he said, 'and this boat isn't nearly as stable as *Our Adriatic*.'

This meant, of course, that the Department's own boat would not pass the regulations for stability that were being imposed on the trawlers. Warden was in no doubt about his own feelings.

'I suppose I'm a bureaucrat myself, but I would still agree that it seems that a lot of people at Whitehall or in the administrative sections of the fishing industry do not have sufficient knowledge of the inshore fishing vessels. The shame of this is that Stan French is one of the most respected fishermen in this area. He's never broken a fishing rule or regulation. He's put his life savings into this boat, which he's got up to standard, and he's got to go to sea in it. But now, according to the Department of Trade and Industry he has to pay about £400 to have the vessel surveyed, then he's told that it won't pass the stability test. So to make a living he's now got to break the law. It's a terrible state of affairs when a man who's been a hard-working, highly-respected fisherman should be put in this ludicrous situation. It would be perfectly in order if he took some visitors out to sea and risked drowning them, according to the DTI, but he is not permitted to take two people fishing in it to make a living. It's a nonsense.'

Marcel Gallin MBE, Chairman of the Brixham Fishermen's Cooperative, agreed. He pointed out that the original design of *Our Adriatic* for use by Belgium fishermen was a 'beamer', operating with a 'leg' over each side supporting the nets. French was using her as an ordinary side trawler. Was this a safer method of use?

'I should say so,' said Gallin. 'And I travel around a lot of English ports, and there are many boats in far worse condition than the ones here. If they're going to get the same treatment they'll all be laid up in the next twelve months.'

Bad though this was, worse news followed. The new regulations were currently being applied to side trawlers. The following June would see the net cast to include the next most commonly used inshore fishing vessels, beam trawlers. According to expert surveyors, these were even more likely to fail the stability test. Leslie Cannington, Chairman of the Trawler Owners Association, drove home the illogicality of the situation.

'French's boat has been made valueless overnight, and he may suffer the indignity of being made bankrupt,' he said. 'All because a group of civil servants with no practical knowledge of inshore fishing formulated a set of regulations without consulting the fishermen themselves. The regulations were recommended by the Holland Martin Committee after an accident to three deep sea fishing vessels in 1968. Three hundred and sixty pages of regulations, blanketing the entire fishing industry. But there's no comparison between the problems of a deep sea fishing vessel and an inshore fishing vessel.'

Cook asked him exactly what was meant by the term 'stability'. Did it mean keeping the mast straight up and down?

'Stability is the ability of a fishing vessel to stand up to all types of weather, tides, sea conditions and loading conditions. It doesn't mean keeping the mast absolutely straight. There are some stable boats that do not roll very much and others that roll violently. A happy medium is needed for a fishing vessel, because men have to work on its decks.'

Cannington told listeners that authorities in Europe were more 'democratic' about fishing regulations.

'They haven't put anyone out of business without compensation, and they didn't arbitrarily stick a set of rules onto the fishermen as they have in this country and deprive some of them of a living.'

He agreed that with some seventy per cent of beam and other trawlers not meeting the requirements the West Country fishing industry would be hit for six . . .

'. . . particularly as the beam trawlers catch most of the country's sole . . . the price of sole, turbots and brills will go sky high . . .'

Cook finally interviewed Stanley Clinton Davis, Under-Secretary of State in the DTI. What did he think of the charges laid by the fishermen that his Department was acting in a ludicrous, high handed, bureaucratic and totally-inflexible manner? There followed a notable interchange.

DAVIS: I cannot accept that, because the rules, which have evolved over a considerable period of time, were in fact the subject of very extensive consultation with the industry (and) they were agreed by the experts. Inevitably there are certain hard cases. Hard cases make bad law, and we have to look at the generality of the situation. I can't ignore something that was said in the Holland Martin Report, that fishermen are alarmingly more at risk than the average male worker.

COOK: But that report dealt with deep sea vessels which don't behave or have to go through conditions anything like inshore vessels.

DAVIS: It's perfectly true that there are different problems, and the rules themselves relate to different problems. But there have to be certain minimum standards, particularly as far as stability is concerned.

COOK: You were talking about consultation, yet the fishermen and their representatives – at least in the area we've been to – said there wasn't any consultation at all.

DAVIS: It's a very disparate industry, spread out all over the country. You can't consult with every single fisherman, but they do have an organisation representing the inshore fishermen. If they say that doesn't adequately represent their interests, they must take action. I can't do that.

COOK: But why are the regulations so stringent and so stringently enforced, as compared with some continental countries where there is, for example, a zoning system so that certain types of boats that might not be fit to go a long way out to sea can at least continue to fish inshore?

DAVIS: Each country has to produce its own particular set of regulations. I can't claim to be an expert in the requirements of some of the continental countries, nor can I accept that proposition as you state it, but the basic requirement is that a vessel must match certain minimum stability requirements, and we stress time and time again that they will be applied and are being applied reasonably and flexibly.

COOK: That's not what the fishermen in Devon and Cornwall have been telling us. For instance, the Devon Sea Fisheries patrol vessel – the one that's used to supervise these people and make sure they are being safe – *isn't* as stable in terms of the

regulations as the boats they're having to put out of business.
DAVIS: Well, thank you for that piece of information. I will instantly have that looked at. . . .

Davis continued by asking rhetorically if it was right to produce laws on the basis of cases that are difficult and hard. If we did, he said, we wouldn't have any Factory Act regulations. But we're not talking about the odd cases, Cook replied, pointing out that a senior surveyor had suggested that seventy per cent of the beam trawlers in the area concerned would fail the tests and that many of them could never be made to meet the regulations. Davis said he was not going to get involved in this 'field of speculation', and Cook brought up the matter of compensation, paid in other countries but not in the UK if a boat is put out of business. Davis explained his reasons for rejecting such a suggestion.

DAVIS: I can't say I would offer compensation for this reason. If a business is carried out on a sort of marginal profitability, which doesn't allow for certain exigencies that might arise, it isn't the survey that's putting them out of business, it's the fact that his business can't sustain an identifiable loss.
COOK: What do you say to people like Stan French, who have been fishing successfully and safely for thirty years, whose boat has been safe for thirty years, indeed went out in Force eleven gales, and went out in bad weather only two weeks ago to rescue another trawler in distress?
DAVIS: I think it's very difficult when certain realities have to be faced up to, and fishermen are peculiarly fatalistic. The worst can never happen to them! But it sometimes does, and I dare say some of the fatalities I could cite to you said exactly the same as Stan French the night before they set sail.
COOK: Are you saying, then, to people like Stan French: Better bankrupt than dead?
DAVIS: I wouldn't want to go so far as to suggest he *is* going to be made bankrupt. However, it's invidious to talk about an individual case when one isn't aware of all the financial implications. All I can be concerned with is the state of his vessel.
COOK: But surely there's a great inconsistency here, because if he chose to de-register the boat, or if he simply chose to take up to a dozen anglers out to sea and then drowned the lot of them, the regulations don't cover him.
DAVIS: There are different regulations that apply . . . We are looking at a scheme to cover more extensively other activities,

such as sea angling and shark fishing, because we think there's a gap that needs to be covered, and I think it's right that we shouldn't relax these situations. I think it's very sad that Mr French and possibly others like him are faced with financial difficulties. I cannot attribute those difficulties to this particular matter of carrying out a survey. I have to look at the generality of cases, because I am concerned with saving life at sea, and that's a hell of a problem.

Meanwhile, continued Cook, as the Minister tries to save lives with what the fishermen say is quite the wrong type of lifebelt, Stan French is trying to save his whole way of life.

'I shall have to keep on breaking the law,' said French. 'I've got to look after my family, not the government. If I have to finish up because I can't use this vessel, you just as well might put me in my grave, because that's my life finished for, isn't it?'

Soon after the programme the new regulations were either modified or withdrawn by the government (some say that the revelation about the Ministry's own boat played a not-insignificant role in this), and Stan French and his colleagues continue to fish in the seas around Devon and Cornwall.

CASE 11
Complaints by Bernard Saltman against the legal system

Broadcast on 10 March and continued on 2 June 1982
Researcher: Dina Gold

Part 1
The case of Bernard Saltman became a *cause célèbre* after this first broadcast, with most of the national newspapers covering the story. It was, by any standards, a frightening account of how justice can go wildly astray in the United Kingdom. As Saltman himself was in prison when the programme was being prepared, his story was told by his wife Lynn, witnesses and friends.

The Saltman family had been operating a furniture retail business in Aylesbury for fifty years. On 21 August 1979 Bernard returned home from work and was chatting to his neighbour Ken Oldham in the garden when his wife took a phone call informing her that the company warehouse was on fire. According to Oldham, 'Bernie looked absolutely pole-axed – no way could that have been acting – Bernie just wasn't that sort of a guy. You could read him like a book'.

The damage to the warehouse turned out to be quite small, being confined to a small area of the building. No one was hurt, but mattresses and bedding were destroyed and some other stock damaged by smoke. Saltman duly filled in claim forms for the General Accident Insurance Company, and on 5 September the insurance company sent a forensic expert, Dr Keith Gugan, to inspect the damage. Before this, the company had instructed Saltman that he could clear the warehouse and sell off fire-damaged stock. On 17 October the Saltmans received a letter from the assessors Cunningham and Hart on behalf of General Accident admitting liability. In two weeks they had a cheque for £50,000 as part payment towards the full claim of £160,000-plus.

'All seemed to be proceeding well,' recalled Lynn Saltman, 'until 17 November when for some unknown reason, absolutely unexplained to us, the police called round to arrest my husband on suspicion of arson.'

Cook emphasised that this shock was all the more intense because of the letter previously received from the assessors which was written three weeks after Dr Gugan had inspected the premises. It was exacerbated because the £50,000 payment had the effect of rendering Saltman liable to a second charge, relating to obtaining money from his insurers by deception. Saltman's works manager John Reed was also very surprised by the arrest. He had previously given a statement to the police about the fire which was, or so he thought, in his employer's favour.

'Mr Saltman and I left the warehouse at 5.40 p.m. together,' said Reed. 'He went his way and I went mine, and there's no way he could have gone back and started the fire and got home by six o'clock.'

Reed told Cook that the police took his statement and asked him to glance through it quickly and to sign it, which he did.

'Now I read it again I see I'm supposed to have said that the company was in financial difficulties, which I know nothing about. I never had access to the accounts, so how would I know? I've worked for Mr Saltman for eight years, and he's not the kind of gentleman that would do that sort of thing to his own business.'

Nevertheless, Saltman was formally charged with arson on 9 April 1980. In searching for a motive, the police claimed that they had witnesses (such as Reed) to the fact that Saltman's company was in financial difficulties and owed a lot of money, both to the Inland Revenue for corporation tax and to the Customs & Excise for VAT. But the company accountant Ben Gemal pointed out that this simply wasn't true. In fact the company had overpaid corporation tax and was entitled to a refund. Not only that but based on the accounts it was improving its profit margins. Suppliers continued to supply after the fire, and the bank was prepared to give an overdraft facility of over £100,000.

'Hardly the hard-headed response one might expect from a bank to a failing company,' said Cook before letting Lynn Saltman drive the point home that there was, by all normal criteria, absolutely no motive for arson.

'We have nothing to gain whatsoever by destroying the business or setting fire to it,' she said. 'We were, in fact, under-insured to the effect that if all had been paid out it would never have replaced the building and the stock involved. The police seem to think we set fire to it. Dr Gugan, working for General Accident, seems to think we set fire to it, but he missed a most vital piece of evidence.'

This evidence was the existence of a power point at the very seat of the fire. Normally a radio was plugged into the point, and John Reed commented that the two pin plug of the radio was set into a three pin socket in a place where beds were regularly moved. Reed believed that this could have shorted the wires and started the fire. Unfortunately, by the time Dr Gugan arrived to inspect the damage, all the evidence had been removed from that spot, except for 'one dirty big black patch on the office wall'.

This patch was examined by another forensic expert, Peter Cook, who was to appear in court on behalf of Bernard Saltman. After his own examination and after questioning witnesses and listening to the evidence of the fire officers who had gone to the blaze Peter Cook came to his own conclusion.

'There was nothing to suggest that this fire had been started deliberately,' he said. 'In fact, the evidence was rather that an accidental cause was more plausible.'

He pointed out that the most likely origin of the fire was that 13 Amp power plug used 'incorrectly' to supply the radio. On the basis of the evidence Peter Cook did not see how the prosecution could conclude that the fire could only have been started deliberately. There was not enough scientific evidence to prove arson 'beyond a reasonable doubt'.

But the prosecution was determined to press ahead with their two charges: of arson and of obtaining money by false pretences. As anyone would, the Saltmans viewed the forthcoming trial with anxiety and trepidation.

'We were petrified,' explained Lynn Saltman, pointing out that they had never been faced with this kind of thing before. 'But our consciences were clear, and we knew we had nothing to fear whatsoever. We were guilty of nothing. We felt confident and clear that the jury and judge would see that there was no motive and no gain to be made from the fire and that it was purely accidental.'

Everything seemed to go well in the trial, as far as the Saltmans could ascertain. They were optimistic about the outcome, and believed that the judge, in his summing-up, seemed anxious to tell the jury to acquit Saltman. And according to Saltman's solicitor, June Ruskin, that is exactly what he was saying. She told Cook that the prosecution's case was based on a number of issues. The first was that their fire expert (Gugan) had reached the conclusion that the fire had been started by a key holder to the premises. There were only two key holders, Saltman and his manager John Reed. Reed had no gain or motive, so the fire must have been started by Saltman. The second issue was that Saltman had a financial motive, the previously mentioned and ficticious shortfalls in corporation tax and VAT, together with the 'substantial' claim he could make on his insurance policy. The defence proved and the judge accepted that these financial motives did not exist.

On the question of Dr Gugan's evidence about the vital power point, the judge had said, 'No expert is so expert that he cannot be wrong, and it may well be that on this score, whatever else you may think of Dr Gugan's evidence, you will be satisfied that he was wrong. Would you also be satisfied that nothing will induce him to admit it?'

The prosecution had in any case agreed not to dispute the existence of the power point and therefore the existence of an alternative cause of the fire. In addition, the judge pointed out that the £50,000 sent by the insurance company to Saltman was sent and paid into his company account a full twenty-four days after Dr Gugan had examined the warehouse, 'in spite of any conclusions he (Gugan) might have reached'.

Thus, at one stage, General Accident must have been satisfied that the claim was valid.

After all this the defence felt that the prosecution case, weak to start with, had been effectively sunk, and Lynn Saltman was elated. As soon as the jury came back, the year and a half nightmare would be over.

'And then the foreman said "Guilty"! We just couldn't believe it . . . I remember collapsing and crying, and Bernard too collapsed . . . The most dreadful thing about all this is to see your husband being taken away from you and led downstairs to a cell.'

Saltman was imprisoned for three weeks and then, unusually, let out on bail. He was at home for a year pending an appeal, and the Saltmans had high hopes that, under the circumstances, this would be successful. Unfortunately, as their solicitor pointed out, things were not as simple as that.

'Although the jury had reached a perverse decision,' she said, 'one cannot appeal against a decision of the jury on the facts. The appeal was based on a misdirection of the judge as to facts and also as to law. Leading counsel (for Saltman) had settled extensive grounds for appeal running to some thirty points. However, the Court of Appeal decided that there had been no misdirection by the judge. In fact they said his summing-up was a model summing-up of which any judge could be proud. The conviction was upheld and the appeal dismissed, and unfortunately there are no further legal avenues that can be explored.'

And so on the 14 January 1982 Bernard Saltman was sent to prison for two years. His accountant Ben Gemal was first on the programme to explain how disastrous this was.

'The business has been completely ruined and, more than likely, Mr Saltman will be ruined. To top it all, the insurance company is seeking to recover the £50,000 that they paid and which the company accepted in good faith. This could lead to Mr Saltman himself being made bankrupt. And his wife, of course, will lose the house and be left with nothing. The whole affair is an appalling, unnecessary tragedy.'

This opinion was shared by Saltman's neighbour Dr Ken Oldham who pointed out that apart from the financial strain and the effect on the family generally, Lynn Saltman's health had suffered badly. She was at the time of the broadcast recovering from a cancer operation.

Cook also interviewed Bernard Saltman's MP, Sir Ian Gilmour, a former Cabinet Minister. He stated bluntly that he thought there had been a miscarriage of justice and that Saltman was innocent. He also criticised the Court of Appeal.

'This judgement, in my view, is tortuous and not at all a credit to the Lord Chief Justice. They admit that the prosecution's case is blown up, both on motive and on the key question of whether or not there was an electrical socket which almost certainly caused the fire, and although they conceded that they still were not prepared to put aside the jury's verdict as unsatisfactory and unsafe. In order to uphold that verdict they went through some very tortuous reasoning indeed, and I cannot believe it's reasoning that they will now be proud of.'

Sir Ian explained that he had been in touch with the Home Secretary. The next step would be to find 'some additional evidence, some new evidence so that we have a stronger case for referring the matter back to the Court of Criminal Appeal.'

In a sad finale, Lynn Saltman explained graphically what it was like to have a twenty-three year marriage devastated by such events. Financial ruin, ill health and a feeling of inadequacy because . . . 'There's nothing I can do to release him. He feels inadequate too because he's locked away and can't help me . . . He writes to me that every day is like a year without me. It's difficult not to get emotional over such a thing like that.'

Yet she stoutly maintained her faith in British justice. 'the fairest in the world . . . We're doing our very best to have faith and to continue believing that one day – very soon – justice will prevail.'

Part 2

The programme returned to 'the disturbing trial and the even more disturbing conviction' of Bernard Saltman almost three months later. By this time the story had been taken up by a number of newspapers, and Greville Janner QC MP had raised the matter in the House of Commons of what he called 'this travesty of justice'. Availing himself of Parliamentary privilege (which enabled him to say things that could have had the programme prosecuted) Janner appealed to other people who had suffered, like Saltman, because of Gugan's reports on fire insurance claims to come forward. He hoped to amass sufficient proof of Gugan's general inadequacies as an expert witness to persuade Home Secretary William Whitelaw to release Saltman.

Checkpoint developed the story by interviewing Lynn Saltman again, and the first part of this second programme on the case was a summary of events. Lynn Saltman reported having received many supporting and encouraging letters from strangers who had heard the previous programme. In particular electronics expert Leonard Stone offered to investigate the circumstances in the company of a representative of MK, the company that made the vital electric socket at which it now seemed certain the fire had started. He introduced an important consideration.

'What Dr Gugan had failed to point out, and it was certainly known to him, was that by the use of a two-pin plug, which does not incorporate a fuse, the equipment was in a circuit controlled only by the 30 Amp fuse in the fuse box. Any break in the insulation of the lead . . . could easily have created considerable heat and arcing and produce flame in the confined space between the wall and the mattress.'

The electrical aspects of the case were expanded by Eric Laithwaite, professor of heavy electrical engineering at Imperial College in London. He pointed out that electrical fires need not necessarily start with a short circuit: a loose connection may be all it takes, such as twisting two wires together.

'Stuffing a two-pin plug into a three-pin socket is another way of getting a not-good connection,' he said. 'There's a chance that the plug will get hot, and the fuse does not protect it, so there are at least two possible sources of fire in this instance – where the plug went into the socket and where the wire went into the equipment.'

Leonard Stone pointed out more inconsistencies in Dr Gugan's prosecution evidence. Gugan had mentioned that if a fire had occured at an electric plug the objects first ignited would be the plug, the socket, the cables attached to it and the nearest combustibles which would include the timbers from which the office wall was constructed.

'It was clear to myself and the gentleman from MK that no timber was employed in the construction of the wall of the office, which was made from breeze block covered in plaster. If someone wished to start a fire it is hardly likely they would choose the most difficult position behind a pile of mattresses and four feet from the floor in preference, for example, to starting the fire on the floor.'

Stone concluded that the probability was for the fire to have started by the electrical socket or the wire near to it, yet despite this and despite the obvious lack of motive, Dr Gugan had insisted that the case was undoubtedly arson. He declined an invitation to appear on *Checkpoint*. Greville Janner returned to his criticism of Gugan, taking the opportunity to widen his appeal for people with experience of Gugan's work to come forward and give evidence so that the Rt Hon. Member for Chesham and Amersham (Sir Ian Gilmour) and he could 'attempt perhaps more successfully to encourage and induce and plead with the Home Secretary to achieve (Saltman's) release'.

Cook, believing that most listeners would now think that nothing could possibly stand in the way of such pressure, read out a letter sent by the Prime Minister (a similarly worded one was sent from the Home Office) to all those who had written of their concern.

> 'I can see that the *Checkpoint* programme will have given many people the disquieting impression that Mr Saltman has been wrongly convicted. However, under our system of law when a person is tried by jury the decision as to his or her guilt or innocence lies with the jury alone. Only when it can be shown that the jury has been misled in some way, for example by a misdirection of the trial judge or some procedural irregularity during the course of the trial, can the verdict be overturned. The Court of Appeal, Criminal Division, had found nothing wrong with the way this case was put to the jury.'

Mrs Thatcher went on to say that, 'it would be wrong for the Home Secretary to intervene,' Cook told listeners. 'However, given the new evidence and a possibly misleading judicial rendering of the defence's forensic evidence it would seem that the criteria for the Home Secretary or the Court of Appeal to reconsider the case have been satisfied.'

Janner certainly thought so: 'We have formed a defence committee. We are trying to mobilise public opinion . . . Sir Ian Gilmour has brought the matter to the attention of the Home Secretary. I have informed the Home Secretary that I, from my side of the House (of Commons), am also deeply concerned. This isn't a Party political matter, and I hope that when we have all the evidence we shall see the Home Secretary.'

A glimmer of hope for the Saltmans, with two Queen's Counsel MPs from opposing Parties on their side, noted Cook. Bernard by now had been transferred to an open prison a few miles from his home. General Accident had written to say it would not press for the £50,000, adding that it would have no hesitation in meeting its obligations if Mr Saltman was shown to have been the victim of a miscarriage of justice. But had the Home Office met its own obligations? Lynn Saltman didn't think so.

'I can't understand in the face of all the evidence we are presenting how they can keep Bernie locked up in prison. Can't the Home Secretary see that justice isn't being done? I'm fighting really hard to have this miscarriage of justice reversed, and we want it reversed quickly. Bernie has been in prison for nearly six months for something he didn't do, and we desperately want him home . . . I didn't think ever that I would have to fight the courts, fight British justice, but I have been helped in this fight by so many people . . . It does help you to continue, and fight we will, because I think that in the end we will win. I'm sure of it.'

Following the two *Checkpoint* programmes, the Saltman case was referred back to the Court of Appeal by the Home Secretary. Bernard Saltman had his conviction quashed on 27 July 1982.

CASE 12
Complaints against Barnett Christie

Broadcast date: 11 April 1979
Researcher: David Perrin

In December 1978 the fringe bank called Barnett Christie collapsed, taking with it £4 million in fixed term deposits made by well over two thousand people through the bank's offices in London and Guernsey. Sadly, the interest rates seemed ideal for elderly people like Gordon and Estelle Hack from Sussex: eleven per cent with no tax deducted. They entrusted their £4,000 life savings to the bank after seeing its advertisement in the *Sunday Express*, and this was money that they, like many others, could ill afford to lose. The first interview was with Gordon Hack, and he quickly put things into perspective.

'I really trusted this firm, Barnett Christie, after seeing it in the *Sunday Express*. I thought it was a good bet, and they were giving a better interest than a building society, which I thought would help me, having so little to invest, so I invested my savings, and now I've lost everything. I feel very low indeed.'

His wife Estelle hammered the point home: 'My husband has been very ill indeed . . . It's really made a mess of our lives . . . We don't go out anywhere, only shopping. We don't go to any amusements, no pictures, and I've been in hospital for a fortnight and a fortnight convalescing, and I'm still under the hospital for a nervous breakdown. My husband as well. We're very disappointed. We were let down, terribly.'

This was a good example of how dreadful the reality behind those sometimes all-too-bland headlines: 'Fringe bank goes under!' More was to follow. Peter Caple from Oxford invested £1,000 on Christmas Eve 1976 and expected, two years later, to have £1,330 due from his Barnett Christie investment. His Christmas present in 1978 was to learn that the company was being wound up.

'The money meant a lot to me. My wife had died from cancer, and I wanted it for a headstone. It was near enough all the available money that I had.'

George Finch took £2,000 out of a building society and invested it in Barnett Christie on the advertised promise of better interest rates paid 'as it comes'. Not only did he lose his money, but insult was added to injury when the Inland Revenue began demanding tax on money that had been lost. 'That's what upsets me!' he commented.

Cook continued the 'upset' theme by reporting how 'pillars of local society' in Guernsey had apparently supported the bank. One executive, Brian Charlwood, persuaded Vera Firth to invest first her savings and then an inheritance, totalling £71,000.

'He was most reassuring, and spoke about his connections with former stockbroking banks. What I did not know then was that they had long since had their licence removed by the State's Advisory Finance Committee. We first heard of the collapse via the *Daily Telegraph*. . . .'

Former school teacher Audrey Phillips had reinvested her savings in Barnett Christie when building work on her cottage was delayed. She lost her money and ended up with an uninhabitable cottage. Derek Hunt believed that he might lose the roof over his own head after losing a total of £15,000, a calamity that was reinforced by his having to dispose of his pet dogs because he could no longer afford to feed them.

Vera Firth and many others lost some or all of their money. Three hundred or so Channel Island investors, worried by the situation and concerned to see Charlwood entertaining lavishly and driving a new Mercedes, formed the Association of Barnett Christie Depositors. The secretary Eric Wadham explained that the situation need not have happened, at least in Guernsey, where there is a Protection of Depositors Act, introduced by the island's 'Treasury' referred to as Advisory and Finance.

'Unfortunately it didn't protect any of the depositors,' he said bitterly. 'It only protected Advisory and Finance, which we have now come to know as Adversity and Fiasco! They decided not to publish the fact that the licence for Barnett Christie had not been removed because, they said, it would cause a run on the bank.'

'To be fair,' Cook told listeners, 'the Barnett Christie empire was, and is, devilishly complicated. It began in the 1960s with a chain of business transfer agencies. In the end there were over a dozen subsidiaries and associates, to many of which the bank made substantial loans. They were involved in businesses as diverse as steam laundries, plastic bag manufacture, property development, Rolls Royce hire and debt collection.'

Cook interviewed the president of the States of Guernsey Advisory and Finance Committee, Peter Dorey, after a debate 'had been discouraged'. Dorey admitted that the Protection of Investors Act did not in its current state offer enough protection, and they were considering revisions. He argued that if they had publicised their withdrawal of the Barnett Christie licence there would have been an immediate collapse of the bank, 'and we might well have been severely criticised for doing just that'.

But the main point was whether or not Dorey and his colleagues knew that the bank was still trading, even without its licence. Dorey denied any such knowledge, but admitted: 'We did hear in the latter part of 1978 that deposits were being "rolled over" to some extent, but we had nothing definite on that.' He argued that there was no way the States could guarantee the large sums of money involved in such banking enterprises (around £800 million was the current level of deposits in the island). And he pointed out that Barnett Christie had given the States assurances that, when their licence was withdrawn, incoming monies would be used to repay deposits. But . . .

'Under the legislation, we have no power to examine or verify if that was the case. To some extent, therefore, I think you can say there is a deficiency in the legislation, but certainly we had assurances.'

The next step was for Cook to seek an interview with Brian Charlwood, who had given Advisory and Finance these assurances. After a number of inconclusive and brief phone calls with Charlwood, Cook attempted a recorded interview, with the standard *Checkpoint* preamble.

COOK: Hello. Mr Brian Charlwood?
CHARLWOOD: Yes.
COOK: My name is Roger Cook from the BBC *Checkpoint* programme. I'm ringing to record an interview with you now following the further consultations you said you'd had with your lawyers.
CHARLWOOD: Yes. I've got people here with me, so you'll have to call back later.
COOK: That means we can have an interview, does it?
CHARLWOOD: No, it doesn't.
COOK: Why don't you want to discuss it? Is there something you

feel oughtn't to be discussed, in your own interests?
CHARLWOOD: My lawyer advises me not to discuss it, Mr Cook.
COOK: And that's as far as you'll go?
CHARLWOOD: Yes. (*Hangs up*)

Both Charlwood and the sometime chairman of Barnett Christie in Guernsey, Laurie Ozanne, referred Cook to the chairman of the bank in London, Christie himself, who was also a director of a number of firms in the company chain that had received substantial loans from the 'parent' bank but that had not always prospered. Cook called on him at his Guildford office, and he denied that the bank was insolvent, despite an asset deficiency of £1.5 million in the UK and a similar deficiency in Guernsey. The crunch had come, he told Cook, over the accounts of a subsidiary called Haper Plastics, which would have been successful if 'the rug hadn't been pulled from under it'. Bearing in mind the disparity between the asset deficiency and the £750,000 of available funds claimed by Christie, Cook put it to Christie that there were those who said his empire was kept afloat only by shunting its cash around.

Christie denied this, saying that until 11 December 1978 none of the companies needed propping up. But he did admit that funds were moved around.

'Of course, as the cash funds were required in one place, they would obviously be made available there, and, if they were required somewhere else, they'd be made available there.'

'But,' Cook pointed out, 'the Guernsey authorities did tell us that they once required you to increase substantially your liquidity there. You did, and then next time they looked it wasn't there any more.'

'I . . . sorry, I'm hesitating now . . . but I'm only hesitating because we're talking about years past . . . Without looking at the records at that time I couldn't give an authoritative answer,' Christie said.

There followed a brief interchange concerning the 'suspicions – to put it no more boldly than that' that some people would have about a business that takes money from investors and puts it into its own business ventures. 'Not something which National Westminster would do,' admitted Christie, 'but even gilt-edged securities can go wrong. We put money into what we believed were sound commercial enterprises. In some of these we had interests, certainly.'

Christie claimed that not all his associated companies had got into trouble, and Cook rejoined that a number of people already interviewed would probably disagree.

'You've been described as having the Midas touch in reverse. It's been said that your investment management record was appalling . . . a history of losses in other companies, of what might appear as financial instability, and that's why the authorities closed you down, because there was a bad track record.'

'I dispute that,' replied Christie, and he went on to say that he thought that authorities such as the Department of Trade had 'interfered' with his businesses: 'and I don't think much of them. I think they took those steps not only to my detriment but to the detriment of depositors and of people who borrowed money off us . . . ordinary, decent people, just the same as you and I.'

After denying knowledge and participation in the high-life of his colleagues of Guernsey, 'Mercedes cars, champagne parties and that sort of thing', Christie insisted that the bank's problems were none of his making, even though Cook confronted him with the accusation that he had continued to take deposits in Guernsey up to two years after his authority to do so had been revoked. This was, according to the States, an illegal act.

Christie claimed that the authorities knew that he was trading but allowed him to continue 'because this was in the best interests of the depositors, the States of Guernsey and ourselves. The authorities were fully aware of the fact that we were continuing to trade.'

'But surely,' Cook replied, 'the point is not whether they knew you were trading illegally, but whether you did.'

Christie stuck to his guns: 'There was no way in which we could suddenly suspend our business and maintain our obligations to the public at large.'

Cook stuck to his: 'But the company went to the wall anyway, and the suggestion is that if you'd ceased trading at that stage fewer people would have lost money. In the interim period £1.4 million was taken in that area (Guernsey) alone.'

Would Christie accept any blame for what had happened? What was his comment on the fact that so many people had lost a lot of their money?

'No. The main thing that went wrong is what went wrong with the banking industry at large. They (the investors) were right to have confidence in us, and, if we'd been permitted to carry on trading, as most concerns are, they would have got all their money back in full.'

Believe him or not, it was a bravura performance. Cook let

Christie have this last word, but made a pointed observation about the Department of Trade, the States of Guernsey and the Bank of England.

'They had been keeping an eye on Barnett Christie for some time. But were they fiddling while Rome burned? And if, in circumstances like this, they were content to watch rather than to act, will the new Banking Act which provides added powers really make the small investor's savings any safer?'

As this book went to press, Christie, having been released from gaol after serving time for his part in the Barnett Christie scandal, had turned to selling Time-Sharing Schemes in holiday apartments.

The States of Guernsey were in discussion with depositors with a view to compensating them for much of the four million pounds invested with Barnett Christie, while, with the full knowledge of the authorities, the company had been allowed to continue as a deposit taker without the necessary licence.

CASE 13
Complaints against Michael John MacDonald Bell and Alan Russell

Programme date: 31 January 1979
Researchers: David Perrin and Maggie Redfern

This programme began with a list of connected companies against which there had been a number of complaints, a complicated business web involving interests as diverse as petrol stations, trade directories, finance and property, spread between the Isle of Man and the Channel Islands and centred in West London. It continued with a number of complaints by aggrieved motorists, and then stretched into the web of intrigue set up by the people involved in their other areas of activity.

'One batch of complaints stood out,' Cook said. 'They concerned a long-established chain of garages called Seagull Autos Limited, which in recent years has spawned three other companies bearing the name Seagull: Seagull Autos (Car Sales) Ltd, Seagull Autos (Forecourts) Ltd and Seagull Economic Fuels Ltd. Peter Mammatt bought a Triumph Spitfire from Seagull Autos (Car Sales) Ltd, but it sounds more like a tank.'

For a few seconds listeners heard the car engine roaring away. Then Mammatt explained his problem. In June 1977 he phoned an agency called Computacar and asked if they had a Spitfire on their books. Eventually they traced one to Seagull Autos in Uxbridge Road, West London. Computacar described the vehicle as being in very good condition, and when Mammatt phoned Seagull Autos he spoke to the sometime company secretary, Michael Bell, who told him the car was in excellent condition. He decided to buy it and paid £699 to Bell and the company sales manager, Alan Russell, who 'waved him off down the road' after assuring him that, as members of the Motor Agents Association (MAA) they would stand by him if anything went wrong.

The car broke down three times, and Mammatt took it back to Seagull Autos each time for repair. Three times they failed to fix it. Mammatt called in the MAA but, said Cook, they didn't seem to be getting very far, either, 'so Mr Mammatt had his grounded Spitfire inspected by an engineer'.

'He appeared to think that it may have been a wreck done up,' said Mammatt, 'so this enforced my resolve to go to court. When the case came up my expert witness unfortunately couldn't turn up, and the garage's barrister argued that they would not accept his written report: he would have to be there in person. So I lost the day. Shortly after that the company I was suing, which was called Seagull Autos (Car Sales) Ltd, ceased trading. It didn't go into liquidation, just ceased trading, and took on the name of Broadway Autos (Car Sales) . . . Mr Russell became the proprietor of the new company. I went to court and got a judgement against Seagull Autos (Car Sales) Ltd, even though it had ceased trading. I immediately applied for the application to be transferred to Seagull Autos Ltd, which was the other company involved. Eventually I found out that a week after I'd made the application Seagull Autos Ltd had ceased trading without going into liquidation and had become Croftball Ltd. The director of Croftball was none other than Mr Alan Russell. In September I was given judgement against Seagull Autos and was awarded £554 against the company which no longer existed. The problem now, having sent the bailiffs to collect my money, is a question of company law, because the company names have been changed, and this has made it extremely difficult to get my money, which I am still fighting for.'

Next came the case of Steven More, who also bought a car from Seagull Autos (Car Sales) Ltd. More described it as a rather nice looking Ford Capri GT, with lots of extras.

'It was being sold by a member of the Motor Agents Association,' More said, 'and I understood from the media that I was supposed to be able to trust such people.'

At the company premises he met Michael Bell who agreed to allow him £200 for his Ford Cortina against the Capri, 'a nice little car'. He paid the balance in cash, together with a fee for a guarantee, a total of £1,028. Then he had to wait a considerable time before he got delivery of the car and put up with bad manners and abuse over the telephone, into the bargain.

'Mr More eventually got his Capri,' said Cook, 'but wished he hadn't. He had it professionally inspected, and on the strength of the report he asked Mr Bell for his money back.'

More described the car, which was rotten with rust, although it had been recently undersealed and resprayed. A second engineer's report valued it at £50, scrap. A dangerous car. More decided that the Motor Agents Association couldn't get anywhere with this garage and that he would sue the company. He was awarded a judgement in November 1978 against Seagull Autos (Car Sales) Ltd, but received treatment similar to Mammatt: no money from the company, which ceased trading and emerged under another name, while he was faced with the loss of his purchase price and solicitor's costs, a total of about £1,500.

'I'm disgusted, annoyed and amazed that these things can go on in these days of consumer laws,' Mammatt said.

'And in the circumstances it is particularly galling for him to see some of the same people in the same premises, still in the same business,' Cook continued. 'It's also galling for the guarantee company that Seagull used. They didn't get their money, or any policy documents, so many people who had paid Seagull for guarantees hadn't actually got them.'

The next question raised by Cook was: how could a company with a reputation as bad as Seagull's be a member of the MAA? He spoke with the assistant director-general, John Boast.

'You've been talking about a group of companies with loose or fixed connection,' Boast said. 'I can only speak about Seagull Autos, because they are the only one of this group that have been members of the MAA, and the only one with whom we've had any dealings.'

Boast pointed out that when the company first joined the MAA there was no problem, but that managements do change. He explained that the MAA had tried on many occasions to follow up customer complaints about Seagull Autos, but their letters were not answered and they could not make contact by telephone with anyone admitting responsibility for the company, particularly with respect to Bell and Russell.

'We were suffering from such a lack of co-operation from this company that their case was brought before our National Disciplinary Committee last year, as a result of which they were expelled from the MAA.'

Not much comfort for those customers who went to Messrs Bell and Russell on the strength of their MAA membership, Cook commented, and the MAA certainly wouldn't be admitting Broadway Autos or Croftball Ltd! But as complaints against these two motor companies began to roll in, so did complaints about the publishers of a series of trade directories that initially covered London and the Home Counties. These were called *Green Guides*, and the publisher was J. Weiner (London) Ltd of Park Royal. And the man behind Weiner was none other than Michael John MacDonald Bell.

Trade directories are useful aids in helping buyers and suppliers meet each other. But in recent years the sharp operators have moved in to exploit the fact that people are keen to buy space in a directory for what is, compared to national advertising, a relatively small sum of money. Jim Raynes of Bexley was first on the programme to explain what happened to his *Green Guide* advertisement.

'In April 1975 I sent off £50 and some copy for my advertisement. My cheque was cashed, but we were unable to get any kind of receipt or any correspondence from the publishers. On 25 January we received a request for advertisement copy for a new issue of the *Green Guide*, and we phoned and asked, "What about the copy and cheque we've already sent?" We were unable to get a reply to this question. Two years later a telephone salesman once more tried to get us to buy space in the *Green Guide*. Again we asked what had happened to our original advertisement. He said he'd phone back, but of course he never did. And all this time, no *Green Guide* had even appeared.'

Raynes knew he would not be the only one with this problem, so he circularised his information around members of the local Chamber of Commerce and wrote to the Trading Standards officer. He learned then that J. Weiner was in liquidation, but he also discovered that it had continued trading after the date of liquidation. At the time of the programme, *Green Guides* were still running, this time under the directorship of the accountant who was supposed to act in receivership of J. Weiner (London) Ltd when it was wound up in 1976, in debt to the tune of £200,000.

Cook gave a swift analysis of this part of the Bell empire. Just before J. Weiner went under it was given a loan of £10,000 by another one-time Bell company, Southern and Suburban Properties Ltd. Yet another Bell company, J. Weiner (Holdings) Ltd, still shared the Seagull address in West London. *Green Guides* new company secretary was a woman called Ann Levy, and her sales adviser was Michael John MacDonald Bell. Once more, as in other *Checkpoint* investigations, the name was changed but the game remained the same, as Bruce Dowell discovered to his cost.

He was approached by a young lady representing *Green Guides* and persuaded to place a small advertisement for his hobby shop in the *Newham Green Guide*. He paid £31.86 to have his advertisement in an issue scheduled for publication in February 1977. When this issue did not appear he contacted *Green Guides* and was told that the issue had been postponed 'for a few months'. After more delay he wrote to cancel the advertisement and ask for his money back. Many letters later he went to the Citizen's Advice Bureau who suggested he pursued the matter through the small claims court.

'After further inconvenience and expense we were given judgement, and, eventually, after having to engage the services of a local bailiff, we were able to get our money back,' Raynes said. 'We feel completely disgusted by the way we've been treated by *Green Guide*, as I believe many other people are.'

'Barry Wilson can vouch for that,' Cook said, continuing the saga. 'He worked for *Green Guides* before leaving in disgust in 1977.'

When Wilson went for his interview he learned that the *Green Guide* organisers were planning to extend their operation to more cities, such as Liverpool and Manchester. The company seemed 'straight' to him, and he accepted the job with enthusiasm. He believed his management team was out to make a fine name and reputation for *Green Guides*.

'And in came Mr Bell, who seemed to take charge of the running of *Green Guides*,' Raynes said. 'He seemed to have a lot of interests, which included property all over London, and his personal secretary, Ann Levy, acted as rent collector, I believe. I knew of the garage in Ealing which was Seagull Autos Ltd. We drove wrecked cars out of it a number of times. And we used to see Mr Bell driving round in his Rolls Royce, which for some reason had Jersey number plates.'

Wilson soon came to the conclusion that, if the amount of

advertising space the company was selling to companies in London and the Home Counties was anything to go on, the company should have been publishing about three *Green Guides* per month. But while he was employed, only one for Harrow was published.

'I asked Mr Bell where the rest of the guides were, and he said they were coming out. I said, how are you going to do it? You need more than two a month to produce enough for the people you're selling ads to. And we had rather a long argument which led to the police coming and asking me to leave the premises. I left the premises and the firm as well . . .'

And he was never paid the commission owed to him, but *Green Guides* carried on operating: 'Collecting money week in, week out, for guides that will never be published as they lead people to believe'.

Now it was time for *Checkpoint* to interview the various people named by the complainants, and as usual this proved to be no easy task. In a preparatory phone call Ann Levy admitted that Bell was indeed the company sales adviser. She said it wasn't worth publishing a guide unless they sold at least £18,000 of advertising space, that they did not promise people anything, and that if anyone had any complaints they could always go to court. However, she flatly refused to discuss matters in a recorded interview.

Piecing together what she had told *Checkpoint* and what informants had said, Cook concluded that Bell must be in both the USA and Jersey at the same time. He reported that Trading Standards officers had been unable to catch up with Bell over a period of years to question him about a string of complaints under the Trade Descriptions Act and to ask why he had been referring his car insurance customers to a brokerage that somehow had a fire while its principals, then under a charge of conspiracy to defraud, were under investigation by the police. Then Cook reeled off a list of Bell's company connections, one of the many labyrinthine empires that *Checkpoint* has analysed over the years with such success.

'He was director of the Seagull Autos group of companies until three years ago, when a controlling interest went to another of his companies, Parkmount Developments Ltd. Parkmount was temporarily wound up in the courts recently at just the time another company in which Bell once had an interest, Yallstone Properties (Alexandra Court) Ltd, were struck off. Parkhurst has passed on its holdings in the Seagull group to a pair of companies registered in the Isle of Man, Bora Investments Ltd, now called Petrol Sales Investments Ltd, and Chrissandra Investments Ltd. These companies are run from a Jersey address and have behind them such concerns as the Gemma Trust and Nominal Limited.

'And if you can follow that,' Cook said, 'you're a genius!'

Checkpoint tried to sort the wood from the trees by telephoning the company secretary of two of the Jersey companies, John Marshall. After the obligatory preamble Cook asked him for information about Bell's involvement with Petrol Sales Investments Ltd and Chrissandra Investments, and about Nominal Ltd and Bora Ltd. Marshall claimed he was not at liberty to give any information and put the phone down.

Next point of call was the premises of Broadway Autos in West London, where Cook hoped to pin down either the elusive Bell or any of his associates, such as Alan Russell. A man answering Russell's description was sitting at a desk. And so began yet another violent confrontation.

COOK: Hello. Can I speak to Mr Russell please?
MAN: He's not here.
COOK: Do you know where he is? (*Pause*) No idea at all?
MAN: What's all this?
COOK: My name is Cook from the BBC *Checkpoint* programme. I've come to interview him about his car sales business.
MAN: Got nothing to say . . . nothing to say.
COOK: It's funny. The description fits you. (*Pause*) Do you deny that you're Mr Russell? (*No reply*) Do you deny you're Mr Russell?
MAN: Would you go . . . would you like to leave . . . or d'you want me to call the police?
COOK: Do. Just call them, then . . .
MAN: (*Sound of scuffle*) Would you like to leave?
COOK: Ah, ah, ah . . . No violence!
MAN: Just out of my office!
COOK: You are Mr Russell?
MAN: Out of my office!
COOK: You *are* Mr Russell, if it's *your* office.
MAN: OUT!
COOK: There are lots of questions to ask about your trading methods.
SECOND MAN: As it happens, it's not his office, it's mine. So out of it!

COOK: So, who are you?
FIRST MAN: Mind your own business, all right?
COOK: Come on, who are you?
SECOND MAN: Just mind your own business . . . Now out!
COOK: Well now, we've had a number of complaints about the way Broadway . . .
FIRST MAN: I don't care what you've had.
COOK: . . . Broadway car sales operate . . .
FIRST MAN: I don't care what you've had.
COOK: . . . and your predecessors . . .
FIRST MAN: I'm not interested in what you've got to say. Out!
SECOND MAN: Mind your own business.
COOK: I beg your pardon?
SECOND MAN: It's got nothing to do with you . . . Out!
COOK: Why?
SECOND MAN: Out!
(*Sound of a struggle and various noises*)
FIRST MAN: You try hitting me . . .
COOK: I'm not hitting anyone. I didn't do anything.
FIRST MAN: OUT!
(*Sound of door banging. General commotion. Dog barking*)

Back in the safety of the studio, Cook explained what happened.

'As they dragged me off, bruised and shaken, with my overcoat in tatters, they let their Alsatian off its leash to deter me from coming back. But that won't stop us from keeping you posted on future developments.'

Another mysterious fire followed the programme and the more visible parts of Bell's empire folded up. A police investigation into the fire, which had destroyed potentially incriminating records, and incidentally risked blowing up much of the surrounding area, resulted in Bell's conviction for arson. He was gaoled for three years and other serious charges were ordered to remain on the file.

CASE 14
Complaints against local authorities

Programme date: 24 October 1979
Researcher: David Perrin

This programme began with the cases of over fifty residents of Celladyke in Fife, on the east Scottish coast, who were fearing for their homes because of actions taken by North East Fife District Council. Eugene Despanemol and Ann Hughes were leading the fight against the council. They told listeners how the population was mainly fisher-people with a long tradition behind them. The village was well kept, homes were clean, tidy and comfortable, and the people were happy – until the council stepped in. Despanemol read out one of fifty closing orders received by villagers.

'Whereas the North East Fife District Council, the local authority under the Housing (Scotland) Act 1966, hereinafter referred to respectively as "the local authority" and "the Act", are satisfied that this house does not meet the tolerable standards and that it ought to be demolished, now therefore the local authority in exercise of the powers conferred upon them by Section 15/1 of the Act hereby prohibit the use of the said house for human habitation as from the expiration of twenty-eight days from the date on which this Order becomes operative.'

Many of the householders actually saw this notice in the local paper before receiving it in the post. Apart from the sheer discourtesy and personal shock, such a public notice made them wonder what other people would think. It made them ashamed of belonging to Celladyke, where many families had lived for generations. As Cook put it, a tenth of the town stood condemned, with many of the population feeling angry and resentful at the way the council were treating them. He visited Maud Walker in her tiny converted cottage, a real 'gem'.

She explained that six years previously her house had been derelict, and a grant was obtained to put it in order. She bought it three years later and made improvements, spending several thousand pounds in the process, 'to make it the way I want'. Now she had the council's letter telling her that her home was not of a tolerable standard. 'I think that's intolerable!' she said angrily. But as far as the council was concerned, the problem was that her bathroom leads off her only bedroom.

Alec Berrell also found the bureaucrats' attitude intolerable. In his neat cottage around the corner the bathroom was next to the kitchen. The fact that he had lived there from the age of eleven to his present seventy-two cut no ice with the council. They wanted him out too.

'I've a lovely view and a beautiful house, well kept inside and outside, and now they're telling me it's a slum. Other people not living here are wondering what kind of houses we're living in. They'll think we're living in hovels, and it's no hovel, this.'

Cook agreed. And neither was Chrissie Allen's house, which the council were actually preventing from being improved. A similar problem was facing John Corbull who had bought a second house and wanted to sell the first house to raise the cash to renovate the second. Both his houses were served with closing orders, effectively blocking all his plans.

A few of the unfortunate fifty received a letter from the council informing them that the sender was regarding the closing order as being suspended 'for the immediate forthcoming period'. Damned gobble-de-gook, scoffed Despanemol. Just an insulting fob-off that does not remove the threat.

Indeed, Ann Hughes saw further possible problems, if the local authority should designate the village as a Housing Action Area. In that case: 'If you don't improve your home, can't afford to, or don't want to, the council can take your house over. People are very frightened that they may lose their homes. And these are not slums, they're happy family homes. The council has no right to come marching in, telling the owners of houses what they should and shouldn't do, or how it should be arranged. The council is being insensitive and unrealistic.'

Many of the alterations being demanded by the council, said Cook, would cost more than the houses were worth. And there appeared to be a certain friction between the council and the Anstruther Community Council (Anstruther is a neighbouring village), which Kenneth Brown joined so that he could become more involved in local affairs. He objected strongly to what he called the 'patronising attitude' of the council and the way council members were 'working behind our backs . . . trying to apply standards for new council houses to seventeenth and eighteenth century fishermen's cottages. The whole thing is quite ridiculous'.

The local councillor for the past twenty years was Agnes Gardner, who was also Vice-Chairman of the District Housing Committee. Unbeknown to the locals she was also a member of the working party that had proposed the closing order scheme. A letter announcing a public meeting and special exhibition related to the scheme had been posted to house owners in the same envelope as the closing orders themselves, and because of this they felt that despite the council's efforts to explain Gardner's work they had been presented with a *fait accompli*. She did not agree, she told Cook. The interview that followed was a classic case of bureaucratic un-logic, not to mention an insight into what some people mean by 'tolerable'.

GARDNER: They ought to have been able to gather from that letter that the closing order was there but it was not to be acted upon.
COOK: But what was the point of issuing it in the first place?
GARDNER: The point of issuing it was for the council to gain control of these houses for the future.
COOK: But the locals say they are their houses, and you've no right to come marching in and telling them what to do.
GARDNER: They are their houses, we fully appreciate that. But they are sub-standard, very sub-standard, some of them. If they are sold to another proprietor, we want to make sure that these houses are brought up to tolerable standards.
COOK: But these tolerable standards apply to new council houses. These are period cottages, some of which I've been in, and I'm most impressed. I mean, they're straight out of *House and Garden*. They're beautiful.
GARDNER: They don't apply to council houses *only*. They apply to all housing. It's provided in the Housing (Scotland) Act 1974.
COOK: But we're talking about cottages that are hundreds of years old.
GARDNER: We're talking about every cottage, and there's nothing to prevent the proprietors of these cottages putting in the tolerable standards mentioned in the Act.
COOK: It depends on what you mean by tolerable, of course. And there is something to prevent them. They cannot afford it, even with a grant.
GARDNER: Well, in that case, if they wish to remain and not put in these necessary . . . If they don't wish to alter their houses to bring them up to a tolerable standard, they will not be forced to do it.
COOK: You see, the people who live in them now think they *are* up to tolerable standards. Take one example. There's a lady who has a beautiful house with what we would describe as an '*en suite* bathroom'. She is a single occupier of a one-bedroomed place. She's been told her house is not up to tolerable standards, and those who've seen it describe that as ludicrous.
GARDNER: Now this is a one-bedroomed house.
COOK: It is indeed.
GARDNER: . . . and the bathroom is off the bedroom.
COOK: That's correct.
GARDNER: And I believe she contends that this is what we have in the best hotels. But then, on the other hand, any other person living in that house wanting to go to the bathroom would have to

go into . . . through her bedroom!
COOK: They couldn't live in the house. There isn't another bedroom.
GARDNER: But there is a living room.
COOK: Well, come on . . . What I'm talking about . . .
GARDNER: **We will not tolerate that kind of thing in Scotland!**

Gardner refused to accept that the issue had been handled in an insensitive manner, insisting that she and 'her' council had done everything in their power to help 'these people'. When Cook asked her why so many people had seen fit to contact *Checkpoint* to say they had been badly treated, she failed to understand how they could do such a thing. After all . . .

'Instead of assisting them, as we have done, we could quite easily have declared an Action Area, which is much more severe. This is not a compulsory order.'

Cook himself failed to understand why the council issued closing orders if it did not, as she implied, intend to enforce them. Why not withdraw them, instead of leaving so many people with a Damoclean sword over their heads?

Gardner insisted the council was only doing what was right and proper, and, after all, the people could come to her and discuss the matter. Cook put it to her that her constituents did not trust her very much, because of her undisclosed membership of the closing order scheme's working party.

'They ought to know that I've never once agreed to anything that was detrimental to their life,' she stated, with a firmness that bordered on outrage.

'Well,' Cook said, 'they think you've done it now.'

At this stage Gardner asserted that if these people could not trust her there was no point in continuing, so a number of Cook's questions remained unasked. But for many listeners, particularly in East Fife, the point had been made.

The second case in this programme dealt with the problems of a small group of residents in the Yorkshire town of Pontefract who, for many years, had been troubled by the Wakefield Metropolitan District Council and a twenty-foot cliff overlooking the main road at the bottom of their gardens. Eighty-five-year-old Frank Holmes explained how, in 1967, the council wrote to the residents to say that they were authorised to acquire 375 yards for the purpose of making a footpath along the top of this cliff. After three years of desultory letter writing by the council, nothing was done, and in April 1970 the residents were told that the council no longer wanted to proceed with the footpath development. For seven years the matter lay dormant, then Holmes was served with a council order to remedy an 'unfenced source of danger'; to wit, his land at the cliff top. The order was dropped when the local council next decided to buy the land. Then they decided to drop the purchase scheme. After more toing and froing it was revived once more, and the county council then asked Holmes and his neighbours to give them the land. Nothing happened for another year. Then unexpectedly, on 7 June 1979, Wakefield Council issued a notice requiring the residents to undertake works of protection. If they failed to comply, the council were empowered to do such works as were necessary and recover the cost from the residents.

'We understand that this cost was about £30,000,' Holmes said. 'I thought this was a staggering demand, because they can't prove that we had done anything towards causing this alleged danger. It's entirely their own work. They made the road, and they made the cutting. Surely it's up to them to protect it.'

Joan and Leslie Mills were also affected. Quite apart from the technical business of being asked to hand over land to the council and the impossible business of being told to pay a proportion of the costly work, Mr Mills, a pensioner, suffered from arteriosclerosis and had had three strokes, with a fourth resulting from the worry of the problem. They managed to sell their home and move away, but Frank Holmes found himself up against the council in a court battle that he defended for himself and on behalf of the other residents. His archival material showed how the road had been developed by successive local authorities since 1779 and how roadworks that widened the road had contributed to the undermining of the cliff. Nevertheless, the magistrates decided that the alleged danger was indeed the responsibility of the residents, even though for the past two hundred years the local authority had been responsible.

Checkpoint checked back to the Wakefield Metropolitan District Council who referred them to West Yorkshire Metropolitan County Council who referred them to Bob Hawkin, the man on their Transportation Committee who was in charge of the situation. Cook asked him whose was the road and whose the cliff? After a perfunctory dismissal of two hundred years of historic responsibility, Hawkin ventured his 'lay' opinion that when the people concerned bought their houses, 'the cliff existed, someone should have told them that they'd bought a problem, and it is their responsibility to make it safe.'

Cook pointed out that the residents disagree with this analysis and emphasised again that the responsibility had been accepted by one authority after another for two centuries.

'I admit there *was* a responsibility,' Hawkin began, but immediately amended this. 'Or apparently there has been, but I don't know how you can carry this responsibility on to the West Yorkshire County Council in 1979. We have gone into this feeling that we are right.'

Cook asked if he thought that even if it was technically right, was it morally right to ask pensioners to pay for the required work on the road and cliff. Hawkin ventured the opinion that it was, because if his own stone wall was falling down dangerously the council could insist that he put it right. Cook went straight to battle stations.

COOK: Have *you* got £30,000? Because these people haven't!
HAWKIN: No, I haven't got £30,000.
COOK: The point is, they haven't got the money. (*Pause*) They haven't got the money.
HAWKIN: Well I don't know. The old age pensioners that I know don't live in palatial houses such as these people live in. I feel that . . .
COOK: I think that's over-doing it a bit, actually. One of the houses is very old and is falling down, and the Mills have had to sell their house because of this threat and move to a tiny cottage up the road.
HAWKIN: I didn't know the Mills had moved.
COOK: They still feel threatened by this huge bill that they can't possibly pay. They're old people with no backing. They couldn't pay.
HAWKIN: If they don't do the work the council will do it and charge it to them.
COOK: But I have to say again: they haven't got the money.
HAWKIN: I can assure you that there are ways and means of helping them, and there would be no pressure at all put on these people by the County Council.

Events proved that to be a rather hollow promise. By the time the programme was broadcast the council had reduced its claim somewhat, but Mr Holmes still could not afford to pay. Moreover he could not see the justification for doing so. So, as a litigant in person, he took the council to the County Court where the original magistrates' decision was overturned. Refusing to admit defeat, the council then mounted an action in the High Court, which they lost. Subsequent threats to drag 85-year-old Frank Holmes as far as the House of Lords came to nothing. The irony is that the costs, legal and otherwise, incurred by the council at the rate payers' expense have far exceeded the cost of doing the original 'works of protection' unjustly demanded of Mr Holmes.

CASE 15
Complaints against Derek Slade, St George's School

Programme date: 8 September 1982
Researcher: Jay Andrews

Cook began by saying the programme was about a most unusual public school supported largely by public funds: St George's School at Great Finborough near Stowmarket, founded by Derek Slade MA.

'This remarkable establishment specialises in educating the children of servicemen, and by all accounts makes Dickens's *Dotheboys Hall* look like a holiday camp.'

Former games master at the school Mark Anderson was one of a number of ex-staff who told *Checkpoint* about repression, brutality and more.

'The school was run on totally autocratic lines. If a member of staff did not agree with the school's policy, he was likely to be asked to leave. The discipline for the pupils was extremely harsh and frequent, even for the young boys. All boys from the age of six to seventeen were punished by being beaten with various implements. The headmaster often set an essay with the title "Whackings I Have Had". You can draw your own conclusions from that.

'The beatings were often harsh and given for very insignificant offences. There were also some very odd goings-on of a sexual nature, some of which resulted in one of the masters leaving the country. All-in-all it's a school to stay away from, and if I had a child I would not send it to St George's.'

'Pupils speaking openly of their experiences are hard to come by,' Cook continued. 'Ninety-five per cent of the 250-odd boarding pupils are children of servicemen, and the Ministry of

Defence pays the school a minimum of £746 cash each term. The Ministry blocked our access to their pupils. Parents, too, can be unco-operative. Some seem to agree with the school's ultra-strict methods, or they're unaware of how far things go, because they are on an overseas posting. Their children are forbidden except in dire emergency to make phone calls home, and all their letters are read before posting. Even when you trace pupils, as we have done, they are reluctant to go on the record for fear of the consequences. This lad only agreed to broadcast if his voice was disguised.'

The pupil began by saying that anyone who did not obey Slade's rules and orders to the letter would be in trouble throughout their school life, and even silly offences incurred serious punishment. Six-of-the-best was common, administered with one of four different beating implements chosen by Slade with regard to how serious he thought the transgression to be: the cane, bat, stick and 'Jasper the gym shoe'. These beatings were administered with the boy's trousers down.

'More often than not boys come out with blood not so much dripping from their behinds but evident . . . Sometimes when two boys have a grudge against each other they'll go to him and have what's called an official fight. He'll officiate and referee as they tear each other to pieces, and it's not stopped until some damage is done – and this can involve big boys against small boys, not often, admittedly, but it does occur.'

The pupil said that most boys are frightened of the consequences of 'getting on the wrong side of Mr Slade', because they felt he could ruin their education, and this was why he wanted his voice disguised.

Aware that the boy's allegations might sound unbelievable to some listeners, Cook pointed out that what he had said was supported by other pupils and by at least nine former members of staff, not necessarily known to each other. Cook first examined the issue of corporal punishment, which Slade was on record as approving.

'. . . but even some supporters of corporal punishment (including, it must be said, the parents of some of his pupils) might feel differently if they knew how far Mr Slade actually went. Former assistant matron Pamela Green recalls how the crunch came for her.'

'A crowd of boys came running to me and said, "Have you seen so-and-so's bottom, Miss?" I decided that I ought to have a look and I was quite horrified. The boy was about eight or nine, and the whole of his backside was covered in bruises of every colour. A few days later another lad walked into the dormitory with two black eyes and a very red face. He said he'd got one from playing rugby and the other from the headmaster. The following day I had a visit from a friend, and I told her how worried I was about what I'd seen. She reminded me that she was a social worker and said she would have to report the matter to her superiors, which she did. A few hours later I had a phone call from the bursar of the school who said my services were no longer required. I was sacked.'

She was also threatened with legal action if she made further public complaint.

Mark Anderson, another ex-employee of the school, took offence at some of the institutionalised violence, particularly the 'official fights', which he felt were extremely dangerous and unfair. But, he said, the headmaster not only seemed to enjoy them but certainly encouraged them. Then there were the so-called reigns of terror, in which the entire school was punished by having all privileges taken away and in which total silence was imposed. No pupil was allowed to leave the premises or to make a phone call for any reason. Ex-junior teacher Jenny Marlow told how the school was tense for days at a time.

'One little boy wrote home and complained to his parents about these reigns of terror, and his parents wrote back to Mr Slade to ask what was going on. In the very next assembly he took the boy in front of the entire school and expelled him for complaining.'

Jenny Marlow told how the food was not nutritious, and she felt that this affected younger pupils worst of all. They didn't get enough vitamins, they were always very tired, they had colds and cold sores. . . . Pupils slept with up to fifty in one dormitory, with older boys walking in and out while younger ones were trying to sleep. Some youngsters were so tired that they constantly fell asleep in class.

One pupil, Nigel Kenton-Barnes, stayed the course and explained that he had managed to adjust to the system. Nevertheless he thought the school was 'not far off' being like a prison camp. He talked about the punishments he had received and how Slade would write the punishment records in a notebook in Greek. One of the 'Whackings I Have Had' essays was read out.

'I was outside the headmaster's study, because I had written on the desk. I was scared. The headmaster told me to come in. I touched my toes. He went to the cupboard and got out a funny looking bat. He raised it, and the bat came down at the speed of sound. The first whack felt like a volcano erupting. Then it felt like stinging bees. Then it felt like a red hot poker with steam coming off as it came down with great force on my bottom. This was agony. I nearly screamed out in pain. The pressure of the whack shoved me forward. There were five more whacks to come.'

Ex-music and dormitory master David Barrett learned to detest these 'whackings', so much a way of life at St George's, said Cook. He told of the long, late night punishment queues outside the headmaster's study.

'I was often told by the boys that they'd actually been beaten with their pants down, punished in their pyjamas or whatever they were wearing at the time. If they happened to be in the shower, they'd go as they were to the headmaster's study. At Christmas there were House parties, and there were games with forfeits. These included a nine-year-old boy drinking a glass of sherry in one go, an eleven-year-old taking his clothes off and acting the role of Tarzan on the table top and another boy, again totally naked, running round the school.'

Nigel Kenton-Barnes went to one of these parties, and he verified that the kind of things described by Barrett did happen. But Barrett had more serious allegations to make. Often, while checking the dormitories, he would notice boys missing from their beds. When he asked the other boys where they were he was told they were in 'such-and-such' a person's room.

'Nearly always it was the housemaster's room,' he said. 'One particular night a ten-year-old boy was missing for the fourth time in succession. I went straight to the housemaster's room, banged on the door and demanded that the boy be returned to the dormitory, which did not happen. So I complained to the headmaster about these boys who were always missing from the dormitory. He refused to comment, and when I pressed the point he flew into a rage and ordered me off the premises. This was half-past eleven at night.'

Cook commented: 'The housemaster, Mr Singer, later fled the country. So while Mr Barrett was summarily fired, Mr Singer was allowed to leave relatively quietly.'

Ex-pupil Nigel Kenton-Barnes recalled that he had seen many teachers come and go, and this brought *Checkpoint* to the next point of criticism: the actual standard of education at St George's School:

'We had about four different maths teachers swopping about,

and we didn't know what we were doing, really. I didn't get a good education. I don't know whether it was his fault or my fault, but I only got six CSEs and one Grade D O-Level . . . Finding it hard to get a job at the moment.'

Teachers told *Checkpoint* about inadequate equipment and inadequate back-up. Monica Schweitzer-Kascher was the fourth teacher in one year to try and teach German at the school. On arrival she was given a timetable and told to get on with it.

'I didn't have any textbooks, no record, no mark books, nothing. Once I started work the children began to complain about discontinuity . . . Their standard of German was absolutely appalling,' she said. She also confirmed the stories of homosexual 'scandal'.

'Similar stories were told about other subjects, such as French and science,' Cook reported, but: 'St George's prospectus gives the impression that good exam results were achieved, long before any of its pupils ever sat a public examination. Success, where achieved, say teachers, is often despite the school rather than because of it.'

Next came the revelation that this educational establishment was, in fact, a limited company called Anglemoss Limited, with Derek Slade as chairman of the board. Teacher Nick Cottham resigned from the school in order to take part in the programme, and he pointed out that as a limited company the school had no board of governors, just Mr Slade setting policies and making all the decisions. There was no 'higher authority' in the school to whom anyone could complain, and Cottham felt that unions would not have been much help in terms of solving the problems faced by staff. The net result was that many teachers were unhappy with things at the school but stayed on to make the best of it, despite a contract that the National Union of Teachers described as 'the most extreme that they had ever seen'. Yet despite the long hours, the low pay and the regular bouts of misery David Barrett told listeners that there was the basis for a good school.

'This whole system is mismanaged,' he said, 'the boys are obviously abused, and the tremendous potential at the school is just not being realised. Taking everything into consideration, it's rather like an episode from *Tom Brown's Schooldays*.'

'And a very bad episode at that!' Cook said. 'The Ministry of Defence has declined to comment. They referred us to the Department of Education and Science, and *they* told us that they'd heard rumours and allegations concerning St George's

School, that HM Inspectors of Schools had visited the place more than once and that the Suffolk police had also been involved. But there had been no formal complaint in writing.'

Cook, with all his experience in reporting, found it difficult to believe that the Ministry could not act without such a letter. He continued the investigation by trying to arrange an interview with headmaster Derek Slade.

'Mr Slade professed amazement at the allegations made against him and his school, and before giving an interview he wanted them spelled out in writing, which we did by telegram. But while we were on our way to see him he had a letter delivered to our office that concluded it was not in the public interest for this programme to be broadcast. So our reception, which involved a rather hefty staff member, came as something of a surprise.'

The confrontation at the school premises was less than satisfactory in terms of information but, as with so many others, it nevertheless revealed quite a lot about the situation, with the staff member refusing to say where Slade could be found and refusing to give his name to Cook.

COOK: Will you give us any assistance whatsoever?
MASTER: No.
COOK: Why not?
MASTER: Because we're told not to, it's as simple as that.

Slade subsequently had his lawyer send a second letter that retracted the first and threatened *Checkpoint* and the BBC with legal action. He also tried to involve his Member of Parliament. But he remained elusive.

'So he won't be giving us his views on education,' Cook said, 'or even contesting the views of David Freeman, author of the soon-to-be-published *Good Schools Guide to Independent Schools*.'

Freeman told how he was alerted to St George's School by an official in the Ministry of Defence who had been worried about it 'for some years'. He went to see the school for himself.

'I formed the impression that the regime of the school was extremely repressive,' he said. 'The standard of teaching gave me severe misgivings. There appeared to be inadequate equipment, inadequate experience among staff, and it worries me very much that the Department of Defence is prepared to spend large sums in maintaining this school – we're talking about £500,000 a year.'

Freeman told Cook that the service authorities could insist on changes, because they could simply withhold allowances, but the inspection of independent schools was no longer obligatory by HM Inspectorate . . .

'But in any case, when an inspection does take place it's always possible for a school to put on a plausible show,' he said.

'I regard this case as exceptional. I haven't come across another school like it this century. It's an unfettered autocracy. A tyranny.'

Following the programme, a significant number of pupils were taken from the school. The episode was subsequently broadcast over the British Forces Broadcasting Service in Germany (funded, as were many of the pupil's fees at the school, by the Ministry of Defence), and more withdrawals followed. Derek Slade attempted to use the national Press to counter the allegations, and most of the major newspapers covered the story during the following week. Ignoring the fact that *Checkpoint* had sent written notice of questions in advance, he told reporters that he had been given no chance to answer the many allegations made in the programme. The Press began digging into his past, and discovered a number of aspects of Slade's life that were not entirely to his credit. Then, on notice from Her Majesty's Inspectorate of Schools that an investigation was planned, St George's school 'revised its corporal punishment regulations' and 'overhauled its organisation and policy'. The Inspectors' report nevertheless criticised the school's approach to discipline and recommended the discontinuance of 'official fights' as a means of settling differences between the boys.

Cook attended the official announcement of the report and was told that the Inspectorate did not investigate any of the original allegations made on *Checkpoint* because, as they put it, they had no power to make retrospective inquiries. Subsequently, education minister Sir Keith Joseph was quoted in the Press as saying that none of the programme's allegations had been supported: a logically correct but nevertheless misleading statement. Officials from the Department of Education and Science had failed to make contact with key complainants. Immediately following the publication of the report, Derek Slade resigned his headmastership.

CASE 16
Special edition on insolvency

Broadcast on 9 June 1982
Researcher: David Perrin

In this special edition Cook began by asking if a remedy was on its way for 'your bitterest and most persistent complaints since *Checkpoint* started . . . the way the law works when companies you deal with go bust'. The programme proceeded to examine a major report on the subject by the Insolvency Law Review Committee under the chairmanship of Sir Kenneth Cork that had been published the previous day. The first interview was with Cork himself who highlighted why the radical reforms it proposed were urgent and imperative.

'The law now does not provide the proper remedies to make directors personally liable or responsible when they have committed fraud. It doesn't make them frightened enough of their own position so as to behave properly. It doesn't stop abuses, such as when one company goes broke and the next one forms the next day, and the next one after that, like the ones you cover in *Checkpoint*. And that must be stopped.'

Cook then described the basis for the Cork Report, commissioned by the government six years previously to carry out the first review for a century of the entire law on personal bankruptcy, company liquidation and receivership.

'In this programme,' he said, 'we only have time to tell you briefly what the report's quarter of a million words have to say about companies. We will not be able to go into its equally radical recommendations on personal bankruptcy. Of course, it's still up to the government to turn the report into new law or to leave it gathering dust on a Ministry shelf. To help you follow the proposals, we offer a brief guide. First, what is a limited company?'

Cork explained that such a company is a vehicle for business, separate in law from the directors who run it. Thus, the directors don't have to pay the company's debts, and that's why it's called a limited liability company. And it is this very protection for the directors, said Cook, that can be exploited and used against the entrepreneur's customers and suppliers.

'It may astound you to know how quickly and cheaply the law allows you to become a company director.'

A *Checkpoint* investigator then visited one of the firms that specialise in selling off-the-shelf limited companies. The conversation revealed that if two people called at the offices with cash (£105, inclusive) the transaction could be completed in about fifteen minutes. The law required only £2 to be put into the company as capital. 'No wonder,' commented Cook, 'that so many people's debts are never paid when a company goes into liquidation.'

There followed a recording of a typical announcement made by a newly-appointed liquidator to a creditors' meeting held under the provision of Section 293 of the Companies Act 1948. The shareholders of the company concerned had decided that it could no longer continue to trade 'because of its insolvency' and had passed a resolution appointing the liquidator, in this case Richard Shaw, a chartered accountant of the firm of Allhusen and Whittle. After such meetings, explained Cook, it is the liquidator's job to take over and to liquidate the company's assets; in other words, to turn them into cash.

After extracting his own fees and expenses, the liquidator has to pay off the company's debts according to a strict pecking order. The first he has to pay include debts to the so-called preferential creditors, such as the Inland Revenue and the Customs & Excise. Then come the banks which loaned the company money. At the end of the queue are the ordinary unsecured creditors, the average customer and supplier. One of the many protests over this has come from the National Federation of Consumer Groups, whose secretary, Janet Upwood, explained why their campaign had concentrated on monies paid by customers in advance, to mail order firms, travel agents, and so on.

She listed a catalogue of sorry stories, including the Laker collapse in which many people had lost thousands of pounds. 'I think it's wrong that such customer's money should go to swell the funds to pay off all the other creditors.'

The Cork Report contains provisions for a new deal for such 'ordinary' creditors, said Cook. Essentially, these will restrict preferential claims to a minimum and ensure that, where there is a receivership, the unsecured creditors should have ten per cent of the net assets reserved for themselves.

'First, this gives them an interest in the receivership,' said Cork, 'and secondly it gives the liquidator a fund from which to take such actions as he thinks appropriate; even to challenge any actions of the Receiver or to question whether the people who appointed the Receiver had the right to do so.'

Cook asked Cork if his committee had gone far enough in this 'key area of complaint'. Cork replied that it was not practical to go further, otherwise they would be interfering with the way companies are financed – 'And that would mean destroying businesses, which we don't want to do.' He felt that his committee had indirectly covered the problem of people sending money in advance to a mail order company by introducing the concept of 'wrongful trading', in which people who do not set aside money to cover money sent in advance could be held personally liable for the money they had received. Other proposals deal directly with the company machinations that exploit the insolvency law, and not before time. Cook introduced a number of examples, one concerning a peer of the realm who used a limited company to order everything for his daughter's wedding reception. When the bills arrived they remained unpaid. The company had no assets, and the lord himself did not have to meet the commitments. And once again there were the many examples of what the *Checkpoint* team had come to call the 'Change-the- name-and-do-the-same game'.

Roy Molyneux owned an engineering company and was doing business with a company operating in Woolwich that went into liquidation owing him £4,000. After two years and much trouble he had not been paid a penny, but the same people were running the same activities in the same premises with the same machinery and the same staff, under a different name. Molyneux commented that it was 'looney that the law lets things like this go on'.

Pride of place was given to Sidney Newman 'whose career of company failure is a by-word for what the law on insolvency allows'. In 1973 and 1977 Newman had two companies put into liquidation when they failed to pay debts. Another of his companies put itself into liquidation owing £13,000. In law he did not have to pay off this sum personally, and meanwhile he was able to stay in business with other companies that he ran. Subsequently two of these were dissolved by the Registrar of Companies and others just stopped trading, one with a loss of £65,000. At that time Newman's biggest venture to date was under way: he was selling the well known Lillibet dishwasher through a company called Lillibet Dishwashers (UK) Ltd. In 1980 this company also ended in liquidation, owing £192,000.

'Once again,' reported Cook, 'Mr Newman didn't have to pay the debts. Around this time he bought himself a new Mercedes. Soon after Lillibet's collapse, Mr Newman was in a new guise, writing to everyone who had previously bought one of his dishwashers. Asking his old customers for yet more money, he offered new service contracts and replacement parts, having bought all the available spares at knock-down prices from the liquidator through another of his companies, Dishmaster Home Counties Ltd.

'And then, for the creditors of all his companies, came the final insult in his tortuous career. . . . Mr Newman changed the name of Dishmaster Home Counties Limited to Dishmaster Lillibet Limited. He got the name Lillibet back, debts of more than £100,000 were left behind . . . and it was all perfectly legal.'

Sir Kenneth Cork explained that his committee's proposals would inhibit anyone playing this change-the-name-and-do-the-same game. 'We're getting at that through the directors. If a director of one company that becomes insolvent becomes the director of another company within two or three years, and if that other company becomes insolvent, the director will be personally liable for the debts. They would also be guilty of fraudulent trading, and that would bar them from being a director of a company for a considerable period.'

Cook asked Cork about under-capitalisation, the only legal liability often being that meagre £2 of share capital necessary for a limited company to begin operations. Cork pointed out that although they would have liked to make under-capitalisation illegal, this would have meant changing company law. However, he said that the new concept of wrongful trading would cover the matter: 'If, with a share value of £2, you lose £5, you're insolvent, so you're liable for debts very quickly.'

He explained that wrongful trading differed from fraudulent trading (in which the prosecution must prove intent) because it covers only the facts of a case: if a company were insolvent and the directors continued trading they would then be personally liable for the debts incurred, and not protected as under existing law.

'So much for directors, but what about liquidators?' asked Cook. He described the 'tiny minority' who seemed to be the last sort of people fitted for such a position of trust, some with no qualifications, some with histories of personal bankruptcies, some even with criminal records. Cork outlined new qualifications proposed for liquidators in his report. Cook then described the difference between liquidations and receiverships.

'Receivers usually act for institutions that have made loans to a company, as for example the Receiver who went into Laker airlines on behalf of a consortium of banks. In most cases a company pledges assets against the value of the loans, and the

Receiver's job is to sell off these pledged assets to pay back the debt.'

All well and good, on the face of it, but Elizabeth Mulholland told how her husband was sent abroad on business, with the family following after. She paid £1,700 to a travel agent, and her cheque was cleared one day after the carrier firm's account had been frozen. 'Our payment had, in effect, gone to subsidise payments to the banks,' she complained. 'Although they must have known what was about to happen, they still took our money. All we can expect is a percentage of what is left after the official groups have had their fill . . . absolutely nothing!'

Cook referred to the many complaints received by *Checkpoint* about the banks' privileged position in this pecking order. What was worse . . .

'Beside their high priority as secured creditors, they have inside knowledge about a company and can choose the timing for putting a Receiver in.' In case any listeners might feel that this was an unjustified slur on their High Street money-shops, Cook referred to a previous *Checkpoint* programme that described how some grain merchants had been heavily overdrawn at the National Westminster Bank, but a Receiver was not called in until after the grain harvest had been collected by the firm from some eighty farmers. 'The Receiver then had the grain to sell, and the bank's debt was met. The farmers, though, are still waiting for their money.'

The Cork Report's recommendations, however, would mean that banks and other so-called secured creditors would not have the impact they do now, and ordinary creditors would be given a better chance to recoup at least some of their money, together with more say in the proceedings. The most important proposals, in Cork's view, were to avoid 'some little chap who only owes a little money' having to go through the rigours of bankruptcy. A serious investigation would be reserved for serious cases.

'To save businesses, we have provided a chap called an administrator, who either the shareholders or the creditors can put in. He'll be able to run the company immediately . . . and this will mean that a large number of businesses that would otherwise go broke will be saved. We also recommend a specialist court for insolvency.'

Cook finally interviewed Dr Gerard Vaughan, Minister for Consumer Affairs at the Department of Trade. What, he asked, will happen to the Cork Report now that it has been submitted to government after six years of preparation?

Certainly it will not be put on a shelf, stated the minister, although it *is* a very large and complicated report.

'I know Sir Kenneth would like to have it looked at as a total package, but that's going to take some time . . . but are there some parts of it which we ought to pull out and try to deal with more urgently? That's one of the things I shall be looking at . . .

COOK: So action could be fairly quick, at least on some parts of it.
VAUGHAN: Well, it is complicated, and we need to talk this over with people who are working in the field.
COOK: It's been talked about, Minister, for six years already.
VAUGHAN: I'm so tired, even in the short period I've been doing this job, of saying . . . 'We must wait for Cork.' Now we've *got* Cork. Let's have a look and see what it means, and what abuses we can deal with. I'm very interested, for instance, in the parts where he's suggesting ways in which firms can be kept trading, (and) I'm very worried about those firms that seem to be able to liquidate, get rid of their debts, and then re-open. Big surprise! A new name, but all the same people. These are the things we need to look into.
COOK: But should we *really* do this piecemeal? Sir Kenneth was telling us earlier today that the government would be, to use his words, 'mad not to implement it all, *now*.'
VAUGHAN: Well Sir Kenneth is a very wise man, and we shall look very carefully at his recommendations, I can tell you. This is not a report that we shall want to ignore, or be able to ignore.'

But, ended Cook, the implementation of the Cork Report could still be a long time coming.

Chronology

What follows is a full list of the major subjects in every *Checkpoint* broadcast since the programme began in July 1973 to the end of the first series of 1983.

The programmes are not given titles but are listed in a kind of crude shorthand, written in *Checkpoint*'s rather eccentric log book to remind the team of the content of individual broadcasts. It gives little indication of how extraordinary some of the stories were.

The few missing dates in the early years indicate that no programme was broadcast. Usually this was for scheduling reasons, but just once there was a legal problem.

Later on the programme was transmitted in series of nine or ten, with a short break in between. *Action Desk*, a magazine programme of short items reported by the research team, was introduced in February 1979 and ran for one edition every three or four weeks until October 1980.

The list reveals how wide-ranging *Checkpoint* inquiries have been from the outset: very little, in fact, devoted to High Street consumerism, and a great deal that was ahead of its time. Chain letters in February 1974, disposal of dangerous wastes the following year, and a hard look at nuclear safety in 1975.

[*Nationwide* co-productions are marked with an asterisk (*). Stories described in detail in the list of Cases are so indicated. When there are two or more separate stories in one programme they are separated by a hatch sign (/).]

Chronological list of main *Checkpoint* stories from July 1973 to December 1982

Date	*Subject*
6.7.73	Opticians: do they sell you glasses you don't need at inflated prices?
13.7.73	'Cowboy' estate agents
20.7.73	Exploited *au pair* girls
27.7.73	The depravations of heavy lorries/The transportation

	of dangerous or toxic loads
3.8.73	Local councillors with vested interests
10.8.73	How manufacturers deny simple spare parts to owners of cars and appliances
17.8.73	Unfair pressure on dealers by British Leyland/ Exploitation of the fuel crisis
24.8.73	Fairground safety/Medical confidentiality
31.8.73	The high cost of dying
7.9.73	Door-to-door encyclopaedia selling
14.9.73	False documents (passports etc): who acquires them, and how
21.9.73	Pyramid selling
28.9.73	Bogus charity collections
5.10.73	Harrassment of tenants: Rachmanism revisited
12.10.73	Induced labour: Your rights infringed and the dangers involved
19.10.73	Computer crime
26.10.73	Social Security sex snoopers
2.11.73	Heavy lorries: the damage and the dangers
9.11.73	Slave workers of the rag trade
16.11.73	Commemorative medallion/Silver ingot swindle
30.11.73	Denial of State welfare benefits
7.12.73	Door-to-door central heating sales/Petrol coupon black market
14.12.73	Child labour scandal
21.12.73	Over-zealous bailiffs
28.12.73	High pressure tombstone selling/Rip-off flat agencies
4.1.74	Doorstep confidence tricks on Old Age Pensioners
11.1.74	Vanity Publishing, Part 1
18.1.74	House extension/Planning problems
25.1.74	Dangerous playground equipment/Children's clothing
1.2.74	Dirty hospitals, Part 1
8.2.74	Exploitation of child models
15.2.74	Adverse drug reactions
22.2.74	A collection of chain letters
1.3.74	Divorce special
8.3.74	Dirty hospitals, Part 2
15.3.74	Adverse drug reactions
22.3.74	Package holiday disasters
29.3.74	Legal Aid (the lack of it!) at employment and housing tribunals
5.4.74	Phoney trade directories/The parking ticket farce

19.4.74	Phoney mortgage brokers
26.4.74	Onerous exclusion clauses (the small print)
3.5.74	Cancer experiments/Illegal child minders, Part 1
10.5.74	Computer dating/Terror of the Tallyman
17.5.74	Shortcomings of the National House Building Registration Council (NHBC), Part 1
24.5.74	High pressure insurance selling
31.5.74	Phoney stammering cure
7.6.74	Bogus model agencies
14.6.74	Dangerous plastic furniture/Vanity Publishing, Part 2
21.6.74	Jewelry franchise swindle/Inflated service charge for flats
28.6.74	NHBC, Part 2
5.7.74	Problems with National Health Service dentistry
12.7.74	Disputes of over-rating assessments: how the machinery fails
19.7.74	Phoney university degrees
26.7.74	Abuses of the Rent Act
2.8.74	Problems with the Post Office etc: faceless bureaucrats at work
9.8.74	Housing special
16.8.74	Dirty pathology laboratories
23.8.74	Investment land sales
30.8.74	Disposal of dangerous industrial wastes (Pitsea etc), Part 1
6.9.74	Welsh roofing swindle
13.9.74	Shady piano dealers/Dangers of dried cat food
20.9.74	Sewage scandal: why pay for a service you don't get?
27.9.74	Travelling 'auction' sales
4.10.74	Is the Automobile Association really a mail order company?
11.10.74	Collapsing mail order companies
18.10.74	Disposal of dangerous wastes, Part 2/Claiming your inheritance, on commission
25.10.74	The children's 'charity' that wasn't
1.11.74	Caravan sites: how you are denied your security
8.11.74	The Wallcoating group of companies, Part 1
15.11.74	Who wants a gravel pit in Oxfordshire?
22.11.74	Planning problems and council secrecy
29.11.74	After the carbon paper racket: Dymo tapes
6.12.74	The perils of renting/Letting holiday flats
13.12.74	More collapsing mail order companies
20.12.74	What can go wrong when you buy a house

3.1.75	The disappearing rural chemist/Outrageous electricity bills
10.1.75	Goods insurance problems/More mail order
17.1.75	Dangerous appliances/Phoney competitions
24.1.75	Dubious trade directories
31.1.75	What price the Master Builders Federation?
7.2.75	Illegal child minders, Part 2/Useless and maddening burglar alarms
14.2.75	High pressure double glazing sales, based on false claims
21.2.75	Holes in the Hire Purchase Act
28.2.75	Inflammable plastics and dangerous furniture foam
7.3.75	More rogue estate agents
14.3.75	Rogue central heating engineers
21.3.75	Demolition Orders – and mistakes
4.4.75	Nuclear safety special (Hunterston)
11.4.75	Dangers of high-alumina cement construction
18.4.75	Fighting the Electricity Boards
25.4.75	Phoney finance company franchise (Glenn Securities)
2.5.75	Steamroller planning at Lambeth
9.5.75	What is a court judgement worth?/Industrial accident compensation
16.5.75	Insurance bungles: house, car, travel
23.5.75	Subsiding houses
30.5.75	Negligent doctors and dentists
6.6.75	Rogue mortgage brokers
13.6.75	The disappearing garage chain (Berners Hill Garages)
20.6.75	Clearing your name after a wrongful conviction, Part 1
27.6.75	More planning problems
4.7.75	Bogus leases/Low flying aircraft
11.7.75	Glenn Securities, Part 2/Mistaken identities
18.7.75	Aircraft safety
25.7.75	The disappearing hi-fi chain (Global Audio)
1.8.75	Investment land sales (Capital Land)
8.8.75	Phoney OAP charity (Senior Citizen's Supplies)
15.8.75	Bogus market researchers
22.8.75	The cost of clearing your name, Part 2
29.8.75	Town planning bungles
5.9.75	Paraquat and other noxious substances, Part 1
12.9.75	More mortgage brokers (second mortgage specialists)
19.9.75	More holiday disasters
26.9.75	Paraquat, Part 2/Over-zealous rent arrears collectors
3.10.75	Banking bungles

10.10.75 The man who sold properties he didn't own (Michael Lohan)
17.10.75 'Heavy' landlords and 'winklers'
24.10.75 Dangerous used cars and mini-cabs
3.11.75 High-handed councils special
7.11.75 Subsiding houses (Manchester)
14.11.75 Family Allowance and Supplementary Benefit bungles
21.11.75 Complaints against the police
28.11.75 Planning blight
5.12.75 Accident compensation
12.12.75 Homelessness, Part 1
19.12.75 Homelessness, Part 2

2.1.76 Christmas holiday disasters
9.1.76 Glenn Securities, Part 3
16.1.76 Car insurance anomalies/Bank evictions
23.1.76 More rogue central heating companies
30.1.76 Bankruptcy special
6.2.76 Dangerous motor cycle crash helmets/Lack of rider training
13.2.76 Has Britain prepared for national disasters?
20.2.76 How the Equal Pay Act is flouted
27.2.76 'Key' money swindles
5.3.76 The Wallcoating companies revisited
12.3.76 More travel horror stories, and how little redress is available
19.3.76 More council secrecy
26.3.76 Lack of accountability of public bodies
2.4.76 Don't treat yourself. Call a doctor!
9.4.76 The man who sold protection from 'Reds under your bed'
23.4.76 Disputes over common land
30.4.76 Long legal delays: how those who can least afford it end up paying
7.5.76 British Rail special
14.5.76 Low paid workers
21.5.76 Sewage special
28.5.76 Burglar alarms/Bogus security companies
4.6.76 Trying to sue a public body (Gas, Council, Water etc)
11.6.76 Blighted houses: who pays?
18.6.76 Compensation problems: consequential damage etc
25.6.76 Insurance fiddles/Defective car tyres
9.7.76 One-parent family special

16.7.76	Insurance assessors versus Loss adjustors
23.7.76	British justice: the man who was tried twice for the same offence*
30.7.76	Dubious old people's homes
6.8.76	Low paid workers, Part 2
13.8.76	Pyramid selling: the role of Cedar Holdings in financing Holiday Magic agents
20.8.76	*Au pair* girls in trouble again/Stolen caravans
27.8.76	Mental health special
3.9.76	Getting compensation from negligent solicitors
10.9.76	Onerous tenancy agreements: victimised tenants and landlords
17.9.76	Squatters special
24.9.76	Senior Citizens Supplies, Part 2*
1.10.76	Noise pollution special
8.10.76	Feudalism in Scotland: Twentieth century serfs
15.10.76	More cases of mistaken identity
22.10.76	Abused apprenticeships: cut-rate training schemes
29.10.76	Problems of being self-employed. More VAT anomalies
4.11.76	The sinking house estate (Fareham)
12.11.76	Unfair treatment of the mentally handicapped
19.11.76	Homes for the disabled
26.11.76	Horse-drawn caravan holidays (Romany Holidays)
3.12.76	Who controls the Water Authorities?
10.12.76	Rogue car dealers (Stewart Motors and Sid West)
17.12.76	Squatters: their rights and yours
21.1.77	The Wallcoating group of companies, Part 3 (the £20 million collapse)*
28.1.77	Dying social clubs: who is taking the money (St Albans, Blacknedge)?
4.2.77	Franchised hairdressing schools (Charles Baron, Harry Hepworth)
11.2.77	What protection is the Court of Protection?
18.2.77	So, you want to be connected to gas or electricity: your rights and their colossal charges/Recorded and registered post going astray
25.2.77	Charity Publishing*
4.3.77	The Harry Hepworth story (Protectaglaze, Protectahome, G. H. Coatings, Charles Baron . . . all defunct)
11.3.77	The hi-fi chain that beats up complaining customers (Saray Electronics)

18.3.77 The taxman's powers, and how they are abused
25.3.77 Would you trust the Public Trustee?
1.4.77 Compensation problems over road and motorway developments
15.4.77 Holiday and investment homes in the sun swindles, Part 1
22.4.77 Holiday and investment homes, Part 2*
29.4.77 Inappropriate fishing regulations and the fishermen bankrupted by them (Stan French). *See Case 10*
6.5.77 More banking bungles
13.5.77 Building societies. 'Red Lining' policies
20.5.77 Rogue mortgage brokers (Accrowhurst Ltd)
27.5.77 High pressure selling, from the inside
3.6.77 Death and the National Health Service
10.6.77 Bank trustees: how they can lose you a fortune
17.6.77 More high-pressure selling tricks
24.6.77 Council house waiting lists, and how they are manipulated
30.6.77 Selected to die: the fate of kidney patients
18.8.77 Complaints against solicitors
25.8.77 Bogus employment agencies
1.9.77 New angles on conning old people
8.9.77 Local Government Ombudsman special: some so-called success stories
15.9.77 The phoney franchise scheme (D. & L. Trading) that promised the earth and gave nothing, Part 1
23.9.77 The ethics of plea bargaining
29.9.77 More worthless court judgements
7.10.77 More phoney franchises/D. & L. Trading, Part 2
13.10.77 Here today, gone tomorrow travel agents (Economy Tours)
21.10.77 The 'cowboy' plumbers
28.10.77 Broken local authority promises: what chance redress?
4.11.77 Who's prepared for the Thames to flood?
11.11.77 Fiddling council house 'swap' schemes
17.11.77 Child custody (Mrs O'Neill: Mr & Mrs Hall)
22.11.77 Mobility allowances: how they are denied to the deserving
1.12.77 Bankruptcy special, Part 2
8.12.77 More high-handed council planning problems
15.12.77 The first 'compilation' programme

12.1.78 Rogue loft conversion firms

19.1.78	Elderly taxi drivers/One man's fight against the Central Electricity Generating Board
26.1.78	Car insurance swindle (Revolution Oil)
2.2.78	Getting justice from the DHSS
9.2.78	Powers of the taxman and the bailiff, Part 2
16.2.78	Unfair dismissal (R. Hall etc): your chance of redress
23.2.78	Defending yourself against defamation and character assassination (Mr Singh etc)
2.3.78	Liquidation special
9.3.78	More homes in the sun (Sun Developments and Paul Prew-Smith)
16.3.78	Property development swindles (Ray Hill)* *See Case 3*
23.3.78	Appealing against your rates and other statutory charges
30.3.78	Sun Developments, Part 2/Revolution Oil, Part 2/Dangerous motor caravans
6.4.78	Greenham Common airbase: the fight to ban air tankers
13.4.78	The disappearing sub-post office/More on Spanish villas
20.4.78	Bargees versus the British Waterways Board
27.4.78	Car rustproofing: who really makes money out of the franchises (Ziebart, now defunct)
4.5.78	The scandal of the Nantes air crash*
11.5.78	Office machine franchise racket (Kencafe Office Services)
18.5.78	Homelessness special: repercussions of the 1977 Housing Act
25.5.78	Bureaucratic bungles over child allowances etc: tragic consequences for the Hall family
1.6.78	Strange planning decisions in Kingston/Ditto in North Wales
8.6.78	Loft conversion disasters (Yorkholme)/The Hall's problems solved (see 25.5.78)
15.6.78	Phoney charity for the deal: sole beneficiary is Mr Mack
22.6.78	Bogus antique dealers, knocker boys etc.
29.6.78	The doctor who stole his patient's inheritance, with a little help from his legal friends (Mrs Bayliss vs Dr Mullen)
6.7.78	Unjustified finance company snatch-backs
13.7.78	Compilation programme
31.8.78	The millionaire who never paid for anything: the

	Newtons and their many companies. *See Case 1*
7.9.78	Rogue central heating firms
14.9.78	The sorry saga of the Embassy Open Pool championships
21.9.78	The villagers of Fishponds versus the CEGB: strange happenings under the pylons
28.9.78	The Nottingham swarm: the house eaten by bees
4.10.78	The Alexandra Palace reggae festival that never happened
11.10.78	More double-glazing rip-offs (Betterwindows, Ideal Homes)
19.10.78	More problems with doctors and dentists
25.10.78	Victims of violence: will nobody help?
1.11.78	Motorway noise/Prison officers injury dispute
8.11.78	More compulsory purchase order horror stories: £30 for your home!
15.11.78	Don't invest in Paraguay*
22.11.78	The farm franchise fraud: Barncroft Milking Services
29.11.78	More so-called homes in the sun (Formula Finance)
6.12.78	British Rail slaves: the level crossing keepers
13.12.78	End of year compilation
10.1.79	Live it up (and die) on holiday (Saga trips for the elderly)
17.1.79	Royston Du Maurier's disappearing fashion show
24.1.79	A crop of crooked car dealers ('Complain, and we'll break your legs!') (Graham Autos, Wharfshaw Ltd, Allingbrook Ltd, Howes Autos)
31.1.79	Michael John McDonald Bell's business empire (The Seagull Auto Group, Green Trade Directories etc.) *See Case 13*
7.2.79	Getting away with murder: why no appeal for the prosecution? Cases of Kenneth Green and David Rogers*
15.2.79	The National House Builders Council revisited
22.2.79	The first Action Desk
28.2.79	Pornography special: Holes in the Obscene Publications Act
7.3.79	Tugs of love: baby snatches*
14.3.79	Action Desk
21.3.79	Local authority maladministration
28.3.79	The Southport connection: the Randall and Sumner kaleidoscope of companies. *See Case 2*

4.3.79 Action Desk

11.4.79 Anatomy of a fringe bank collapse (Barnett Christie). *See Case 12*

18.4.79 Wrongful arrest/Police treatment of suspects

25.4.79 Action Desk

2.5.79 The problems of foreign litigation

9.5.79 Insurance anomalies: he who makes the rules bends them

16.5.79 Action Desk

23.5.79 Pyschic surgery: miracle or fraud?* *See Case 7*

30.5.79 Divine Light Mission special

1.6.79 Action Desk

13.6.79 Liquidation special: John Eidemak, Robert E. Howes

20.6.79 Casualties of the NHS*

27.6.79 Action Desk

4.7.79 Australian land deals: want to buy a swamp? (Alfred Grant companies)

11.7.79 Mid-term compilation

29.8.79 How safe are our safety standards?

5.9.79 Action Desk

12.9.79 The case of the disappearing Dane: Bjorn Lindahls's construction empire

19.9.79 More home workers on slave wages

26.9.79 Action Desk

3.10.79 *Fawlty Towers* was never like this: Bytermill Hotel

10.10.79 The Victoria Carriage Company, Part 1

17.10.79 Action Desk

24.10.79 Local Authority lunacy (Celladyke and Pontefract). *See Case 14*

31.10.79 Mobile homes special

7.11.79 Action Desk

14.11.79 Beauty and the ballroom: extraordinary complaints against the Barbara Daly School of Beauty/The Arthur Murray School of Dancing

21.11.79 The non-union Trade Union country club (Plaw Patch Hill)

28.11.79 Action Desk

5.12.79 Mr Harris's non-existent building businesses (Premier Glass, Premier Engineering, Tudor Stone)

12.12.79 Greaseaters: the company that 'eats' its agents, despite being *The Money Programme* company of the year

19.12.79 End of year compilation

16.1.80	Victoria Carriage Company, Part 2
23.1.80	Action Desk
30.1.80	The story of 'Tom the Conner' (Tom O'Connor: Equimos Ltd, Commercial Freight & Marketing, Rennowise Ltd, Whitegates Ltd, the Blue Note Night Club)
6.2.80	Childline: Samaritans for kids?
20.2.80	Beyond the fringe of fringe medicine (Mrs Janet Pitman's miracle cures) *See Case 6*
27.2.80	The West Indian 'Mr Fixit': dubious dealings of Guy Elleston
5.3.80	Action Desk
12.3.80	The Great Grain swindle (Taylor & Wilson)
19.3.80	David King's business empire (Cavern Jewelry, Judie Summers International, Sandmore Construction Ltd, Yorkshire Properties, Yorkshire Music Ltd)
26.3.80	Action Desk
14.5.80	Phoney antique auctions (Kings Auctions), Part 1
21.5.80	Action Desk
28.5.80	Kings Auctions, Part 2/Whatever happened to the Scottish Custom Car Show?
4.6.80	Another dubious mortgage brokers, and the disasters they left behind (Criteria Mortgage Company)
11.6.80	Action Desk
18.6.80	The neighbours dispute to end them all, and how the police made things worse (Weymouth)
25.6.80	Homes in the sun revisited (Michael Rutt: Laird & Co)
2.7.80	Action Desk
9.7.80	Mid-term compilation
13.8.80	The Thanet School of English and its remarkable proprietor (Salaam Blackmore)
20.8.80	Action Desk
27.8.80	Kings of the Cowboy Plumbers (the Hetmanski brothers: Ever-ready Plumbing, Citywide, Destaton, Alice & Watergate). *See Case 4*
23.9.80	The rogue Belfast builder and IRA kneecapper (Sean Mallin) *See Case 5*
10.9.80	Action Desk
17.9.80	Company insolvency special
24.9.80	Personal bankruptcy special
1.10.80	Action Desk
8.10.80	Ivor Cavarllo's pornographic publishing empire

(Landsdown Distribution Company, Archoak Ltd, Troydeck Ltd, Associated Magazine Distributors Ltd, Graderest Ltd, Lofthane Ltd, Reapglen Ltd, Eurap Publishing Company (London) Ltd, Concord Supply Company etc, etc.)

12.11.80 A touch of the *Sun*: how the *Sun* newspaper reported and allegedly created a Skinhead problem in Tilbury

19.11.80 Action Desk

3.12.80 Denis Kendall's miracle cure (DMSO)*. *See Case 8*

10.12.80 Final Action Desk

17.12.80 End of year compilation

21.1.81 The bogus security firm and its equally bogus staff union (Security Taskforce)

28.1.81 The Photographers Institute of Great Britain (Sunil Agawalla)

4.2.81 A special on the Companies Act (1981)

11.2.81 Heart transplants: the debatable use of scarce medical resources in East Anglia to support Papworth Hospital's national programme. *See Case 9*

18.2.81 Mark Promotions: they make money, even if you don't

25.2.81 The business bungles of Marcus Jones, barrister-at-law

4.3.81 Property sharks (Burlington Investments)

11.3.81 The dangers of system-built housing (Bison Wall-frame)*

18.3.81 The cowboy company liquidators (Chancery Lane Registrars: Messrs Caplan, Davis and Pepler)

22.4.81 Local authority corruption (Surrey County Council, Elmbridge Borough Council, Mr Baker and Miss Bowden)

29.4.81 More collapsing mail order firms (Collonade and Asset)

6.5.81 Harrassed tenants

20.5.81 The use and abuse of Closing Orders on houses

27.5.81 Aspects of advertising: the suppression of competition

3.6.81 Chequebook journalism special

10.6.81 How the Masons control the London Borough of Newham

17.6.81 Mid-term compilation

22.7.81 Abdul Shamji 'rescues' Stonefield Vehicles etc.

29.7.81 The Royal Insurance Company versus the Durrants: a case of arson?

5.8.81	Dr Benjamin Cohen, 'company doctor' (Federal Consolidated Investments, British & Overseas Insurance, Pinnock Finance)
12.8.81	The actors' agent who didn't pay up (Jan Dutton/Kirby)
19.8.81	The Moores versus Guardian Royal Exchange Insurance: another case of arson? How the police fudged the evidence
26.8.81	Homes in the snow (Silvercoast Properties Overseas Ltd)
2.9.81	Brooklands Nursing Home (A Fawlty Towers for OAPs)
9.9.81	Saray Electronics revisited
16.9.81	Mansion block landlords (Freshwater group, again)
21.10.81	The further exploits of William Patrick Dowling (or Kelly): financier and car dealer
28.10.81	The Shimna Valley Clinic. Robert Boyd's 'cures' for cancer and multiple sclerosis
4.11.81	Back pay for RAF ex-prisoners-of-war. Why won't Britain pay this debt of honour?
11.11.81	'Investments' in electronic gaming machines (Barry Freeman: Cashflow Investment Services, Jobed Ltd, Star Grange Ltd)
18.11.81	Collapsing houses in Exeter and Manchester
2.12.81	Mail order special
9.12.81	On the trail of UK horse rustlers
16.12.81	End of year compilation
20.1.82	Racial discrimination in the Lancashire Fire Brigade: the victimisation of Roland Steven
27.1.82	Slave wages in the launderette and laundry business
3.2.82	The national barter scheme that wasn't (Peter Stanley and the Great Lakes Trade Exchange)
10.2.82	Bogus university degrees revisited: the world of Raymond Young (St Giles University College, Harley Private College, London School of Beauty Therapy etc)
17.2.82	The Grange Academy of Theatrical & Associated Arts (David 'Spider' Taylor)
24.2.82	A tale of two planning tangles, including 'The Great Wall of Burbage'
3.3.82	Are building societies run as they should be?
10.3.82	The trial of Bernard Saltman: a miscarriage of justice?

	Part 1. *See Case 11*
17.3.82	Disappearing landlords (Mason/Martin, Nicholas Van Hoogstraten)
21.4.82	A phoney animal charity (National Society for the Protection of Animals: sole proprietor, Herbert John Kirby)
28.4.82	Cashflow Investments, Part 2
5.5.82	Great Lakes Trading, Part 2
12.5.82	The great trailer fraud (John Edwin Clarke)
19.5.82	Andrew Fox's media schools (TV Training Centre etc)
26.5.82	Mobile homes again (Rusty Well Park, Yeovil)
2.6.82	The Saltman Case, Part 2. *See Case 11*
9.6.82	Special on the Cork Report on insolvency. *See Case 16*
16.6.82	Mid-term compilation
21.7.82	Tru-Tu-Form horse racing investments (the Beilby family)
28.7.82	More on Closing Orders/The Saltman conviction quashed. *See Case 11*
4.8.82	Close Encounters introduction agency
11.8.82	The energy-saving system that doesn't (Potex Pirhana)
18.8.82	Medical confidentiality revisited: serious breaches
25.8.82	The church commissioners as landlords
1.9.82	Mr Shah versus the DHSS/The house built on thin air
8.9.82	St George's School, Stowmarket. Mr Slade's latter-day Dotheboys Hall. *See Case 15*
15.9.82	Medical mistakes that kill or maim
21.10.82	The insurance sales sharks (Bond Street Investments)
28.10.82	Another holiday homes swindle (Caravilla Ltd, George Ley)
4.11.82	The Cork Report on Insolvency revisited
11.11.82	The Nigerian Connection. The business world of Chief Francis Nzeribe
18.11.82	Double-dealing landlords/Heron Books
25.11.82	How to get a £500,000 company for only £22,500. Allegations by the Newlove family
2.12.82	Unsound planning laws/Unsafe bicycles
8.12.82	More scandalous legal delays
15.12.82	End of year compilation

19.1.83 Tony Fitzgerald – The bankrupt who lived like a millionaire for 10 years at other people's expense

26.1.83 The Starch Blocker franchise swindle. How Goodscale Ltd sold expensive franchises for a worthless slimming aid

2.2.83 The scandal of Britain's remand prisons. How people awaiting trial can wait up to 2 years in dreadful conditions and then be acquitted without compensation

9.2.83 A solicitor's role in a brokerage fraud/Mr McCafferty's many fitted kitchen companies

16.2.83 University Village – an example of the awful plight of the single homeless

22.2.83 Another bankruptcy special. The train driver made bankrupt by mistake, and the solicitor trapped in bankruptcy by his trustee

30.2.83 The Court of Protection and the Official Solicitor How they manage/mismanage the affairs of the mentally ill

9.3.83 McDonald Dempsey Insurance – Where have the two and a half million pounds gone?/Housing Catch-22 in Gateshead

16.3.83 The other side of the privately rented housing coin: The tenants who cheat and terrorise their landlords

EPILOGUE

No final word . . .

More than four years have sped by since that London taxi driver and I sat together and listened to *Checkpoint*. Each time I thought I had captured the essence of the programme, something new turned up to change things. I must confess it has not been an easy exercise. One of the worst problems has been the natural wish to follow up all the harrowing and disturbing stories, to find out what happened to the people concerned. Occasionally this proved to be possible. More often not, because some of the people had moved on, because a case was still *sub judice*, or because there simply wasn't time. Then again, I have been dealing with a number of people concerned with the programme who have at least one thing in common: a very strong personality. Their perceptions of what has happened over the years do not always coincide. That is why I have included as fully as possible the views of so many people on, for example, the origins of *Checkpoint* and its ethics. The book, like the programme, is full of loose ends, and the reason is simply because life is full of loose ends. I made efforts to contact some of the villains who have featured in the programme over the years. Not surprisingly perhaps, I failed. Persistence may have led me to meet the cowboy plumbers, but logic told me that getting my head smashed in by a lump of four-by-two would not necessarily result in a better book. Anyway, I'm a coward.

On the other hand I did get responses from other contributors to the programme. The wealth of respect and gratitude expressed by so many people is summed up in the following letter, sent to me by the wife of Bernard Saltman.

> The entry in my diary reads: '27th July 1982 – We have won!' Words that brought an end to three years of anguish for my family. Sharing the joy with me at the end of a long and arduous campaign were not only my husband Bernard, our three children, members of our family and many close friends

but also three people who had, in a short time, become both friends and supporters. Without their help I am convinced we could never have achieved what at one time seemed unachievable.

I refer to the team from the BBC's Radio 4 programme *Checkpoint*: John Edwards, the producer, Dina Gold the researcher, and Roger Cook the presenter.

I became involved with *Checkpoint* when I wrote to them in February 1982. This was one month after my husband's appeal against his conviction had failed in the Court of Appeal (Criminal Division). My husband had been imprisoned on a charge of arson, a crime he did not commit and for which he had been wrongfully accused and arrested. The summing up by the Crown Court judge at my husband's trial in 1979 clearly implied his innocence and threw doubt on the evidence of the prosecution's only forensic witness. Nevertheless, the jury brought in a verdict of Guilty. I knew that I had to campaign for his release and to prove his innocence. This campaign was to be the sole purpose of my life in the subsequent years, and I knew that I must enlist the help of as many people as possible. For example, I approached our Member of Parliament, Sir Ian Gilmour, and found him to be a courteous and sympathetic ally who studied the file on the case most carefully and promised me his complete attention and support.

After my husband's appeal was rejected I recalled that he had often relayed to me stories he had heard on the car radio on his way to work, how an investigative programme looked into cases of grave wrong-doings, miscarriages of justice and fraudulent deals. But I could not recall the name of the programme. Then a neighbour told me of a builder in Wales who had suffered an experience similar to ours and how the *Checkpoint* programme had assisted him. At about the same time I received a letter from an Old Age Pensioner who had read of our case in the excellent coverage we had received in the local Press. Once again I was pointed in the direction of Roger Cook and *Checkpoint*.

I wrote as short a letter as possible, condensing the years of misery into a brief outline, and a week later I received a telegram asking me to telephone Dina Gold in the *Checkpoint* office. We arranged a meeting, and Dina spent a whole day with me, asking, probing, inspecting and reading the many documents. Finally she left with an armful of papers, both of us completely exhausted. I knew she would have to present her material to her colleagues, and they would all have to decide if I was telling the truth, and if they could achieve anything by putting our story on the air.

My family and I were given new hope when, on 4 March, Roger Cook came to our home to interview me. I had been nervous when Dina called, and I was now strained and tense. It is one thing to write a letter to someone or to talk face to face. But it is entirely different to speak into a microphone, conscious of the programme's audience of perhaps two million people. But Roger was very kind and sympathetic and extremely professional. I was soon put at my ease and made to feel that I was speaking only to him.

The programme was broadcast on 11 March. As a result, many people came forward to offer their sympathy, financial assistance and support. Most important of all were offers of practical help and advice from professional people. The programme had beyond doubt opened that elusive door, whose handle I had been rattling, turning and pushing without effect for so long.

Eminent and expert people were interviewed in a second programme broadcast on 12 June, including Sir Ian Gilmour, Greville Janner QC, MP and Sir Eric Laithwaite. They and others helped us to unearth aspects of the story of which, at the time of the first broadcast, we had been unaware. This ultimately led to Home Secretary William Whitelaw granting bail and referring the case back to the Court of Appeal.

And so, on 27 July 1982, almost three years after the start of a trail of events that shattered our lives and ruined our business, we finally got the justice for which we had fought so hard. An innocent man, wrongfully imprisoned and parted from his family had been given back his liberty, his self-respect and his dignity.

We thought at the time that this was the end of all our problems, yet sadly in reality they continue. We are still fighting an insurance company for restitution. The company so far refuses to acknowledge that they or any of their agents are in any way responsible for the loss of a family business that had been operating for over 60 years.

Where is the moral obligation they have to restore the livelihood of our family? Or does that question raise still more questions? Another case for Roger Cook and *Checkpoint*, perhaps!

LYNN SALTMAN October 1982

Bibliography

A short bibliography

ARLIDGE, A. and EADY, D. *Law of Contempt* Sweet and Maxwell, 1982.
COOTE, A. and GILL, I. *Women's rights: a practical guide* Penguin Books, n.e. 1981.
CURRAN, J. and SEATON, J. *Power without responsibility: Press and broadcasting in Britain* Fontana, 1981.
EVANS, E. *Radio: a guide to broadcasting techniques* Barrie and Jenkins, 1977.
EVANS, H. *Editing and design* Book 1 *Newsman's English* Heinemann, 1972.
GATLEY, C. *Libel and Slander* 8th rev. edn. P. C. S. Lewis. Sweet and Maxwell, 1981.
GOODE, R. M. *Commercial Law* Penguin/Allen Lane, 1982.
GRANT, L. et al. *Civil liberty: the National Council for Civil Liberties guide to your rights* Penguin Books, n.e. 1978.
HERBERT, J. *Techniques of radio journalism* Black, 1976.
MCLEISH, R. *The technique of radio production: a manual for local broadcasters* Focal Press, 1978.
MCNAE, L. C. J. ed. *Essential law for journalists* Butterworth, 8th edn, 1982. (Including 1981 Contempt Act).
MOLLENHOFF, C. R. *Investigative reporting* Collier Macmillan, 1981.
'READER'S DIGEST' *You and your rights: an A to Z guide to the law* Reader's Digest, n.e. 1982.
RICHARDS, A. *Law for journalists* Macdonald and Evans, paperback 1977. op.
STREET, H. *Freedom, the individual and the law* Penguin Books, 1972.
WILLIAMS, P. N. *Investigative reporting and editing* Prentice-Hall, 1978.
'WHICH?' *Guide to your rights* Consumers' Association, n.e. paperback 1981.

Index